Working at RELATIONAL DEPTH *in* Counselling *and* Psychotherapy

DAVE MEARNS *and* MICK COOPER

Los Angeles | London | New Delhi
Singapore | Washington DC

First published 2005

Reprinted 2010, 2011

SAGE Publications Ltd
1 Oliver's Yard
55 City Road
London EC1Y 1SP

SAGE Publications Inc.
2455 Teller Road
Thousand Oaks, California 91320

SAGE Publications India Pvt Ltd
B 1/I 1 Mohan Cooperative Industrial Area
Mathura Road
New Delhi 110 044

SAGE Publications Asia-Pacific Pte Ltd
33 Pekin Street #02-01
Far East Square
Singapore 048763

British Library Cataloguing in Publication data

A catalogue record for this book is available from the British Library

ISBN 978-0-7619-4457-7 (hbk)
ISBN 978-0-7619-4458-4 (pbk)

Library of Congress Control Number: 2005901773

Typeset by C&M Digitals (P) Ltd., Chennai, India
Printed and bound in Great Britain by CPI Antony Rowe
Printed on paper from sustainable resources

PRAISE FOR THE BOOK

'The importance of the relationship between the client and their counsellor or psychotherapist has long been recognised as constituting the cornerstone of effective therapeutic work. However, in recent years there has been a tendency to take the significance of the therapeutic relationship for granted, and to understand the dynamics of this relationship in terms of an alliance between the practitioner and person seeking help, in which each participant negotiates and agrees how best they can work together. In this book, Dave Mearns and Mick Cooper provide a fresh and challenging new perspective on the therapeutic relationship. By using the concept of relational depth, they are able to move beyond a vision of the relationship as merely a backdrop to therapeutic work, and to begin to explore the moments when the possibility of being able to relate more fully to another person can have a life-enhacing impact. Grounded in a person-centred approach to counselling and psychotherapy, the book articulates the meaning of relational depth by drawing on ideas from psychodynamic, postmodern, existential, cognitive, developmental and social psychological theory and research. The authors powerfully combine vivid case material and careful conceptual analysis to examine different aspects of relational depth and to show how it may be facilitated, and weave in a fascinating discussion of the interaction between therapeutic context and the types of relationship that can be created between therapist and client. This is an important book. It integrates concepts and practices from a range of approaches to therapy, and offers a convincing and original perspective that has the potential to inform practice, training and research for many years to come.'

*John McLeod, Professor of Counselling
Tayside Institute for Health Studies,
University of Abertay Dundee*

'Timely, informative, challenging and a delight to read ... Mearns and Cooper have provided a valuable template with which to consider and reconsider the dialogical qualities of the therapeutic encounter.'

Professor Ernesto Spinelli, Senior Fellow,
School of Psychotherapy and Counselling,
Regent's College, London

'This is one of those rare books which will attract a wide readership because it operates at so many different levels. It is, by turn, scholarly, dramatic, challenging, prophetic, practical, intensely personal and yet with implications which, if taken seriously, could transform the whole field of counselling and psychotherapy.

Dave Mearns and Mick Cooper are courageous enough to proclaim boldly that the heart of therapy lies in the real meeting and connection between human beings and then undertake the task of putting into words the nature of encounters which can often feel beyond language. They explore the profound implications of conceptualising human nature as essentially relational and what this means both for the development of the person and for the work of the therapist. They dare to employ such words as intimacy and love and to take us into the moment-to-moment process of therapeutic relationships which demand every last ounce of a therapist's integrity and commitment.

This is a book which has about it an inspirational quality which will leave few readers unmoved. It also raises disturbing questions about many current trends both in society at large and in the profession of counselling and psychotherapy itself. Do not read this book if you want a quiet life and undisturbed sleep.'

Professor Brian Thorne, co-founder of The
Norwich Centre, Norwich

CONTENTS

PREFACE

Mick: One evening, at the age of about nine or ten, my parents dragged me round to one of their friends' houses for supper. I did not like the friends very much, and liked being dragged away from my evening's television schedule even less, but soon became engrossed with one of the games that they had put out for my sister and me. It was a plastic board with spokes on it, and the game was to slot some plastic cogs onto the spokes such that the cogs meshed together; and when they did so, the turning of one cog would lead to the turning of them all. I can still remember that feeling of all the cogs turning together – that sense of engagement and connection – and how it contrasted to the looseness of just one cog spinning on its own. When I started counselling, I was reminded of that experience, because of the sheer sense of connection that I experienced with some of my clients. It was not all the time, but at some moments, I would have this sense of my client and I being deeply connected to each other: engaged, enmeshed, intertwined. It was as if, when I 'turned' I affected my clients, and, when they 'turned' they affected me; and although, at these times, the pace of the therapeutic work was much slower, I had a profound sense of genuine human contact. Generally, after such meetings, I would come out of the sessions exhilarated, partly out of a relief that I actually seemed to be enjoying my new-found career but also out of a sense that, at these moments of meetings, I seemed to be helping my clients in a very profound way. Many years later, and after many theoretical and empirical excursions, I am aware that this desire to connect with my clients is still at the heart of my therapeutic work: nothing, it seems to me, has more healing potential.

Dave: 'Will you stop fuckin' loving me!' bellowed Peter, not quite loud enough for anyone to hear because, on that Saturday morning, the 'List D' school[1] was empty of anyone but some domestic staff, me and Peter, a boy who had become 14 years old that morning.

I had known it was his birthday and he would 'celebrate' it, alone, apart from my greeting and the box of sweets I had bought him. All the other 94 boys were on weekend leave – 75 per cent in the parental home and the others with relatives or friends. Some of the boys had nowhere to go but went with other boys. Peter used to be invited but he had always refused, so they stopped asking him. 'I don't like families – stuff their families', he said. His view about families wasn't surprising – his father was serving life for killing his mother.

Bringing the sweets was a misjudgement, and yet it wasn't. Peter had experienced it as 'loving' him and he didn't want that, or at least part of him didn't want it. The other part of him got stuck into the sweets and offered me one.

That began what, for both of us, was 'Peter's Day'. I told him that he was stuck with me for the day and that I was stuck with him because I was the only staff on duty and he was the only boy. I asked him what he wanted to do that day, knowing that he would give the stock response, 'dunno' – anything else would be to give too much. 'No, seriously', I said, 'we'll do *anything* you want to do today, providing it's possible, and legal'. It was as well to add the 'legal' because, despite his slender age, Peter had 27 previous convictions and those only recorded his 'failures'.

He looked me straight in the face – in truth he liked me a lot and I liked him. But the secret was not to openly *show* it, that's why the sweets partially annoyed him. 'Anything?', he repeated. 'Anything', I confirmed. 'OK', he said, 'first we'll go to your Students' Union and play snooker then we'll go to the pub at lunch time'. I saw the smallest smirk at the edge of his mouth. 'OK, the cafe', he said. 'Then, we'll go to the game.' For a moment I wondered if he would be prepared to accept the idea of watching my football team play but that was a false hope – it had to be Glasgow Rangers, of course. That raised a slight problem because their game was against Celtic and it would be a sell out. 'After the game we can have dinner in a posh restaurant and go on to the casino… OK, I'll settle for a fish supper and back to school!' One of the things Peter and I used well together was our humour.

The day, in the words of the local vernacular, was 'pure dead brilliant'. Some of the students in the Union looked down their noses at this raucous 14 year old but they kept looking over at our table admiring his skilful play. He beat me by seven frames to one – 'I gave you one', he said, 'I felt sorry for you'. 'I won it fair and square', I retorted, 'I was brilliant in that frame'. The café meal was great, particularly our competition to see who could eat most bowls of ice cream – again Peter won – but this time only by four to three and a half.

It was at the football game that I surpassed myself and earned admiration even from Peter. We walked past all the normal turnstiles to one marked 'complimentary tickets' where we collected two tickets in my name. Early in the morning I had phoned a friend who played for the football team I supported and asked him to fix two tickets for me, but not for his game – he phoned another friend, etc. The tickets were for the Centre Stand, right beside the Directors' Box. Peter's mouth fell open as soon as we went in and it stayed open most of the afternoon as he kept pointing out injured heroes a few feet away in the Directors' Box.

His team won 4–2 and we got our 'fish suppers' on the way back to the school, eating them from their newspapers as they should be eaten. Back in the school I took him to the staff room and we had tea together – it was special for boys to be in there.

I was with him at the side of his bed at the end of the day as I had been at the beginning. 'Good night Peter', I said. 'Thanks, Dave', said Peter and smiled at me. I smiled back at him and left quickly before the frog in my throat reached my eyes.

People like Peter taught me a lot about psychotherapy before I even became a therapist. No matter how 'damaged' they are there is always a part of them – sometimes a very small part – that does indeed want to be in relationship, even wants to be loved. The secret is to meet them on their terms.

Across time and place, and under various different guises, philosophers (e.g. Buber, 1947) psychotherapists (e.g. Laing, 1965; Schmid, 2002) and numerous other thinkers (e.g. Bohm, 1996) have attempted to describe an in-depth mode of relating in which two individuals experience a great sense of connectedness with each other. Martin Buber, the Jewish existential philosopher, for instance, has written about moments of 'genuine dialogue' in which 'each of the participants really has in mind the other or others in their present and particular being and turns to them with the intention of establishing a living mutual relation between himself and them' (1947: 37). Similarly, Judith Jordan, the feminist psychotherapist, has written about times of 'mutual intersubjectivity' in which:

> [O]ne is both affecting the other and being affected by the other; one extends oneself out to the other and is also receptive to the impact of the other. There is openness to influence, emotional availability, and a constant changing pattern of responding to and affecting the other's state. There is both receptivity and active initiative toward the other. (1991a: 82)

This is a book about such contact, as manifested in counselling and psychotherapy. It is about those experiences of real engagement and connection that, as our autobiographical extracts suggest, have come to be seen by both of us – as well as by many other contemporary therapists (for instance, Ehrenberg, 1992; Friedman, 1985; Hycner, 1991; Jordan, 1991a; Schmid, 2002; Stern, 2004) – as the heart of a healing relationship.

Such experiences of engagement can be very difficult to put into words. How does one describe, for instance, those moments of connection and intimacy with a client when each person's words seem to flow from the other's and all self-consciousness is lost? Such an encounter can feel beyond language, and to put words on to the moment can feel like cheapening the depth and profundity of the experience. And yet, to not talk about such experiences because of their indefinability would be like the drunk who searches for his keys under a lamppost even when he has dropped them further down the street, on the grounds that that is where the light is! Without doubt, it is easier to talk about and operationalise such aspects of therapy as 'homework compliance', 'levels of therapeutic alliance', or even 'frequency of self-disclosures', but none of these components, it seems to us, captures the essence of what therapy is all about. For us, therapy is about a real meeting and connection with another human being, and even if such experiences are difficult to put into words, the attempt seems eminently worthwhile.

The term that we will use in this book to describe these in-depth connections with others is 'relational depth'. This is a term that Dave Mearns has developed in earlier texts (Mearns, 1997c; 2003a). He gives a background to the term from a recent lecture:

> In 1989 Windy Dryden and I published a book entitled *Experiences of Counselling in Action*, looking at the experiences of both counsellors and clients. In the research for that book I was amazed to find how much of the experiencing of both parties was kept hidden from the other, even in work that both saw as 'good'. When I began to look at the material that was in this 'unspoken relationship' (Mearns, 1994; 2003a) I found that most of the *really* important stuff for the client was in there. The next step was to explore the circumstances where the client might bring it out. There was only one answer to that – the client only brought the really important stuff out when they experienced 'relational depth' with their counsellor or therapist. While this is an exciting quest – to explore and to develop relational depth – the corollary to the discovery is somewhat tense: that much of what 'normally' happens in counselling and therapy hardly scrapes the surface (Mearns, 2004c).

For the purposes of this book, our working definition of relational depth is as follows:

> A state of profound contact and engagement between two people, in which each person is fully real with the Other, and able to understand and value the Other's experiences at a high level.

In using the term 'depth' here, we are not wanting to imply an object-like model of the 'self' in which a person is seen as having some deep 'inner core'. Indeed, from a phenomenological and intersubjective standpoint (see Chapter 1), the idea that experiences reside 'inside' a person is deeply problematic (see Boss, 1963; Cooper, 2003a: 37–9). Rather, what we mean by 'deeper' is those things that are, phenomenologically speaking, 'truer' and more 'real' for a person: that coincides more fully with the actuality of their lived experiences. What we should also state here is that we do not want to attach any value judgement to the term 'depth'. In other words, we do not see it as superior to more 'presentational' ways of being or relating. Clearly, both have an important place in human lives. What we will argue, however, is that *some* depth of relating is essential for optimal human functioning, just as it is often key to the therapeutic process.

In this book, we will be using the term 'relational depth' to refer both to specific *moments* of encounter and also to a particular *quality* of a relationship. In other words, just as we might use the term 'intimacy' to refer both to a specific experience (e.g. 'I felt really intimate with John last night') and to a particular type of relationship (e.g. 'My relationship with John has always been very intimate'), so we will use 'relational depth' in both senses. This first sense we will generally write as 'moments', 'times' or 'experiences' of relational depth. In this respect, what we mean by moments of relational depth is similar to what Stern (2004) has termed 'moments of meeting', and also has many parallels with Buber's (1947; 1958) notion of 'dialogue' and the 'I–Thou' attitude. In the second sense, however, relational depth describes not just a specific moment of encounter, but an *enduring* sense of contact and interconnection between two people. Here, there will be many *moments* of relational depth, but there are also likely to be times when there are less intense moments of contact. Furthermore, where a relational depth exists between two people, there will be a connection with each other that exists outside of specific times of physical proximity. So, for instance, if a relational depth exists between my sister and myself, I may keep her in mind as a valuing and understanding presence – indeed, I may actually feel her warmth and understanding even when she is not there.

Given our definition of relational depth, it should also be noted that we are seeing this as a phenomenon relevant to the whole spectrum of human encounters and not just limited to the therapist–client relationship. Hence, while this book will focus primarily on relational depth as manifested in therapy, we see this as just one context within which such in-depth meetings can take place.

The aim of this book, then, is to explore the nature of relational depth, and to outline a form of practice that has such relating at its heart. Though, as authors, we come from the fields of person-centred and existential therapy, we see the notion of 'relational depth' as central to the work of therapists from a great many approaches and this book is written with that diversity in mind. Indeed, it is fascinating to see the increasing numbers of psychodynamic and cognitive practitioners (see Chapter 1) moving in this same direction.

Viewed from within the person-centred approach our aim is to outline and develop a particularly *dialogical* approach to person-centred therapy. This is a *two*-person-centred therapy', or what Godfrey Barrett-Lennard (2005), the distinguished person-centred researcher and author, has recently termed a 'client-centered relational psychotherapy'. This is an approach to person-centred therapy in which the primary focus of the work is neither on maintaining a non-directive attitude (cf. 'classical client-centred therapy', see Grant, 2004; Merry, 2003) nor on facilitating emotional change (cf. 'process-experiential therapy' and 'emotion-focused therapy', see Elliott et al., 2004; Greenberg et al., 1993), *per se*, but on encountering the client in an in-depth way and sustaining such a depth of relating.

While such a way of working may already be implicit to the practice aims of many person-centred therapists – particularly, perhaps, in the UK – we believe it is high time to make such a stance more explicit, as person-centred therapists like Peter Schmid (2001a) and Godfrey Barrett-Lennard (2005) are doing. Finally, in developing such a dialogical approach to person-centred therapy, we believe that we can incorporate some of the most exciting contemporary developments in philosophy, psychology, psychotherapy and psychoanalysis into the person-centred world, as well as creating valuable bridges with other, relational and postmodern, approaches to counselling and psychotherapy.

The book itself is divided into nine chapters. In Chapter 1, we will present an array of contemporary findings from the psychotherapy research field, as well as recent developments in the fields of philosophy, developmental psychology and psychotherapy itself, which suggest that the quality of the therapeutic relationship, for the majority of clients, is likely to be a key factor in the success of the therapy. In Chapter 2, we will argue a similar point, but from the perspective of 'psychopathology'.

Here, we suggest that many forms of psychological distress are brought about – or compounded – by a lack of close interpersonal engagement, such that in-depth relational encounters in therapy, again, may be a critical element of therapeutic success. In Chapter 3 we will then go on to look at what these moments of in-depth therapeutic contact may be like; and in Chapter 4 we will turn our attention to the kind of therapeutic relationship that is characterised by an enduring sense of relational depth. Chapters 5 and 6 will then illustrate therapeutic work at a level of relational depth through two case studies; and in Chapter 7 we will look at how therapists might facilitate such an encounter. In Chapter 8 we will broaden this out to look at the wider personal development agenda for the therapist, and in Chapter 9 we will conclude by discussing some of the implications of our analysis.

As authors, our relative strengths, interests and backgrounds meant that we have taken the lead on different aspects of the book. Dave Mearns, with his long-standing experience as a person-centred therapist, trainer, supervisor and writer, first drafted the more practical Chapters (5, 6 and 8) as well as our final discussion (Chapter 9). Mick Cooper, on the other hand, with his background in existential therapy and his interests in dialogue, intersubjectivity and psychotherapy research has taken the lead on the more theoretical and empirical Chapters (1, 2 and 3) as well as Chapter 7. Interestingly, Chapter 4, which suggests that relational depth can help clients explore their existential issues and concerns, was first drafted by Dave Mearns. Each of the chapters was then revised by both of the authors several times, so that the end product is an entirely joint effort.

As part of the preparation for this book, we conducted in-depth qualitative interviews (Kvale, 1996) with eight experienced person-centred therapists and trainers. We asked them about their experiences of meeting clients at a level of relational depth, and also related questions such as how they experienced their clients at these times and what they saw as the therapeutic value of these encounters. Data from this study is presented primarily in Chapter 3, although the responses of our interviewees have informed numerous aspects of this book.

To ensure complete anonymity, all identifying features of the clients presented in this book have been changed, and in some instances, the 'clients' are actually an amalgam of several different case-histories. Where a person's 'story' is extensively used, in all but one case we consulted the person and invited them to choose an alternative name. We emphasise the fact that all names are changed, lest people falsely recognise themselves.

We have used female pronouns throughout this book to refer to therapists and male pronouns for clients. This convention allows for more direct language and reverses the normal power imbalance. We do not distinguish between the terms 'counselling' and 'psychotherapy' because everything we say in this book could apply to either activity under most distinctions between them. For our part we are equally happy to be known as 'counsellors' or 'psychotherapists', recognising that the different labels tend to refer to different contexts rather than differentiated operations.

We are extremely grateful to Helen Cruthers, Suzanne Keys and Gill Wyatt for their feedback on a first draft of this book, and to Tessa Mearns, Rachel Owen, Heather Robertson and Norma Craig for their outstanding administrative support throughout the writing of this book. The time and effort that our interviewees gave to take part in our research is also greatly appreciated. We would also like to thank our many supervisees, students and clients over the years, who have played such a major part in helping us develop the ideas and practices presented herein. Finally, we would like to express our thanks to Alison Poyner, Louise Wise, Joyce Lynch and other members of the SAGE Publications team who, as always, have provided an indispensable level of support, encouragement and professionalism throughout the writing of this book.

Dave Mearns and Mick Cooper
February 2005

Note

1. A 'LIST D' school in Britain is a residential school for young offenders.

1 TOWARDS A RELATIONAL THERAPY

This book is about moments of intense relational contact and enduring experiences of connectedness within the therapeutic relationship. Such experiences of relational depth can be striking in the significance they have for the people involved. That they are striking reflects how far the existence of the human being is predicated upon relationship – we are born into a powerful, usually intensely loving, relationship; we learn to define ourselves through relationship; and throughout our life our evaluation of ourselves is especially influenced by relationship. Equally, it is relationship that can be most destructive to us. Criticism hurts most because it comes from another person and abuse is particularly damaging when it comes from someone who should love us. There are over 20 clients mentioned by name in this book. Almost all of them had been damaged in relationships and continued to be hurt. Some had been so damaged and were so hurt that they had sought to separate themselves from relationship. Human beings are skilful in relationship and ingenious in trying to protect themselves from relationship. They can try to close off from relationship – either by avoiding it altogether or by not 'getting involved'. They can pre-empt the attack they fear from the other by first attacking themselves in a fashion that diminishes self-esteem to a degree that inadequacy in relationships becomes a self-fulfilling prophecy. They can also protect themselves from relationship by figuratively, if not literally, 'killing' the other person that would threaten them with relationship. All these people are in this book – all of them had found themselves engaged in the potentially dangerous situation of being a client in counselling or psychotherapy. Why on earth did they do that? Perhaps because hope and despair are close neighbours. Perhaps because we are *so* grounded in relationship that even though we have been thoroughly damaged we see the best hope of change as through relationship. Yet, that 'hope' can be faint and the task of the therapist delicate: can she offer 'encounter' without 'invasion' and can she do it in such a way that she will be believed? Therapeutic working through relationship is challenging for both people, but it is a logical way to work – if damage is caused through relationship, cannot healing too? Over the past half a century, the work of numerous psychologists, psychotherapists and philosophers has pointed towards this healing potential of the therapeutic relationship and in this introductory chapter we look at the arguments and evidence that have unfolded.

Empirical Evidence

In 2002, the American Psychological Association (APA) set up a task force to review all the available data on the link between therapeutic outcomes and the therapeutic relationship. The principal finding of the task force was that 'the therapy relationship...makes substantial and consistent contributions to psychotherapy outcome independent of the specific type of treatment' (Steering Committee, 2002: 441); and it recommended that practitioners should 'make the creation and cultivation of a therapy relationship...a primary aim in the treatment of patients' (p. 442).

The research reviewed by the APA Task Force was extremely rigorous. For example, a study by Krupnick and colleagues (1996) looked at the relationship between the outcomes of therapy and the quality of the therapeutic relationship for depressed clients who had undergone either cognitive-behavioural therapy, 'interpersonal therapy', drug treatment, or a placebo control. Between the two therapeutic groups, researchers had found no significant differences in outcome (Elkin et al., 1989), but what they did find was a significant association between the quality of the therapeutic relationship – as rated by clients – and therapeutic improvements. In other words, in terms of outcomes, it did not seem to matter much whether therapists practised from a cognitive-behavioural or interpersonal standpoint but what did matter was how allied the clients felt they were with their particular therapist. One other interesting finding from this study was that the link between outcome and the therapeutic relationship was as strong for those clients experiencing cognitive-behavioural therapy as it was for clients experiencing the more 'relational' interpersonal therapy (and, indeed, was also as strong for those clients experiencing drug treatment and the placebo conditions!) In fact, there is some evidence to suggest that relational factors may actually be *more* important – or, at least, more closely related to outcome – in the more technique-orientated approaches. Bohart et al. (2002), for instance, found that a higher correlation existed between levels of empathy and outcomes in cognitive-behavioural therapies than in psychodynamic and experiential/humanistic approaches.

While some cognitive-behavioural therapists, then, see their techniques and skills as the primary motor of therapeutic change (for instance, Reinecke and Freeman, 2003), it may be that even in these approaches the principal 'curative' factor is the quality of the therapeutic relationship. At least with some clients, the research suggests that this is the case. Keijsers et al. (2000), for instance, reviewed five studies in which cognitive-behavioural clients were asked about the most helpful aspects of their therapy and concluded that clients consistently reported that 'the relationship with their therapist [was] more helpful than the cognitive-behavioural techniques that were employed' (p. 267). Keijsers and colleagues go on to state that, 'when patients who have completed cognitive-behavioural treatments are asked to indicate what had helped them to overcome their problems, they will answer, "talking with someone who listens and understands"' (p. 291).

Findings such as these have led to the increasing acceptance of a 'common factors' model of therapeutic change (e.g., Hubble et al., 1999; Lambert, 1992). Advocates of this approach argue that therapeutic change is not, primarily, the result of specific practices being implemented by practitioners of different orientations. Rather, they argue that there is a common set of factors responsible for therapeutic change across the whole spectrum of psychotherapeutic and counselling approaches. First among these factors, according to Asay and Lambert (1999), is 'client variables and extratherapeutic events'. These are variables such as the client's level of motivation, or events that happen to them – such as the birth of a child – during their time in therapy. But second, and drawing on an extensive body of empirical data, is the quality of the therapeutic relationship. Asay and Lambert calculate that this accounts for approximately 30 per cent of the variance in therapeutic outcome. 'Except what the client brings to therapy,' then, say Hubble and colleagues, relationship factors, 'are probably responsible for most of the gains resulting from psychotherapy interventions' (1999: 9).

While not all researchers in the psychotherapy field agree that the association between relational factors and outcome is of this magnitude (see, for instance, Beutler et al., 2004; Sachse, 2004), there is general agreement that 'relationship quality is one of the stronger correlates of outcome' (Beutler et al., 2004: 292). But what sort of therapeutic relationship are we talking about here? Based on the empirical evidence, the APA Division of Psychotherapy Task Force categorised relational factors into those that were 'demonstrably effective', and those that were 'promising and probably effective' (Steering Committee, 2002). In terms of individual therapy, three factors fell into the first of these categories, one of which was the therapist's level of empathy (Bohart et al., 2002). A second demonstrably effective factor was the therapeutic alliance: the 'quality and strength of the collaborative relationship between client and therapist in therapy' (Hovarth and

Bedi, 2002: 41); and a third factor was the level of agreement between the therapist and client on the goals of therapy (Tryon and Winograd, 2002).

Seven relational variables were found to be 'promising and probably effective' (Steering Committee, 2002). The first of these was the familiar person-centred condition of positive regard (Farber and Lane, 2002). A second promising and probably effective factor was the therapist's level of congruence and closely associated with this were two other factors: the quality of the *feedback* that the therapist provided to the client regarding their behaviours (Claiborn et al., 2002), and the therapist's level of self-disclosure (Hill and Knox, 2002) (where the self-disclosure was not overly frequent, and where it focused on 'non-intimate' topics). A fifth promising and probably effective factor was the therapist's willingness and ability to repair breakdowns, or 'ruptures,' in the therapeutic alliance (Safran and Muran, 2000); and a sixth one was the therapist's ability to manage 'countertransference' issues (Gelso and Hayes, 2002): i.e. their willingness and ability *not* to act out towards their clients. Finally, it was concluded that the 'quality of relational interpretations' was also a promising and probably effective element of the therapeutic relationship, provided that these interpretations were infrequent and that they were predominantly focused on the way that the client was with the therapist (cf. feedback) (Crits-Christoph and Gibbons, 2002).

The Intersubjective Turn in Philosophy

Alongside developments in counselling and psychotherapy research, developments in the field of philosophy over the last century or so also point towards the idea that the client–therapist relationship is absolutely central to the outcomes of therapy.

Up until around the mid-twentieth century, a particular understanding of human existence came to dominate the western mind. Exemplified in the thinking of the French mathematician and philosopher, René Descartes, this 'modern' worldview understands human existence in fundamentally individualistic terms. Here, each human being is conceptualised as a sovereign, autonomous, individual monad, fundamentally distinct and separate from other people around him. And while, from this modernist standpoint, human beings are seen as having the capacity to relate to each other, these relationships are seen as little more than the meeting between these two separate entities – like two billiard balls knocking together – within which, and from which, the two entities can retain their individual status.

Such has been the pervasiveness of this model of the human being that, to a great extent, most of us simply accept it as a given. Indeed, even relational theorists like Carl Rogers (1959) have a sizeable foot in the individualistic camp: construing human beings as separate and unitary entities, with the capacity for an autonomous and inner-directed existence (see critiques by Barrett-Lennard, 2005; Holdstock, 1993) and the right to *self*-determination (Grant, 2004; Witty, 2004).

But are we really so separate from other human beings? Over the course of the twentieth century, many philosophers and psychologists have challenged this assumption: arguing, instead, that we are fundamentally and inextricably intertwined with others, and that our being is first and foremost a 'being-in-relation'. In other words, what these authors have suggested is that we do not exist as individuals first and then come together with others to form relationships. Rather, what they have argued is that we exist with others first, and only after that come to develop some notion of individuality or separateness.

This 'intersubjective' standpoint (see Crossley, 1996) has been reached from a number of different directions. Existential philosophers like Martin Heidegger (1962) have started from the assertion that human existence is not an object-like thing in the way that a table or a molecule is, but an ever-changing flux of experiencing (see Cooper, 2003a: 12–13). And if we conceptualise human existence in this way, other existences become much more central to the essence of who we are. In other words, at the level of lived-being, we are constantly interacting with others, or thinking about others, or imagining doing things with others, or using tools that have emerged from an interpersonal matrix. So, for instance, although I might be physically on my own as I (in this chapter, the first person refers to Mick Cooper) write these words, my whole being, my 'writing-these-words-now', is oriented towards an imaginary other: the you that is reading this. At the level of lived-being, then, I am as infused with the existences of others as I am with the air that I breathe: others circulate around me and within me and are an integral part of who I am.

In my writing and relating to you I am also using language. That language – a socially constructed medium – is so fundamental to who we are and what we do is a major reason why the notion of separate, individual selves has come to falter in the last century or so. Contemporary philosophers like Derrida (1974) and Wittgenstein (1967), as well as psychologists like Vygotsky (1962) and Gergen (1999), have all argued that language is at the root of all our thoughts, something that we cannot 'stand outside of', and something that is intrinsic to our sense of who we are. Hence, even notions of 'individuality' or 'self' cannot be seen as ultimate and given truths, but constructs that emerge out of a particular sociolinguistic context.

This is a point of view shared by many feminist and cross-cultural theorists, who have also challenged the idea that individuality is a given truth of human existence (see Gergen, 1999). Social psychological researchers, for instance, have shown that many non-Western cultures have a much more 'interdependent' view of the self in which the 'I' is not seen as an isolated entity, but something that is defined in terms of relationships with others (see Aronson et al., 1999). When asked, for instance, to complete statements beginning with 'I am...' people from Asian cultures are more likely to define themselves in terms of family or religious group than people from Western cultures (Aronson et al., 1999). Similarly, feminist theorists have argued that the notion of individuality is a particularly male view of human existence, and that females tend to have a more interdependent and relational understanding of who we are (see Jordan et al., 1991). Indeed, from these standpoints, modern individualism is seen as much more than just a benign set of beliefs, but as an ideology that legitimises a very specific set of social relations: western, patriarchal, late-capitalism; for instance, by implying that competition between human beings is the 'natural' state of affairs or that people should not be subverted by socialising influences. Perhaps this is why Rogers (1963) gained wide popular appeal 40 years ago, when he presented the positive value of the actualising tendency against the forces of society and conformity.

Although these developments in our understanding of what it means to be human may seem relatively abstract, they have important implications for the theory and practice of counselling and psychotherapy. However a-theoretical we may consider ourselves to be, our therapeutic practice will always be based on certain assumptions about what it means to be human. If, for instance, our practice is orientated around helping clients to revise their cognitions, then at some level we must believe that cognitions are an important mediator between how a person feels and how they respond to their world. Similarly, if the emphasis of our therapeutic work is on trying to change what is 'inside' a client – perhaps through offering them interpretations or a set of conditions to help them actualise their individual potential – then at some level we must conceptualise human beings as separate, discrete entities, *within which* the key psychological processes take place. A move towards a more intersubjective understanding of human existence, then, is likely to entail a significant shift towards a more relational form of therapeutic practice. Here, where a client is conceptualised *as* their relationships to others, the therapist–client relationship becomes a cauldron in which the most integral aspects of the client's being can be healed. Furthermore, through an exploration of the client–therapist relationship, the client can begin to reflect on, and revise, those elements of their being that are absolutely central to their existence: their relationships with others.

Developmental Perspectives

Not only has the idea that individuality precedes relationship been challenged in a philosophical sense, but it has also been challenged in a developmental sense. Here, a range of developmental psychologists, psychoanalysts and philosophers have argued that human infants do not begin life as separate, isolated individuals, but as part of a fundamentally relational matrix. One of the first of these, the Jewish existential philosopher Martin Buber, writes that 'the ante-natal life of the child is one of purely natural combination, bodily interaction and flowing from the one to the other' (1958: 40). This is very similar to the view expressed by psychoanalysts such as Margaret Mahler (Mahler et al., 1975), Hans Loewald (see Mitchell, 2000) and D.W. Winnicott, the last of whom was well-known for his statement that 'there is no such thing as a baby, only a nursing couple' (quoted in Curtis and Hirsch, 2003: 73). It was Margaret Mahler, however, who probably developed the most complex model of this early state of 'fusion'. Drawing on detailed observations of infant and caretaker behaviour, she argued that, from about four weeks to five months, the infant goes through a 'symbiotic phase' in which he 'behaves and functions as though he and his mother were an omnipotent system – a dual unity within one common boundary' (Mahler et al., 1975: 44). Here, Mahler argued, the infant does not differentiate between 'I' and 'not-I': external forces which satisfy the infant's needs (such as the mother's breast) are not experienced any differently from internal forces (such as burping). Only later, according to Mahler, does the infant develop some sense of self and other. And while, for Mahler, the infant learns to differentiate herself from others as she develops, for Hans Loewald, this symbiotic sense of being-with-others continues throughout life – in fantasy and imagination – existing 'beneath' the more differentiated and conscious sense of self and other (Mitchell, 2000).

Not all developmental psychologists agree with this: indeed, both Daniel Stern (2003) and Colwyn Trevarthen (1998), leading advocates of an intersubjective standpoint, question the idea of this primordial fusion. Nevertheless, within the field of developmental psychology, an increasing number of researchers and theorists have been questioning the idea that human beings are first and foremost discrete individuals; arguing, instead, that infants come into the world fundamentally orientated towards, and attuned to, others.

Within the psychoanalytic field, one of the first theorists to develop such a perspective was John Bowlby. Bowlby (1969) argued that, for evolutionary reasons, infants are born with a predisposition to become attached to their caregivers, and that they will organise their behaviour and thinking in ways that maintain these attachment relationships (Mitchell, 2000). Evidence for such a hypothesis is abundant. Any parent who has tried to walk around an unfamiliar house, for instance, with a toddler strapped to their leg because they are afraid of the other grown ups will know the true meaning of attachment theory! Infants also seem to be equipped with one of the most powerful tools for attracting the attention of caregivers when they are frightened or distressed: an ear-piercing shriek!

Of more direct relevance to this book, however, are recent advances in the field of developmental psychology and child observation which would suggest that human beings have an inborn desire and capacity, not only to bond with others, but also to interact and communicate with them (see, for instance, Beebe et al., 2003b; Stern, 2003; 2004; Trevarthen, 1998). In other words, while human infants may want affection, security and unconditional acceptance – particularly in unfamiliar or frightening situations – they would also seem to have a basic desire for something more engaging. They want to be loved, but they want to interact with that other and that love, to give as well as to receive, and to experience an immediate and engaged contact. Indeed, person-centred therapist David Brazier (1993) goes so far as to suggest that the fundamental human need may not be to *receive* positive regard, but to *provide* it to others. The fact that children often behave in ways that they know others will disapprove of, but which earn that other's attention and engagement, suggests that the desire for interaction is sometimes stronger than the desire for acceptance or approval. When my two-year old daughter Ruby, for instance, sticks her fingers in her yoghurt and smears it all over the dining room table, she would not seem to be primarily looking for approval. Rather, she would seem to be looking for something much more engaging (at least, for Ruby): getting mum and dad's attention, interacting with our pleas for 'a nice calm dinner time' and generally turning a dull meal time into a much more interactive affair.

This basic human desire for contact and engagement with others is so all-pervasive that it is easy to overlook, yet empirical research with adults suggests that it is one of the most basic human needs. A majority of people, for instance, say that the thing that matters most to them in life is relationships (Duck, 1998), and that being left out of social interactions is one of their biggest fears (Csikszentmihalyi, 2002). Human beings also spend an inordinate amount of their day making contact with others: whether face to face, or through emails, text messages or telephone calls. Indeed, anyone who has witnessed the young people of today furiously thumbing out text messages on their mobile phones cannot doubt the enormous human drive to relate to others.

There is also evidence that levels of health are connected to the experience of having others to engage with (Duck, 1998), such that the presence of one or two close confidants can be critical to an individual's physical well-being (Duck, 1998). We will explore this more fully in Chapter 2.

With respect to the person-centred approach, the position being outlined here does not contradict the Rogerian hypothesis that human infants have a powerful need for positive regard (Rogers, 1959; Standal, 1954). Nevertheless, in suggesting that human beings *also* have a need for something more interactive, bidirectional and mutual, we are outlining a model of human development that has subtle yet significant implications for the practice of person-centred therapy. If we start from the classical Rogerian (1959) position that the need for positive regard is a key driving force in human development – leading people to deny and distort those self-experiences that are inconsistent with the 'positive regard complex' – then it makes absolute sense that the therapist's practice should revolve around the provision of unconditional positive regard to the client. If we also hold, however, that human beings have a fundamental need for something more interactive, and that psychological difficulties arise when a person's capacity to engage with others becomes disrupted (see Chapter 2), then this points towards a therapeutic approach in which dialogue and interaction take more centre stage: one in which it is the *encounter* between the therapist and client, rather than the *provision* of a particular set of conditions *for* the client, that is conceptualised as being key to the healing process. This means that, in a dialogical approach to person-centred therapy, there is more of an emphasis on the therapist bringing herself fully into the encounter, and interacting with the client in a mutual and transparent way. She is not simply there as a 'container' for the therapeutic work or as an embodiment of a particular set of conditions. Rather, she is there as a real and genuine human being, and it is the process of the client being real *in relation to* a therapist being real, that is conceptualised as the crux of the healing process.

Not only would we suggest, however, that human beings have an inherent *desire* to interact with others. Drawing on recent advances in the field of child observation studies and developmental psychology research, we would suggest that babies are born with an inherent *capacity* to engage in such interactions. Studies with babies as young as 42-minutes old, for instance, show that they have the capacity to imitate such actions as sticking a tongue out, opening the mouth, and making surprise expressions (Meltzoff and Moore, 1998; Trevarthen, 1998). What is all the more remarkable is that, if an adult sticks out his tongue at a baby and then waits patiently, the baby may, even after two or three minutes, 'deliberately poke out the tongue to "provoke" another response from the attentive adult' (Trevarthen, 1998: 30). More remarkable still, by the age of six weeks, infants can reproduce gestures after a day's interval, and specifically towards the person who had made those gestures in the first place! This suggests, then, that these imitative behaviours are not simply reflex actions, but volitional attempts by the baby to engage with another, perhaps as a means of testing that person's identity (Trevarthen, 1998).

Furthermore, the fact that new-born infants can imitate the gestures and movements of another indicates that human beings are born with some capacity to compare the actions of another to their own. That is, they must have some innate ability to know whether another person is 'like them'. This means that human beings must come into the world with some rudimentary-yet-complex ability to understand other people (Trevarthen and Hubley, 1978): some in-built readiness to know another's state (Trevarthen, 1980). Trevarthen (1998) refers to this as an 'effective interpersonal intelligence' and he suggests that this sensitivity to other human beings exists long before the development of cognitive skills for thinking about inanimate objects (Trevarthen, 1980). Beatrice Beebe and colleagues (2003a) refer to this intelligence as an 'innate sympathetic consciousness'. As further evidence of this interpersonal intelligence, Meltzoff and Moore (1998) cite research which shows that infants, by the age of 18 months, are already able to perceive another's intentions behind their action. If, for instance, they see someone try to do something but fail halfway through, they will imitate what the person was *trying* to do (i.e. the intended behaviour) rather than what they *actually* did (i.e. the failed behaviour). By this age, then, infants must have developed some notion of 'other's minds' – that others have thoughts and intentions behind their actual, overt actions.

Not only is it the case, however, that babies seem to come into the world with an interpersonal intelligence; they also seem to be born with an innate attraction towards human-like features. Research shows, for instance, that infants, only minutes old, are more interested in a set of shapes when they are organised in a face-like arrangement than when they are scrambled up (Dziurawiec, 1987; Goren et al., 1975); and they show a particular interest in the human organs of communication such as eyes, hands, and mouths (Trevarthen, 1979). Very young infants also react to speech sounds with particular interest and show a preference for the pitch characteristics of the voice as against non-voice sounds (Trevarthen, 1979).

As we have already seen with respect to imitation, however, it is not simply the case that very young infants respond to the actions and characteristics of others in passive and reflexive ways. Rather, infants seem to come into the world with an innate capacity to take a *proactive* role in interpersonal interactions. In other words, they are not only designed to elicit care, but also to affect those caretakers intimately (Trevarthen, 1980). Studies of gazing between infants and caretakers, for instance, show that babies 'exert major control over the initiation, maintenance, termination and avoidance of social contact' (Stern, 2003: 21). Two-month-old infants can stop and start activities with caretakers, and may also make moves to recover communication if a caretaker fails to display affection (Trevarthen, 1979). This is powerfully demonstrated in studies where a mother is instructed to freeze her expressions in the midst of a happy communicative exchange. Here, babies will respond with a range of complex emotional responses: sudden waving of the arms or grimaces of excitement while staring at the mother's face, as if appealing for re-engagement (Trevarthen, 1979). In terms of having an innate capacity to communicate with others, photographic and video evidence also shows that infants are born with the ability to make almost every facial expression that is present in adults, as well as the mouth and tongue movements associated with speech (Trevarthen, 1979).

Hence, in terms of human interrelating, babies would seem to come into the world with some ability both to receive and transmit interpersonal communications; and by ten to 11 months they can be considered highly competent communicators (Newson, 1978). More than this, what the developmental research shows is that very young infants have an ability to *synchronise* their behaviour with adults in a mutually regulated, cooperative and 'co-intentional' (i.e. towards the same goal) exchange. Based on observations of a young infant's exchanges with her mother, for instance, anthropologist Mary Bateson described how, 'the mother and infant were collaborating in a pattern of more or less alternating, non-overlapping vocalisations, the mother speaking brief sentences and the infant responding with coos and murmurs, together producing a brief joint performance similar to conversation' (quoted in Trevarthen, 1998: 23). Bateson termed these interactions 'proto-conversations', and they would seem to be the precursors for subsequent 'proto-language' at nine to ten months (Trevarthen, 1979) as well as the many different forms of dialogue and interpersonal exchange that human beings enter into in later life.

At the heart of this proto-conversation is the infant's ability to take turns and empirical research suggests that some kind of synchronicity is inherent to even the youngest of infant's functioning. Right from the first days of life, for instance, babies seem to cycle between periods of interest/attention and avoidance/inattention, and it has been proposed that these alternations may be the precursors to subsequent interpersonal exchanges (Shaffer, 1996). Such ability to turn-take can also be seen in the endless capacity that young infants seem to have to play games such as peek-a-boo, where the cyclical movement between action, response and counter-response mirrors the dialogical structure of later adult communications.

Evidence from child observation studies thus seems to be suggesting that the human brain is specialised for mutual regulation of joint action (Beebe et al., 2003b), and very recent discoveries in the neurobiological field provide some tentative support for this. Here, researchers have discovered a special type of cell in primate brains, termed 'mirror neurons', which are activated when a particular activity is observed as well as when that activity is performed (Wolf et al., 2001). This discovery suggests that the human capacity to imitate, understand, empathise with, and synchronise with others may, indeed, have a biological and innate basis.

As with the philosophical advances discussed earlier, the intersubjective developments discussed here have important implications for the practice of counselling and psychotherapy. If human beings come into the world fundamentally orientated towards others then, again, it would make sense to suggest that the therapist–client relationship is often of paramount importance in therapy, because it is the crucible in which the client can explore, revise and heal that which is most central to who they are. Moreover, if human beings come into the world with a need for engagement with others, then the therapeutic relationship is one context in which this need may be met at a very deep level. We will explore this more fully in Chapter 2.

The Development of Relational Therapies

Given the developments outlined above, it should come as no surprise that recent years have witnessed a growth in relational and intersubjective approaches to counselling and psychotherapy. Drawing on the work of Martin Buber, for instance, Maurice Friedman (1985) has developed a 'Dialogic Psychotherapy' which considers the meeting between therapist and client as the central mode of healing. Likewise, feminist psychodynamic therapists, such as Judith Jordan (1991b; 2000), have been involved in the development of relationally orientated therapies in which empathic attunement is considered the key to the developmental process. In recent years, the field of psychotherapy has also witnessed a rapid growth in 'interpersonal' approaches to therapy (e.g., Stuart and Robertson, 2003), which focus on helping clients to reflect on, and revise, their specific modes of relating to others.

Alongside this, relationally orientated variations of many of the more established therapeutic approaches have begun to spring up. In the field of gestalt therapy, for instance, Richard Hycner (1991; Hycner and Jacobs, 1995) has developed a dialogical form of practice that, drawing on the work of both Martin Buber and Maurice Friedman (1985), aims to help clients develop the possibility of a mutual encounter with their therapist. Relational approaches have also emerged within Transactional Analysis (Hargaden and Sills, 2002). Even in the cognitive-behavioural field, traditionally regarded as one of the least relationally orientated therapies, interpersonal factors are increasingly being considered as change elements in their own right and not just the vehicles for different techniques (Giovazolias, 2004). Here, there is also a growing recognition that cognitive-behavioural techniques are only ever effective if they are grounded in a good working alliance between therapist and client (Grant et al., 2004).

It is within the psychodynamic and psychoanalytic fields, however, that some of the most striking movements towards a relational, intersubjective therapy have been made (see Mitchell (2000) for an excellent overview). Here, writes Daniel Stern, current thinking 'has moved a great distance in the recent past from a one-person to a two-person psychology' (2004: 77). Mitchell refers to this as a 'relational turn' (2000: xiii). Such are developments in this field that there now exists an International Association for Relational Psychoanalysis and Psychotherapy, and a journal of relational perspectives, *Psychoanalytical Dialogues*. Moving on from classical psychoanalytic thinking, relationally orientated psychoanalysts such as Darlene Ehrenberg (1992), Daniel Stern (2004) and Robert Stolorow and colleagues (1987) all argue that psychotherapists should not be seen as 'blank screens' on to which the client projects their subjectivity, but as real human beings who interact with their clients in a bi-directional way. Such developments have also led to changes in the conceptualisation of therapeutic practice, with a greater emphasis on exploring here and now interactions and the creation of a warm, collaborative and mutual relationship. Such is the extent of these changes that, in some instances, psychoanalysts have been ready to reject some of the central tenets of psychoanalysis. Ehrenberg, for instance, writes that: 'For some patients, the fact that someone is willing to listen, interested in their experience, interested in knowing them, able to enjoy being with them, and willing to hang in there even when the going is rough, may have greater significance than any interpretation' (1992: 23).

From a person-centred standpoint, it is encouraging to see so many therapists make this relational turn (though the infrequency with which person-centred writings are referenced or acknowledged can be frustrating; see Bott, 2001). To a great extent, person-centred therapy can be considered the original relational therapy: one in which it is the quality of the therapist–client relationship that is deemed to be the primary source of therapeutic change (Rogers, 1957). At the same time, however, as already discussed in this book, there are elements of a classical approach to person-centred therapy that are less consistent with an intersubjective, dialogical standpoint. Rogers' ideas were inevitably embedded in the modernist outlook of his time and culture, and many of his beliefs, for instance that self-development involved a move towards greater autonomy and self-direction (Rogers, 1961), betray a strongly individualistic starting point. Within the person-centred field, there is also a tendency to focus on the therapist's experiences and communications *towards* the client (e.g. empathy, positive regard) (Rogers, 1957), rather than the bi-directional, mutual encounter *between* therapist and client. (This is one reason why much of the research in the psychotherapy field has moved away from an investigation of the core conditions, because it is actually the therapeutic alliance *between* therapist and client that is generally a better predictor of positive therapeutic outcomes.) Recent years, however, have seen some important advances towards a more intersubjective, dialogical person-centred therapy. At the forefront of developments here is the Austrian therapist Peter Schmid (2001a; 2001b; 2002; 2003) who draws on the work of Martin Buber, as well as the French philosopher Emmanuel Levinas (1969), to propose that the heart of a person-centred approach is a dialogical *en-counter*. Dave Mearns and Brian Thorne (2000) have also initiated a move away from an emphasis on individual actualisation, towards a greater acceptance of the need to actualise social and interpersonal needs. At the same time, Mick Cooper, (2005), like one or two other person-centred and experiential therapists (e.g., van Kessel and Lietaer, 1998) has begun to examine interpersonal dynamics from a person-centred standpoint. Dave Mearns' work on relational depth (1997c; 2003a) is, of course, another attempt to develop the relational and intersubjective dimensions of person-centred practice; and, in this book, we hope to make the most serious foray yet towards a *two*-person-centred therapy.

The picture in the field of existential therapy is somewhat similar. To a great extent, founders of the existential therapy movement, such as Rollo May, Medard Boss and R.D. Laing, were among the first practitioners to suggest that a genuine meeting between therapist and client lay at the heart of a truly healing relationship (see Cooper, 2003a). At the same time, the writings of many of the existential therapists – particularly American existential-humanistic therapists such as Irvin Yalom (1980) – carry a deeply individualistic sentiment, emphasising the 'inexorable aloneness' of human beings and the need for people to disentangle themselves from others. In recent years, however, existential therapists like Ernesto Spinelli (1997; 2001) in the

United Kingdom have developed a more intersubjective form of practice, in which therapists are encouraged to enter into their clients' relational worlds and to use the therapeutic relationship as a means of exploring how the client interacts with, and experiences, others. Interestingly, in more recent times, existential therapists like Irvin Yalom also seem to be placing more emphasis on human interrelating and the therapeutic encounter (see his excellent collection of 'tips' for therapists, Yalom, 2001), and less on the 'ultimate aloneness' of human beings.

Where Next?

Based on the above review of research, theory and practice, we can be relatively certain of a number of things. First, it would seem clear that the quality of the relationship between therapist and client is a key factor in determining the effectiveness of the therapeutic work. Put simply, the better the relationship, the better the outcome seems to be. Second, it seems possible that human beings are less individual than modern Western society has led us to believe; and third, human beings would seem to be inherently motivated towards, and capable of, forming, relationships with other persons. Third, many therapeutic approaches would seem to be moving in a relational, intersubjective and dialogical direction. All this would suggest, then, that if we want to help our clients as much as possible, we should pay attention to the quality of the therapeutic relationship.

But what actually happens between therapist and client? Despite all the research on the particular therapeutic variables correlating with positive outcomes, the reality is that we still know very little about the actual processes and dynamics that take place between therapist and client, and how these might lead to significant therapeutic change (Bachelor and Hovarth, 1999). Indeed, in many respects our understanding of the key relational variables and the kind of change they might bring about has developed little since Rogers' (1957) first assertion of the necessary and sufficient conditions for therapeutic personality change. Thus, there is a need to develop our theories about what happens in therapeutic relationships, and develop models of how particular relational processes may bring about particular types of psychological benefit. Furthermore, given that much of the research tends to focus on relatively surface-level therapeutic variables, like levels of collaboration, what needs exploring and theorising about is the much more intensive and in-depth feelings of connection, intimacy and encounter that can emerge within the therapeutic relationship. Here, we know virtually nothing; and yet, as we shall see, these experiences of connection are absolutely central to many therapists' accounts of how therapy works.

Before we examine the phenomenon of relational depth in more detail, however, we want to develop our argument for why such a relationship may be so important in therapy. In Chapter 2, therefore, we will look at a range of psychological problems and show how they may be intimately related to difficulties that people have in establishing in-depth connections in their lives.

2 PSYCHOLOGICAL DISTRESS: A RELATIONAL UNDERSTANDING

Dennis

Dennis, a client of mine [in this chapter, the first person will again refer to Mick Cooper], was a fifty-something head librarian who was trapped in a particularly vicious spiral of conflict with his wife, Tsui. Dennis was highly stressed at work, but did not feel that he could tell Tsui about his difficulties because he did not want to 'burden' her with all his problems. He also did not want to appear weak and vulnerable. Unfortunately, the effect that this lack of openness was having on his wife was quite the opposite of what Dennis wanted. She knew something was going on because he was so irritable all the time, but because he would not say what was happening, she felt confused, not trusted and excluded from his life. Consequently, she got frustrated and angry with him, and even threatened to have an affair with a colleague of hers at work. This, then, further compounded the situation. Dennis got furious with Tsui, could not sleep, got less work done, and consequently became even more stressed and irritable; which then led Tsui to feel even more confused.

Rebecca

Rebecca, a chef in her twenties, was another of my clients. She came to therapy hoping to overcome her feelings of depression and her growing addiction to alcohol. In the first session, Rebecca talked 'at' me almost without a break: about her problems at work, about her interfering mother, and most of all about her 'useless lump' of a boyfriend, Ewan. Session two was something similar. For me, it was like being bombarded by words: an incessant

(Continued)

(*Continued*)

stream of opinions and character assassinations – all delivered in an affectless, monotonic way – with which it felt almost impossible to engage. In session three, Rebecca slowed down a bit and started to talk more about her relationship with Ewan, about the fact that he never did anything, that she had to organise all their holidays and social events and that he seemed to be more interested in his games console than her. In this session, Rebecca began to verbalise some of her frustration and anger towards Ewan, but in session four, after Ewan had spent the whole weekend playing his console games, the wall of words returned. At the receiving end of this, I felt powerless, silenced and frustrated, and finally decided to share with Rebecca something of what I was feeling. 'Rebecca', I said, 'I'm really trying to get a sense of what's going on for you, but I'm finding it hard to engage with, to find a way of communicating something of my sense of it all to you'. To my surprise, Rebecca took my feedback quite calmly, and said, 'that's what Ewan always tells me. He always says I never listen to him or let him talk'. When we explored this further, Rebecca came to acknowledge that her relationship with Ewan had got into a vicious cycle whereby the more he withdrew, the more she talked *at* him, and the further he withdrew. Rebecca felt that this cycle was mainly Ewan's fault, but she also accepted that she was often much better at telling other people what to do and talking at them, rather than listening to them. 'I think I'm scared that if I start letting people tell me what to do I might be out of control', she said.

In many respects, the difficulties faced by Dennis and Rebecca are very different. What links them, however, is that both clients seemed to find it difficult to relate to others at a level of depth. In the case of Dennis, the problem seemed to be that he found it difficult to express his true feelings to his wife and others. In the case of Rebecca, the problem seemed to be less one of expression and more one of 'receptivity', of not really being able to take in others and engage with what they were saying to her.

This chapter builds on the arguments presented in the previous chapter, providing further evidence for why a meeting at relational depth may be so important to our clients' development. Here, we will argue that many of the psychological difficulties that our clients come to see us with are, as in the cases of Dennis and Rebecca, rooted in a difficulty with relating to others in an in-depth way, or an absence of such relationships in their lives. Such an argument is consistent with wider moves within the fields of psychology and psychotherapy to understand psychological problems in interpersonal, as well as intra-personal, terms: a 'relational', or 'dialogical' model of psychological distress (e.g., Birtchnell, 1999; Segrin, 2001; Stolorow et al., 1987; Stuart and Robertson, 2003).

Loneliness

Perhaps the most obvious psychological problem that has, at its core, a lack of relationally deep contact with others is loneliness. This problem is more common than we believe (Duck, 1998). A large-scale study, for instance, found that around a quarter of people had felt 'very lonely' recently (Bradburn, 1969, in Duck, 1998). Loneliness may also be much more painful than many people assume. Studies of people's hour-by-hour thoughts and feelings, for instance, suggest that 'most people feel a nearly intolerable sense of emptiness when they are alone, especially with nothing specific to do' (Csikszentmihalyi, 2002: 168). A preado-lescent's description of loneliness powerfully conveys this sentiment: '[Loneliness is like] being in a deep dark pit, with nothing in sight, and no way out. It feels like a dark rainy day. Just there, just sitting there lonely. It's like a blue, a dark blue, almost a black, but then it's also a light blue, washed out and dingy. It's a deep empty pit in your stomach' (quoted in Moustakas, 1961: 40). Research also shows that lonely people report greater feelings of desperation, impatience, boredom, and self-depreciation, are more likely to suffer from depression and general medical complaints and to attempt suicide (Duck, 1998).

As most of us will know loneliness is about much more than just being on your own. Indeed, for many people, solitude is a profoundly rewarding experience. Equally, one can feel lonely in a crowd. Gavin, for instance, a handsome 20-year-old client of mine, said that he felt most alone at the pub with his mates. 'I sit in the corner', said Gavin, 'and just listen to the conversation going on around me. It's not that no one will talk to me, it's just that I can't really talk to anyone about what's going on for me, like the fact I feel so awful about myself or the fact that I can't get up in the mornings'.

For people like Gavin, then, the pain of loneliness is much less to do with the physical absence of others and much more to do with a lack of genuine human contact. As the American Professor of Communication, Chris Segrin writes, 'what the lonely person appears to long for are meaningful and intimate friendships' (2001: 41). Like many other lonely people, Gavin has a deep sense that others do not really know who he is, that others have not really touched down to the depths of his being and witnessed the hidden world that is there. Indeed, Gavin was well aware that others held a particular *image* of who he was, but the fact that this image was so incongruent with his own sense of himself made that loneliness all the more painful. People knew his mask, but no one had ever seen the face behind the mask, and this was profoundly upsetting and disturbing to him. Gavin also had a sense that he, alone, was shouldering the difficulties and challenges that he was facing in his life, that no one was there to help him, because no one knew what his struggles were. Furthermore, because he rarely encountered others at a level of depth and intimacy, he had a deep sense of alienation, of being outside of the nexus of everyday social interactions. For Gavin, everyone else seemed to know what was going on; everyone else seemed to talk to each other. But he was on the sidelines, alone, unknown.

Gavin's loneliness also evoked in him a profound sense of frustration and loss. While he was aware that he kept others at arm's length, he also desperately wanted to be seen and known by those that he cared about. Such psychological misery makes particular sense if we posit, as we did in Chapter 1, that human beings have an inherent need for contact with others such that to be without this closeness is to frustrate one of the most powerful human desires. 'Even in the deepest retreat', writes Hycner, 'there is a vague *restlessness of the soul yearning for a genuine meeting with others* ... It is as if the capacity for genuine dialogue and meeting has been lying dormant, in wait, for someone to seek out the real self' (1991: 65, emphasis in original).

Interpersonal Conflicts

As in the case of Dennis, interpersonal conflicts are one of the most common problems that clients bring to therapy; and here, the kind of relating styles that clients have are often the very antithesis of an open, intimate, reciprocal way of engaging with others. In the case of Dennis, for instance, his difficulties with Tsui seemed to be closely related to his tendency to hide his true feelings away from her – as he tended to do with everyone – and to engage in an incongruent and indirect manner. This had a number of consequences. First, because he did not tell Tsui how he was feeling, she was left to make inferences from observing his behaviours, and what she saw here – his irritability and aggressiveness – was only one very small part of what was going on for him. But because this was all she knew, this was all she could respond to, and consequently she acted towards Dennis in a way that left him feeling misunderstood and hurt. In a way, the real problem here was not that Dennis did not tell Tsui (as well as others) what was going on for him, but that he did not tell her and others, *and then assumed that they would know about it anyway.* So he assumed, for instance, that Tsui would somehow know that his irritability was benign and not directed towards her, such that his fury in response to her frustration and anger was based on a feeling of 'how can she be so insensitive to me when she "knows" how tough things are for me right now'. Interestingly, within the cognitive and interpersonal therapy fields, this belief that others can somehow read our minds – the 'myth of self-transparency' – is seen as a key cognitive distortion, associated with marital disputes (Stuart and Robertson, 2003) and with avoidant and paranoid personality types (Kaslow et al., 2003: 233). I have also written about it extensively in a recent journal article (Cooper, 2005).

Another problem is that, because Dennis does not tell Tsui what he needs, he does not get what he wants. This failure to 'assertively' communicate one's needs is, perhaps, one of the main reasons why some people do not get what they want in life; and, again, partially relates to people's assumptions that others will instinctively know what they want. Lucy, for instance, was sick and tired of her boyfriend going to the pub every night. When she talked about it in therapy with me, she explained how she would try and get back at him by going out with her mates, or by telling him he was drinking himself into an early grave; but the idea of honestly and directly saying to him, 'I wish you would spend more time with me' simply had not occurred to her.

At the heart of Dennis's problems with his wife, however, was not just the fact that he could not be open with her about what was going on for him. As we will discuss more fully in Chapter 3, to meet someone at depth requires a *receptivity* to them as well as an *expressivity*; and Dennis, like Rebecca, seemed to really struggle to hear what the other person was saying.

This inability to receive and acknowledge others may be as much a source of interpersonal conflicts as the inability to assert oneself: something which is likely to fuel resentment, frustration and rejection in the other. A person, for instance, who talks endlessly in conversations without allowing others a turn is likely to receive powerful negative responses from others. Jim, for instance, was a man in his mid-fifties who dearly loved his only daughter. He was immensely proud of everything she did, and would often tell his friends about her achievements – the medical career, the two grandsons – but whenever she would come to visit him and his wife, he would end up feeling rejected and hurt, as if he never quite got the affection he craved from her. His daughter Sandra's side of the story was this: she loved her dad, but whenever she was with him she never felt that he really listened to her. Whether they would talk about politics or her work, it always felt like he *had* to know better, had to show her and her mum how clever he was, like a little boy. It was as if he was closed to her, and although she sensed that he desperately craved her love and attention, she felt that she just could not give it. She resented it too much. She tried talking to him about how she felt, but he seemed closed to that too – he became very defensive and told her that she was just 'too sensitive'. Without really being able to respond to and take in another, then, Jim found that others would not respond to, and take in, him.

Other therapists have also highlighted the importance to psychological well-being of being able to 'receive' another. Yalom (2001), for instance, states that the ability to empathise accurately is as essential for clients as it is for therapists, and that we should help our clients develop this ability towards others. Similarly, Jessica Benjamin (1990), the feminist psychoanalyst, states that the aim of therapy should be that the client can experience others as *subjects*, rather than *objects*. Hycner (1991), relating this specifically to the therapeutic relationship, suggests that one of the indicators that a person is ready to end therapy is that they can see therapy from the therapist's side, as well as their own.

Another way of looking at this issue is to say that Jim, like some clients who come into therapy, does not seem to be able to engage with the actual person who is there in front of them. It is as if they are talking to someone from the past (transference), or someone who is highly critical of them, or perhaps, in the words of Buber, 'a fictitious court of appeal whose life consists of nothing but listening to [them]' (1988: 69). Mikael Leiman (2004), a Finnish psychotherapist, has done some interesting work here, showing how our talk (whether external or internal) is always *towards* someone, but the question is, is it towards the actual person we are *with*, or is it towards someone entirely different? If the latter, the chances of interpersonal misunderstandings and conflicts would seem relatively high.

Anxiety

'Solitude…is the mother of anxiety' states E.S. Wolf (quoted in Stern, 2003: 109) and it seems possible that many forms of anxiety may also be related to an absence, or inability to form in-depth connections with others. An individual, for instance, may be worrying that they are shouldering all their burdens on their own, and this may be because they have never really shared their problems with others, or formed the kind of relationship in which they feel supported or cared for. We can see this in the inordinate sense of relief many people experience just talking about their problems with someone else and having a sense that others know what they are going through. Indeed, it would seem that simply being on your own increases feelings of anxiety, and perhaps this is because, as Csikszentmihalyi (2002) suggests, when we are involved with others and doing things together, we are not thinking so much about our own problems and difficulties. Perhaps this is why so many of us experience our greatest anxieties at four o'clock in the morning, the time when even a partner may be asleep. What is more, without some external perspective on our problems to 'ground' us, our anxieties can easily spiral upwards, turning the most minor worry into the most major catastrophe.

One form of anxiety that may be particularly rooted in a lack of in-depth relationships is social anxiety. This is the most prevalent of the anxiety 'disorders' (Segrin, 2001) and can be defined as 'anxiety that results from the prospect or presence of personal evaluation in real or imagined social situations' (p. 44). Difficulties in establishing in-depth relationships may be a precursor to social anxiety for a number of reasons. First, if individuals do not experience mutually affirming relationships with others, then their views of social interactions are likely to be more negative. And, indeed, evidence shows that socially anxious individuals hold strong representations that interactions with others will go badly (Stuart and Robertson, 2003). Second, and closely related, if an individual does not experience honest and open encounters with others, then he may be unlikely to have much sense of how others perceive him. And because he is missing out on relationships in which others are likely to perceive him positively, he is likely to misconstrue others' perceptions of him in a negative direction. This is, indeed, the case. Research shows, for instance, that socially anxious people tend to underestimate their overall likeability and also the interest that they convey to a partner, while overestimating the visibility of their anxiety (see Segrin, 2001). Of course, it should also be noted that the relationship between social anxiety and difficulties in encountering others at a level of depth is a bi-directional one, as people who are afraid of social contact are unlikely to find it easy to become close with others. Social anxiety is also closely linked to the experiencing of loneliness (Stuart and Robertson, 2003) and it is likely that all three of these ways of being compound and aggravate each other, as well as themselves.

Depression

Of all the forms of psychological distress, depression is the one in which a lack of close interpersonal contact is most clearly implicated. Empirical studies demonstrate, for instance, that depressed people have less intimate, more distanced, and poorer quality relationships

(Birtchnell, 1999; Segrin, 2001) and, in many cases, lack close relationships altogether (Segrin, 2001).

The reason that this correlation between depression and the lack of close interpersonal relationships exists is likely to be due to a number of factors. First and most basically, as indicated earlier, human beings seem to be happiest and most alive when they are with others (Csikszentmihalyi, 2002) and this is particularly the case when the contact is intimate. As American Professor of psychology Mihaly Csikszentmihalyi states: 'There are few things as enjoyable as freely sharing one's most secret feelings and thoughts with another person' (2002: 188). Hence, if someone does not have such contact in their lives, they are likely to experience lower levels of happiness, as well as a sense that they are missing out on something and possibly also envy towards others. Second, there is the fact that people who do not relate closely, or well, to others, are likely to experience higher levels of interpersonal conflict, and the evidence suggests that this is closely linked to feelings of depression. Fifty per cent of women who are depressed, for instance, are in distressed marriages, where caustic and poor communication processes often exist, and where there is a lack of synchrony and responsiveness between partners (Segrin, 2001).

Not only is it the case, however, that the presence of poor relationships can be a precipitating factor for depression, but the lack of positive ones can be one too. Brown and Harris's (1978) classic study on depression in women, for instance, found that the absence of close, confiding relationships was a key 'vulnerability factor' making the women more susceptible to depression. In other words, people who do not have close relationships may be as happy as others when things are going well, but when problems start to emerge, they do not have the social support to help them through their difficulties. Hence, sadness, grief or feelings of loss may be more likely to descend into a deeper depression.

Of course, the reason that a correlation exists between depression and the quality of a person's interpersonal relationships may also be because depressed people find it more difficult to become intimate with others or have a tendency to push others away. Indeed, Segrin (2001) suggests that one of the key dynamics here is that depressed people have a tendency to seek out reassurances from others, requests which are initially met by sympathy, but which are increasingly met with irritation and rejection in the face of incessant demands for reassurance. Here, we cannot say that the lack of close interpersonal relationships has *caused* the depression, but it may still serve as an important mediating factor, making it subsequently more difficult for the person to re-establish a level of psychological well-being for the reasons discussed above.

Psychosis

Over the course of the twentieth century, several existential psychiatrists have also proposed that the development of schizophrenia may be attributable to an absence of close, dialogical relationships with others (Laing, 1965; Trüb, 1964; Von Weizsäcker, 1964). Their starting point, as suggested in Chapter 1, is that human beings have a basic need to interrelate. From this, they have argued that, without such encounters on the external plane, human beings will tend to encounter *themselves* on the internal plane, thus creating intrapersonal splits and fragmentations. Buber, on whom much of this work is based, puts it like this:

> If a man does not represent the *a priori* of relation in the living world, if he does not work out and realise the inborn *Thou* on what meets it, then it strikes inwards. It develops on the unnatural, impossible object of the *I*, that is, it develops where there is no place at all for it to develop. Thus confrontation of what is over against him takes place within himself, and this cannot be relation, or presence, or streaming interaction, but only self-contradiction. (1958: 93–4)

Buber is suggesting, then, that an individual who cannot reach out to a true Other and engage with them will strive to create some kind of Otherness on the internal plane. From this perspective, hallucinatory dialogue could be understood as a desperate attempt by the psychotic individual to attain some level of meeting, to encounter something even if it has no concrete form. The German psychiatrist Viktor Von Weizsäcker uses a similar approach to explain a schizophrenic individual's hallucination of a double of himself standing by his bed. He writes:

> [T]his delusion of a double is nothing more than the hallucinated restoration of a two-ness, after one has reached the unbearable loneliness. It is a representation of a misplaced synthesis of I and Thou, the cleavage of the I represents – for a moment – the relationship of the I to the Thou which has become unattainable. It is a substitute for the latter. (1964: 409)

A similar understanding of psychosis was developed by the Scottish existential psychiatrist R.D. Laing (1965). Laing argued that people who are predisposed towards psychosis have often experienced communication patterns in which their experiences were invalidated, distorted, entangled or 'mystified' – the absolute antithesis of an authentic, relationally deep encounter. For instance, when one of the young female schizophrenics in Laing and Esterson's (1964) *Sanity, Madness and the Family* tells her mother that she experiences her as domineering, the mother consistently ignores this and instead tells the daughter that she and her 'get on very well together' (p. 94). Such denial, Laing (1967) suggests, becomes even more ominous when it, itself, is denied; for instance, the mother tells the daughter that of course she is listening to her, but then goes on to repeat that their relationship is entirely perfect. Drawing on the work of the American anthropologist Gregory Bateson (Bateson et al., 1956), Laing also argued that the experiencing of 'double-binds' may be a particularly significant precursor of later psychotic onset. These are situations in which an individual is threatened with punishment if they do one thing, but also told – often at a more covert level – that they will be punished if they *do not* do that thing. For instance, a young boy is told, 'why don't you come and kiss your daddy?' but when he approaches him is told, 'now, don't be such a soppy boy' and when he moves away again is berated with, 'what's the matter, don't you love your dad?'

Under such circumstances, in which there is a 'constant shifting of meaning and of position' (Laing and Esterson, 1964: 96) and where the individual feels that they 'cannot make a move without catastrophe' (Laing, 1969: 146), Laing suggests that the person may withdraw into their own 'inner world'. In other words, they retreat into a private citadel of the mind and 'pull up the drawbridge', such that they no longer fear that others will annihilate them, and thereby have some sense of control and certainty. According to Laing, what they leave on the external plane is an empty, false shell – often a highly compliant persona – which they project out into the world to keep others off the scent of the 'real' self. As Laing writes, however, the tragic paradox is that the more the individual tries to protect their real being in this way, the more that it is destroyed. '[T]his shut-up self, being isolated, is unable to be enriched by outer experience, and so the whole inner world comes to be more and more impoverished, until the individual may come to feel he is merely a vacuum' (1965: 75). In Trüb's terms, by turning in on itself, the individual cuts itself off from the deep 'soul nourishment' of others (Hycner, 1991: 61). The person, holed up within their 'inner' world, experiences an increasing sense of deadness and desolation and, because their interactions with others are always at a level of detachment, they are experienced as meaningless and futile. Moreover, as discussed in the anxiety section of this chapter, because the self is never qualified by another, and does not experience the kind of reality checks that human interrelating can provide, it is in increasing danger of losing all touch with 'reality', descending into a world of fantasy and hallucination.

Empirical support for these existential models of psychosis remains sparse; and, indeed, in recent years, a growing body of evidence suggests that there is a strong biological component to schizophrenia (see, for instance, Plomin et al., 2001). Nevertheless, contemporary research also indicates that 'interpersonal communications and relationships play a vital role in this most serious mental health problem' (Segrin, 2001: 65). In his review of the evidence, Segrin identifies three particular factors, across which there is much overlap. First, as hinted at by Laing (1965), families of schizophrenics do seem to communicate in 'odd, idiosyncratic, illogical and fragmented ways' (Segrin, 2001: 71), with blurred foci of attention and meaning, and abrupt changes or drifts in conversation. This style has been labelled 'communication deviance'. There is also evidence that schizophrenia is associated with high levels of 'expressed emotions' in families in which communications tend to be critical, overinvolving, overprotective and emotionally reactive (Segrin, 2001). Empirical research suggests that a third communication style associated with schizophrenia is a negative 'affective style', in which critical, hostile and unsupportive messages are communicated directly to the psychotically predisposed individuals during conflicts. From such research, there is no suggestion that any of these communication styles *cause* schizophrenia, but it would seem that such disrupted forms of interpersonal engagement make some individuals more likely to develop this difficulty, as well as making it more likely that they will relapse after discharge.

Developmental Perspectives

So far in this chapter we have argued that a range of psychological problems may have at their core, or be compounded by, an inability to experience relationally deep connections with others, or a lack of such connections in one's life. Attentive readers will note, however, that in Chapter 1 we argued that human beings have an inherent capacity to relate to others in just this way. This begs the question, then, of how it might happen that human beings fail to develop this capacity to engage deeply with others, or how that ability might become suppressed.

In the previous section on psychosis, we already explored some ways in which this might happen. More recent and more empirically based, however, is the work of Stern (2003) (and see also Gerhardt, 2004) which has outlined a range of ways in which an infant may come to develop negative representations of interactions with others, and may therefore choose to avoid close interpersonal contact. Stern refers to such representations as 'RIGs': Representations of Interactions that have been Generalised.

First, suggests Stern (2003), is the possibility that the child will experience intolerable levels of *overstimulation* when interacting with their caretakers. For instance, if a child's mother constantly plays with him even when he does not want to, perhaps out of her own need for closeness and affection, then he may develop a representation of inter-actions with others that says 'relationships with others are too demand-ing for me'. Consequently, he may tend towards avoiding interpersonal contact, or else become resigned and compliant when interacting with others. Where a parent is overbearing and takes too much space in interactions, it is also possible that the child will not be able to suffi-ciently develop their own capacity to communicate and interact with others, such that this potentiality fails to grow (Trevarthen and Hubley, 1978). At worst, if a child experiences a parent as overstimulating or overbearing, they may come to fear that their very selves will be *engulfed* by this other. Here, suggests Laing, 'the individual dreads relatedness as such, with anyone or anything or, indeed, even with himself, because his uncertainty about the stability of his autonomy lays him open to the dread lest in any relationship he will lose his autonomy and identity' (1965: 44).

Alternatively, the child may experience interactions with others as intolerably *understimulating*, perhaps because their caretaker is unre-sponsive, depressed or disinterested in them. This may then lead them to form representations of relationships as unrewarding and rejecting. As a consequence of this, they may then tend towards avoiding close contact because they feel that there is little that they can get from interactions with others. Alternatively, suggests Stern (2003), they may go in the opposite direction, becoming 'little performers' as a means of trying to get the interaction, closeness and attention that they crave; and perhaps, as adults, people who are unable to receive others because they are so desperate to have their own experiences received.

A third possibility discussed by Stern (2003) is that the caretakers may *selectively attune* to some of the infant's behaviours and emo-tions. For instance, they may fully engage with their daughter when she is bright and bubbly, but leave her to her own devices whenever she is sad or grumpy. This is similar to Rogers' (1959) idea that the behaviour and experiences of infants is strongly shaped by the condi-tional positive regard that they receive from their caretakers. Here, then, the infant may learn that it is only rewarding to interact with others when she is in a good mood; and that when she is feeling grumpy or depressed, she is better off on her own. Alternatively, through this selective attunement, an individual may come to develop a very rigid and narrow sense of self (Safran and Muran, 2000) – for instance, 'I am always a happy person' – as a means of trying to be the kind of person that others would like to interact with. This, again, is similar to Rogers' (1959) thinking: in this case the notion of a 'self-concept' that is inconsistent with the actual 'self-experiences'. Later in life, such a person may then find that they only tend to engage with others when they are in certain states of mind.

A fourth possibility suggested by Stern (2003) is that the caretakers may *misattune* to the child. This is a form of response in which the caretakers may match to some extent, but in a way that is still quite unaligned with the child. An example of this might be a father who responds to his daughter's squeals of delight by softly smiling, but then trying to dampen down her exhilaration with words like, 'now do not get too excited'. Stern suggests that such forms of mismatching may be particularly detrimental to the infant because the partial level of matching means that they gain entry into the infant's world, before distorting and undermining it. Here, infants can end up feeling that relationships with others are confusing or frustrating, or even that their experiences seem to be 'stolen' in such interactions, and hence they may tend to protect themselves by withholding their actual experiences from others.

Finally, there are *unauthentic attunements*, which are very similar to the kinds of deceitful forms of communication discussed by Laing (1965). Here, infants may develop the idea that relationships with others are profoundly disorientating, because others' overt expressions will be experienced as incongruent with what they seem to be conveying at a covert level. Total withdrawal into the self, then, can be a result of such a RIG.

Of course, in suggesting that problems with relating start to come about when caretakers fail to accurately attune to their children, we are not in any way suggesting that caretakers must be perfect mirrors at all times. Indeed, it is interesting to note that both Beebe et al. (2003a) and Safran and Muran (2000) emphasise the point that the issue may be less about the degree of matching or mismatching, and more about whether or not there is the potential to repair interactions when they will inevitably break down. So, for instance, if a baby smiles at her father and the father is so caught up in work concerns that he does not smile back, the question is whether he is able to acknowledge this lack of responsiveness and make up for it, or whether the infant's attempts at interaction are lost forever. Where the parent can repair the interaction, not only may the child develop a more positive RIG, but the infant may also begin to learn that failures of communication are manageable, as are *differences* in how people feel and respond. But where each breakdown in communication leads to an unbridgeable gulf between self and other, infants may come to dread any lack of matching or attunement, for fear that this signifies a total loss of connection. Later in this book there are numerous examples of therapeutic meetings at relational depth where a key ingredient is not that the therapist gets it 'right' all the time but that they can strive to repair the interaction when they get it wrong.

With respect to how RIGs develop, it is also important to point out that we are not suggesting here that these are laid down in concrete at an early age, determining the person's way of being in irreversible ways. Rather, RIGs are undoubtedly modifiable, if not, what would be the point of therapy! But often, what may happen is that particular RIGs come to reify themselves through feedback loops. A person believes, for instance, that interactions with others will lead to feelings of rejection and hurt, so they avoid contact with others and this means that others will tend to avoid making contact with them. And then, of course, because they see others avoiding them, their belief that interactions with others will lead to feelings of rejection and hurt becomes reinforced.

Before concluding this section, a final point can be made. Like numerous other models of psychological distress, what we are suggesting here is that children, at an early age, internalise certain representations of their world, and that these representations – where they are inconsistent with the actual world that the adult inhabits – may then be the basis for later psychological problems. What is different about the model proposed by Stern (2003) and outlined here, however, is that we are not suggesting that infants primarily internalise representations of another person, or of parts of another (as in internal objects), or even some generalised sense of what others will approve of (as in Rogers' (1959) 'positive regard complex'). Rather, what we are suggesting is that infants primarily internalise some understanding *of how interactions with others will be played out.* In other words, the child's primary learning is not that 'my mother is a disapproving person', but 'I experience hurt when I try to get close to someone like my mother'. Such a way of conceptualising things has a number of advantages. First, it is a less abstract and more 'experience-near' model of how people make sense of their world: that we do not think so much in terms of what other people are like, but more in terms of what will directly happen when we interact with them. This also means that it is an expectation, not just of how others might be at a conceptual level, but of a real, concrete encounter with another person. Such an understanding also makes it clearer why it is so easy to 'transfer' experiences from one person to another: because we are not primarily holding a sense that 'so and so is like this', but that 'when I engage in this particular way, these particular things seem to happen'.

Modes of Self-relating

Up to this point in this chapter, we have talked about relationships at an entirely interpersonal level. As Rogers points out in his dialogue with Buber, however (see Anderson and Cissna, 1997), we can also talk about a person's relationship *with themselves*; and also about *the relationships between different 'aspects' or 'facets' of a person*. What we will suggest in this section, then, is that psychological distress may be related to difficulties in *intrapersonal* encounter, as well as in inter-personal encounter.

Before doing so, however, a brief digression may be useful. Within the person-centred world, as well as within many other areas of psy-chology, psychotherapy and counselling, an increasing number of theo-rists and practitioners have come to suggest that human beings can be conceptualised as a constellation of different 'parts' – or 'configurations of self' (Mearns and Thorne, 2000), 'modes' (Cooper, 1999) and 'selves' (Barrett-Lennard, 2005) – as well as a unified whole. (See Cooper et al. (2004) for a recent dialogue among self-pluralistic theorists in the person-centred and experiential world; and Hermans and Dimaggio, 2004; Rowan, 1990; Rowan and Cooper, 1999 for broader overviews.) In other words, while Buber (1958) and the existential thinkers discussed above have tended to see self-plurality as an inherently problematic state, many theorists would now argue that it is a basic quality of human exis-tence. What these authors have also tended to suggest, however, is that there are certain forms of self-plurality related to psychological well-being and certain forms related to psychological distress, and what makes the difference is the level of communication and relatedness among the different 'parts'. More specifically, psychological well-being has been associated with open and dialogic relationships among the dif-ferent ways of being, while psychological problems have been associated with competitive, unempathic and abusive 'intrapersonal' relationships (see Cooper (2003b) for a summary).

Drawing these arguments together, Mick Cooper (2003b; 2004) has suggested that it is possible to talk about two specific modes of intra-personal relating: the first is called an 'I–I' mode, and the second an 'I–Me' mode. The I–I mode is a transposition of Buber's (1958) I–Thou attitude to the intrapersonal level, and can be essentially thought of as *self*-relational depth. Here, a person communicates to themselves – or from one configuration to another – in an empathic and affirming way, recognising different feelings, behaviours, thoughts or configurations as valid and human ways of being. In other words, in this form of self-relating, the person is open to their own 'Otherness' – in Rogers' (1986) terms, they are in touch with the unknown in themselves – they allow themselves to be impacted by it and to learn from it, while also recognising that that Otherness is ultimately part of them. For instance, a person who has had an angry outburst at a work colleague may feel bad about reacting to them in this way, but they are also able to stand in the shoes of their 'angry mode of being' and understand how they came to react with such venom. This is similar to what Jordan (1991b) refers to as 'self-empathy' and to the way in which 'self-acceptance' is used in Chapter 8.

The opposite of this I–I form of self-relating is what Mick (Cooper, 2003b; 2004) has referred to as an 'I–Me' self-relational stance. This is equivalent to Buber's I–It attitude towards others. Here, the person makes little attempt to try and 'get inside the shoes' of themselves when they behaved in a particular way and to understand how they came to act in that manner. Rather, the self, or a part of it, is criticised and objectified, or the person may attempt to fully disown that particular way of being: for instance, 'it was the alcohol/society/my parents/ my unconscious/and so on that made me do it'. Here, the relationship from self to self is more monologic than dialogic: a diatribe delivered to the self in which there is no interest in hearing back from that other way of being, or in acknowledging the legitimacy of that other part's needs.

With respect to psychological well-being, Mick (Cooper, 2003b; 2004) has argued that this I–Me form of self-relating is linked to the existence of psychological difficulties for a number of reasons. Most obviously, if a person primarily relates to themselves in a critical, or disowning I–Me way, then their sense of self-worth is likely to be relatively low, as well as their mood state. Second, such a way of self-relating is likely to be associated with a high level of internal conflicts, which are liable to absorb large proportions of the person's 'mental space', thus making them less able to achieve their in-the-world goals. Third, I–Me self-relations are likely to be associated with the creation and maintenance of 'subjugated' (Hermans and Kempen, 1993) or 'disowned' (Stone and Winkelman, 1989) ways of being. This is problematic for several reasons. First, because each of the configurations of self contains a valid need (for instance, to be heard or to be respected), the subjugation of this configuration will also entail the suppression of a legitimate and healthy desire. Moreover, because this need is part of them, it will not go away; and this means that it can create anxiety in the more dominant configurations, as it consistently bangs on the door of awareness, demanding repatriation. There is also the problem that the more the person tries to deny or disown a particular way of being, the more difficult it becomes to control it. So, for instance, in the earlier example, if a person disowns her angry outburst and says that it was caused by her colleague, then she will feel that she has no possibility of controlling it – after all, she did not create it in the first place! Finally, if a person does not create a communication bridge to the subjugated and disowned modes, then when these modes take over – and they will, because they are a legitimate part of the total organism – the person has no way of communicating 'back' to the more 'adult' configurations. In other words, when the office worker is in her raging mode, she cannot hear the voices of her inner adult or even her inner critic, because no bridges of communication have been built.

The hypothesis that psychological problems are related to difficulties in the way a person communicates to themselves has been developed very recently by other psychologists and psychotherapists interested in a pluralistic model of the self (e.g., Semerari et al., 2004). John and Paul Lysaker (2002; 2004), for instance, an American philosopher and psychologist respectively, have suggested that people with schizophrenia have a disrupted or suspended internal dialogue, such that they can only talk to themselves or others in monologic ways. Similarly, the Italian cognitive therapist Giancarlo Dimaggio has suggested that many clients with dissociative 'disorders' and some personality 'disorders' may experience a 'disorganised' form of internal dialogue, in which 'their mind's theatre is inhabited by a multitude of characters, each chaotically occupying centre stage and begging urgently to speak, without waiting for the question posed by another to be solved or the latter's desires to be attained' (Dimaggio et al., 2004: 192).

Discussion

In this chapter, we have suggested that many forms of psychological distress may have at their root a lack – or absence – of in-depth relating, either with others or with oneself. Furthermore, it seems likely that the forms of psychological distress discussed here are just some of those in which difficulties in in-depth encounter may be implicated. With the autistic spectrum disorders, for instance, an inability to empathise with others and poor communication skills would seem to be a common part of the syndrome (Comer, 1998); and some theorists are now beginning to link autism to interpersonal difficulties through the mechanism of mirror neuron deficits (Williams et al., 2001; Wolf et al., 2001; see also Chapter 1). Also, Segrin (2001) outlines a range of other psychological problems in which interpersonal difficulties may play a role, and this includes bipolar disorders, personality disorders, substance abuse problems and eating disorders.

Furthermore, as well as being causative and predisposing factors, it may also be that difficulties in interpersonal relating moderate and mediate the relationship between early childhood difficulties and later psychological problems. Whiffen et al. (1999), for instance, found that survivors of child sexual abuse were better protected from depression when they perceived their relationships to be of a high quality and more vulnerable to depression when they did not. This leads Segrin to suggest that 'childhood sexual abuse may cause later depression because it sets people up for interpersonal difficulties that interfere with establishing intimacy with others' (2001: 40).

Before concluding this chapter, however, it would seem important to put a few caveats in place. First, while we are suggesting that psychological problems may be related to difficulties in establishing or experiencing close connections with others, we are not suggesting that people should consistently and exclusively relate to others and themselves in this way. As Buber and many other theorists have suggested (e.g., Birtchnell, 1999; Greenberg, 2005; Safran and Muran, 2000), human beings have a need for interpersonal *distance* as well as *intimacy* and a healthy level of psychological functioning would seem to involve both. We are not suggesting here, then, that separation from others, or from oneself, is inherently problematic; simply that, when this is the only way in which a person relates to themselves and others, psychological difficulties may be a likely corollary.

In this book, we are also not suggesting that all forms of psychological distress can be reduced down to difficulties with intimate relationships. Hence, there is no suggestion here that relational depth is a therapeutic cure-all. Clearly, some clients' problems are more connected to relational difficulties than others, such that an in-depth therapeutic encounter will be of differing value to clients. A client, for instance, who has numerous close friends but cannot decide what he wants to do with his future may need less of an in-depth therapeutic encounter and more of a cognitive exploration of his various possibilities. Nevertheless, what we are suggesting in this chapter is that problems with encountering others and oneself at a level of depth may be more prevalent than we assume and may be implicated in a whole range of psychological difficulties. Hence, while a relationally deep encounter is not the be-all and end-all of therapy, it may be a crucial element in helping clients to overcome the difficulties that they bring to therapy. In the following chapter we will explore in much more depth what this encounter can be like.

3

THE NATURE AND EXPERIENCE OF RELATIONAL DEPTH IN COUNSELLING AND PSYCHOTHERAPY

What is it like to meet another human being at a level of relational depth? How does it feel for a therapist to really engage and connect with a client? Drawing on the interviews with person-centred therapists mentioned in the Preface, this chapter will explore these questions, focusing primarily on therapists' experiences of *moments* of relational depth. Towards the end of this chapter, we will also address the question, 'what is the therapeutic value of such moments of meeting?'

A Single Core Condition

From a person-centred perspective a relationally deep meeting in therapy is one in which all six of Rogers' 'necessary and sufficient conditions' for therapeutic personality development are present, with the 'core conditions' (3, 4, and 5 below) in high degree. These six conditions are:

1. Two persons are in psychological contact;
2. The first, whom we shall term the client, is in a state of incongruence, being vulnerable or anxious;
3. The second person, whom we shall term the therapist, is congruent or integrated in the relationship;
4. The therapist experiences unconditional positive regard for the client;
5. The therapist experiences an empathic understanding of the client's internal frame of reference and endeavours to communicate this experience to the client;
6. The communication to the client of the therapist's empathic understanding and unconditional positive regard is to a minimal degree achieved. (1957: 96)

Rogers (1973) was later to expand the sixth condition also to emphasise that the communication of the therapist's congruence should be received to a minimal degree, a dimension that is critical to the offering of a therapeutic meeting at relational depth.

Put succinctly, then, we would suggest that a therapist's experience of relational depth can be described as follows:

> A feeling of profound contact and engagement with a client, in which one simultaneously experiences high and consistent levels of empathy and acceptance towards that Other, and relates to them in a highly transparent way. In this relationship, the client is experienced as acknowledging one's empathy, acceptance and congruence – either implicitly or explicitly – and is experienced as fully congruent in that moment.

In response to the demands of the science of his time, Rogers had to break up his holistic concept of the therapeutic relationship into more operationally definable sub-variables. For therapeutic personality change to occur, however, he did require *all* of the therapeutic conditions to be present. This shows that Rogers did not believe that the absence of one condition could be compensated for by the presence of others in high degree. However, he did allow for some partiality in relation to the *degree* to which each condition was present: 'If all six conditions are present, then the greater the degree to which conditions 2–6 exist, the more marked will be the constructive personality change in the client' (1957: 100). In other words, while all the conditions had to be present to some degree, he did accept that, for example, the therapist's empathy, unconditional positive regard or congruence might vary in degrees and that the outcome would consequently vary.

Our assertion, however, is that the full power of the therapeutic relationship – as manifested in relational depth – is best regarded as a gestalt comprising the core conditions in high degree and in mutually enhancing interaction. This is a view shared by many other leading figures within the person-centred field (e.g. Lietaer, 2002; Merry, 2004; Wyatt, 2001), and is supported by empirical evidence which suggests that a high degree of correlation is often found among the three 'core' conditions of empathy, unconditional positive regard, and congruence (see Bohart et al., 2002). In other words, while many person-centred therapists have been trained to conceptualise these three conditions as discrete variables, in reality it may be more appropriate to think of them as facets of a single variable: relational depth. More specifically, as Bohart and colleagues suggest, we might think of empathy, congruence and unconditional positive regard as analogous to the hue, brightness and saturation of a colour. 'While in principle any given color can be dissected into these three qualities, the impact of that particular color depends on all three' (2002: 102). In this sense we are not deviating from Rogers' grounding but we are trying to re-emphasise its integrative power. In the following sections, then, while we will talk about different components of the relationally deep encounter, it is important to bear in mind that we are not talking about separate or additive components but facets of a single whole. That is, we are not saying that 'relational depth = empathy + involvement + etc.' but that 'relational depth' = an 'empathic-involved-etc. way of being'.

Our description of moments of relational depth starts from the standpoint of the therapist and we will talk about therapists' experiences of realness, empathy and affirmation towards their clients at these times. As we will emphasise throughout this book, however, an encounter at relational depth is not something that a therapist can create, or experience, alone, and the next part of this chapter goes on to look at the client's contribution to a relationally deep encounter in terms of openness. We then draw these two sides of a relationally deep meeting together by looking at the mutual, interactive and bi-directional nature of this encounter. Finally, we will say something of why such meetings may be so important for therapy.

Presence

When two people come together in a wholly genuine, open and engaged way, we can say that they are both fully *present*. Rogers (1986) wrote about this experience of 'presence' in some of his later works, describing it as a time when he is closest to his inner self, in a slightly altered state of consciousness and behaving in 'strange and impulsive' ways that seem to be of great value to the client. The concept of presence has also been discussed and researched by person-centred and experiential therapists such as Brian Thorne (1992) and Shari Geller (Geller and Greenberg, 2002), as well as by American 'existential humanistic' therapists (e.g. Bugental, 1976; Schneider, 2003; Yalom, 2001). James Bugental (1976: 36), one of the foremost writers on this phenomenon, has described presence as being 'totally in the situation' and distinguishes between two, wholly interrelated, aspects of presence: an intake side that he refers to as 'accessibility' and an output side that he refers to as 'expressivity'. For Bugental, accessibility is the willingness to allow what happens in a situation to matter to oneself and to be impacted by it, while expressivity refers to the willingness to share oneself in a situation. This is very similar to Jordan's (1991a) suggestion that at times of mutual intersubjectivity people have a stance of both 'receptivity' and 'initiative' towards each other (see Preface).

Realness

From the therapist's standpoint, perhaps the most fundamental aspect of a meeting at relational depth is a complete genuineness and transparency in the encounter. As one of the therapists we spoke to put it, 'there's something about being absolutely there just as a person'. Here, the therapist is not play-acting the role of 'counsellor' or 'psychotherapist', but is simply being herself in the meeting. As Mearns (1997c) writes, at this level of relating, the therapist has done away with 'lace curtains' and 'safety screens': defences that she may have developed to give the appearance of intimacy while at the same time protecting herself from the reality of a genuine human encounter. So, for instance, the therapist does not adopt the persona of a cold, detached and dehumanised blank screen – as some therapists may have mistakenly understood Freud to urge them to do so (Wolitzky, 2003) – and neither do they play the part of the overly effusive and ever-smiling caricature of a 'person-centred' counsellor. Rather, in these moments of relational depth, there is 'a willingness and ability to reveal one's own inner states to the other person, to make one's needs known, to share one's thoughts and feelings, giving the other access to one's subjective world' (Jordan, 1991a: 82). Here, there is also a naturalness, a spontaneity and a willingness to take risks: a trust that by being most fully human, the client can be most fully helped.

In relation to being real, Geller and Greenberg (2002) emphasise the way that, at these times of presence, the therapist is in touch with their experiencing on a multitude of levels: the physical, emotional, mental and visceral. This means that their mode of engagement with their client is not just cognitive, but also brings in their feelings and even their physical sensations. Mick Cooper (2001) has referred to this latter way of being as 'embodied empathy', in which the therapist is able to be fully responsive to their clients as a cognitive-affective-embodied whole (see Chapter 7).

At these times of relational depth, the therapist is also in touch with their vulnerabilities, uncertainties and confusions, and may well bring these aspects of themselves into the therapeutic relationship. Indeed, as we shall see in Chapter 7, it is often through articulating such aspects of their experiencing that the door to an in-depth encounter is opened.

From an intersubjective standpoint, then, a person-centred approach to therapy in no way requires therapists to 'shed' their personalities or to fuse or merge with their clients, as is sometimes assumed. Nor does it require therapists to become sounding boards for their clients; or, worse, nodding dogs! Too often, people's image of the therapeutic conditions is of a relationship where the therapist is a passive recipient of the client's expressions and is active only in equally passive reflection. This caricature is sometimes reinforced by therapists who actually do endeavour to hide their personhood and who, generally, have an inadequate understanding of congruence, seeing it only as a dramatic event trying to retrieve systematic earlier incongruence rather than a constant process of presenting the client with a different human being to reflect their experiencing (Mearns and Thorne, 1999: 92). A meeting at relational depth requires the therapist to be the unique, genuine human being that they are: a solid and grounded 'Otherness' with which the client can interact. In Stern's terms, the encounter must carry the therapist's 'personal signature' (2004: 168). This is because, if the therapist were to 'become' the client, then any form of relating would be impossible: you cannot relate to something that you are! Relationship requires difference (Schmid, 2002) and a meeting at relational depth can be understood as a very special encounter in which two human beings meet each other in a full and intense way, all the time holding on to their uniqueness and individuality.

Empathy

While the therapist's genuineness is an essential facet of the relationally deep encounter, we are not talking here about an inwardly focused self-interest. Rather, it is an honesty and responsiveness 'in the service of' the client: a responding *to the core of the client* from the core of oneself. Here, Peter Schmid (2002), adopting the terminology of Levinas (1969), talks about the 'Thou–I' relationship – a re-orientation of Buber's (1958) 'I–Thou' attitude, and one that may be more appropriate for the context of therapy, in which the experience of the client comes first and the therapist endeavours to perceive and understand (Schmid, 2003). In this relationship, the therapist's Otherness is called forth by the Otherness of the client, and this requires a deep, empathic understanding of the very essence of the client's experiencing. In his encounter with Rogers, Buber could not accept that an 'I–Thou' relationship could pertain in therapy where there was an obvious nominal power difference between the participants (see Anderson and Cissna, 1997). Perhaps this reframing in terms of a 'Thou–I' encounter might have helped.

Therapists that we interviewed described these in-depth experiences of empathy in very vivid terms. One, for instance, talked about seeing into the windows of the client's soul; and another likened it to walking into the same room as the client and really knowing that both of them were in the same place, even though they had both walked in through different doors. What also came through from these interviews was that, at these times of in-depth encounter, the therapists experienced an empathic attunement with the *whole* of the client's being. So there was an empathy, for instance, with both who the client was in the present and also who they had been in their past; or there was an empathic engagement with the client's different modes of being (see Chapter 2). Here, in particular, the therapists talked about the experience of being both with the part of the client that yearned for intimacy and the part of them that was terrified of closeness; or the part of them that wanted to be emotionally expressive and the 'gatekeeper' that wanted to stop any feelings getting out. In other words, at these times of relational depth, the therapists were not only attuned to that part of the client that was open, expressive and 'growthful', but also that part of them that was wary of the whole therapeutic encounter, in Mearns and Thorne's terms (2000), the 'not for growth' configurations of self (see Chapter 7).

Such an empathy with the whole of the client means that, at these moments of relational depth, the therapist is as attuned to the client's physicality and emotions as they are with the client's thoughts. Here, one might think of the analogy of the tuning fork, the therapist's body and feelings resonating with the client's own physicality. One of the counsellors we spoke to, for instance, said that, at these times of encounter, they were 'almost feeling like a mirror for what's happening inside the other person'. As was mentioned earlier, Mick Cooper (2001) referred to this whole-bodied empathy as 'embodied empathy'. He writes:

> In this mode of embodied attunement, the therapist is not resonating with specific thoughts, emotions or bodily sensations, but with the complex, gestalt-like mosaic of her client's embodied being, that initial primal thrust of the client's experiencing as it emerges into the world. At this level, the whole of the therapist's body is alive in the interaction, moving and vibrating in tandem with the client's experiencing. She experiences an all over unity and a most basic sense of being there in the world with another. (p. 223)

Such is the depth of this empathic attunement that it is quite common for therapists to experience themselves as highly 'immersed' and 'involved' in – or 'focused' and 'engaged' with – their clients and the therapeutic work at these times. Here, there is a minimal experiencing of distractions: thoughts that were previously invading the therapists' minds or external noises suddenly become irrelevant. Indeed, such can be the level of immersion that approximately half of the therapists we spoke to described their experience of relational depth in ways that would suggest that they were experiencing something of an altered state of consciousness, as hinted at by Rogers (1986) earlier. For instance, one of the therapists likened the experience of relational depth to being in a stupor, another talked about feeling physically lighter, and two talked about changes in their perception of time, for instance, 20 or 30 minutes seeming to pass instantaneously. At these times, therapists also described feeling very 'alive', 'energised', 'excited' and 'stimulated'; and one of the therapists likened his experience of relational depth to 'suddenly being wide awake'. Another therapist likened it to putting on her glasses: suddenly everything seemed so much clearer. Terms like 'more satisfied' and 'feeling right' were also often used to describe the experience of this in-depth encounter.

Interestingly, these descriptions of a relationally deep encounter bear many similarities to the experience of 'flow' described by Csikszentmihalyi (2002): a state of 'optimal experiencing' that can occur in any situation when a person's skills and abilities match the challenges facing them. Here, as Csikszentmihalyi reports, people experience feelings of enjoyment, effortless involvement, an absence of self-consciousness and transformations in the experience of time. At these times of relational depth, then, the therapist experiences a deep sense of resonance with, and immersion in, the client's world; but just as such an encounter requires the therapist to hold on to her own Otherness, so it requires her to be fully open to the Otherness of the client. In other words, at these times of encounter, the therapist is not simply assimilating the client's experiences into her own pre-existing conceptual frameworks and understandings. She is not thinking, for instance, 'this is horribly reminiscent of when I split up with my partner', or 'she really sounds like she's got a borderline personality disorder'. Rather, at these times of relational depth, the therapist is in touch with something unexpected and enigmatic (Schmid, 2002), something 'alien outside-of-oneself', something which always overflows the images and concepts that the therapist holds of it (Levinas, 1969). Not surprisingly, therefore, therapists will often feel awe and wonder at these moments of relational depth, struck by the sheer novelty and beauty of the world that is disclosed to them.

As an example, some years ago, Mick Cooper was working with a young female client, Paula, who was diagnosed with a potentially fatal illness. Paula came to therapy experiencing a deep sense of disorientation in her life, but what frustrated her most was her apathy and lack of enthusiasm for things. One session, as she talked about this with Mick, Paula described the way in which it often seemed so pointless to make a start on things, as the spectre of death meant that she might never be able to complete the projects that she began. And how frustrating and awful it would be to have her hopes and aspirations cut through like that. Mick, being an existential therapist, had read extensively about the anxieties that death can evoke (e.g. Heidegger, 1962; Sartre, 1958); but as he sat there listening to Paula, the real meaning of what it must be like to live with such devastating uncertainty came to life. It was a moment of awe in the face of such a totally unfamiliar, yet totally coherent, way of seeing the world, like finally seeing the three-dimensional image on one of those Magic Eye® stereograms.

Put another way, we can think of the relationally deep encounter as a meeting with something that is fundamentally 'counter' to the self (Schmid, 2002). Paraphrasing the German philosopher Romano Guardini, Schmid states:

> encounter means that one is touched by the essence of the opposite. In order for this to happen, there must be a non-purpose oriented openness, a distance which leads to amazement, and the freedom of initiative. In inter-personal encounter, both affinity and alienation can be experienced at the same time. So, encounter is an adventure which contains a creative seed, a breakthrough to something new. (p. 60)

Along these lines, many of the therapists that we spoke to said that, at those times of relational depth, they felt 'moved', 'touched', and 'impacted upon' by their clients; and it is interesting to note that, for the German psychiatrist Viktor von Weizsäcker, such 'touch-ability' is the most important quality of an effective therapist. He writes: 'It always seems to me to be of the utmost importance that in a comprehensive therapy the doctor lets himself be changed by the patient; that he lets the profusion of excitations that emanate from the patient have an effect upon him' (1964: 407).

Hence, there is no guarantee that the therapist who encounters her client at a level of relational depth will be exactly the same person as she was when going into the encounter. Like an abseiler who jumps from a cliff, the therapist who meets her client with the whole of her being – and in a spontaneous and unpremeditated way – no longer has any firm, external foothold from which to control or determine the encounter; no external position which can guarantee her absolute certainty and safety. Buber describes the I–Thou attitude, which has many similarities to a relationally deep meeting, as one that is 'perilous' and 'unreliable', in which 'the well-tried context' is 'loosened' and one's 'security shattered'. Yet in this loosening of one's security lies an enormous potential for growth. Buber goes on to state that 'the human being who emerges from the act of pure relation that so involves his being has now in his being something more that has grown in him, of which he did not know before and whose origin he is not rightly able to indicate' (1958: 140). As one of the therapists that we spoke to put it: 'maybe in a way you can say that I learnt something from them too, or– in a way, maybe it's a moment of change…in me as well. I'm a bit different'. Another therapist simply said: 'I take something huge from it'.

Affirmation

Not only, at those moments of relational depth, is there a reaching out to the client's Otherness, but there is also a profound valuing, appreciation and acknowledgement of their Otherness. Buber's (1958) term here is 'confirmation': 'an act of love through which one acknowledges the other as one who exists in his own peculiar form and has the right to do so' (Friedman, 1985: 134). One of the therapists that we spoke to said that, at these times, 'it's almost as if your heart opens'; and another, like Friedman (1985), spoke of 'love'. Here, as with the empathic component of relational depth, the therapist's affirmation is not extended to just one part of the client, but to the totality of her being: a 'multidirectional partiality' (Mearns and Thorne, 2000).

Our use of the term 'affirmation', rather than 'acceptance' or 'unconditional positive regard' is a deliberate one. What we want to emphasise here is that, at these times of relational depth, the therapist is *actively* 'prizing' (Rogers, 1957) the client (Rogers' favourite term for unconditional positive regard): it is far more than simply refraining from judgement, or holding an attitude of 'however you are is alright by me'. Here, there is a positive affirmation of the client down to the very essence of their being, a confirmation of their uniqueness, individuality and humanity. At these times, as discussed earlier, the therapist has a real sense of the intelligibility and wonder of the client's way of being, a deep valuing of how they are in the world.

Client Openness

Up to this point, we have talked about relational depth in terms of the therapist's way of being with a client, but a meeting at relational depth is not something that can be defined solely in terms of one individual. Nor is it something that the therapist, in isolation, can construct (Stern et al., 1998), for a meeting at relational depth requires two people, and a therapist can do no more than offer her client the possibility of such an encounter. Hence, we can distinguish between 'presence' as a coming together of congruence, empathy and acceptance at high levels in the therapist; and 'relational depth', which requires both the presence of the therapist, and *some form of presence or responsiveness from the client*. Presence is something that the therapist can offer to her clients – indeed, may need to offer – as a means of establishing a more in-depth relationship, and we will explore how she may do this in Chapter 7. But presence, in itself, is not the same as relational depth, for how the client responds to the therapist's presence will be a crucial factor in determining its quality. This is something that has historically been overlooked in the person-centred field, where an emphasis on the core conditions of empathy, congruence and unconditional positive regard – taken out of context from the other three conditions (see earlier) – can lead therapists to assume that it is their sole responsibility, and capability, to construct a therapeutically beneficial relationship. Indeed, it is paradoxical that *client-centred* therapy has, in its research and writing, focused so much on the work of the therapist. In recent years, this imbalance has been addressed, with some important explorations of the first and sixth conditions (e.g. Wyatt and Sanders, 2002) and a greater emphasis on the client's role as active self-healer (see the ground-breaking text by Bohart and Tallman, 1999). In fact, Rogers acknowledged this in a letter to Dave Mearns dated 4 January 1987, exactly one month before his death, stating, 'we have spent so much time looking at the part played by the therapist, and not enough at the part played by the client'.

Just as relational depth, then, requires the therapist to let down her lace curtains and safety screens, so it requires this from the client too: to share with his therapist those things that are most essential to his being. As one of the therapists we spoke to said, 'there's something about stripping down and paring away and coming to the core of something', and this often involves a willingness on behalf of the client to express those aspects of himself that are most vulnerable and frightening. At these times of relational depth, the client is also doing far more than talking about his difficulties in a rational and emotionally neutral way; he is there with them, living them, feeling them, sensing them, conveying them to the therapist in an alive and powerfully evocative manner (see 'Dominic' in Chapter 5).

In rolling up the lace curtains and safety screens, however, the client is not only expressing his real feelings and needs to the therapist, he is also 'receiving' the therapist's responses. Hence, just as relational depth requires the therapist to allow herself to be impacted by the client, so it requires the client to allow himself to be impacted by the therapist; and while a relationally deep level of contact will sometimes be achieved immediately, clients vary enormously in how far they will let the therapist engage with them. Indeed, this may be one of the primary sources of frustration for many therapists: that a client does not seem to be really 'letting them in' or engaging with what they are saying. Chapter 4 will explore this client variation in more detail, appreciating those clients whose systems of self-protection offer a sophisticated and stoic resistance to an encounter that carries a danger of exposing them to the judgement of others and, indeed, to the judgement of themselves as well as pointing to the demands this places upon the therapist to 'earn the right' to encounter.

In terms of letting the therapist in, what seems most central to the experience of a relationally deep encounter, as Rogers suggests in his sixth condition, is that the client allows himself to experience the therapist's warmth and empathy (and later congruence; see Rogers, 1973), at least to a minimal degree. This has many parallels to the idea of 'accepting acceptance', developed by the Christian existential philosopher Paul Tillich (2000). Here, Tillich writes about finding the courage and faith to say 'yes' to that which values and believes in us even if we cannot be totally certain of its existence. At these moments of relational depth, then, the client takes in the therapist's affirmation; he trusts the therapist and allows himself to encounter the affirmation that the therapist extends towards him. There is an acknowledgement that he is being acknowledged and a fundamental sense of knowing that he is known. One of the therapists that we spoke to described it as the client having their 'eyes wide open': 'they can perceive me and know that I am responding to them'.

Clients have also described this powerful sense of knowing that they are known. Emily reflects on her counsellor:

> It is an amazing feeling to feel so understood. I knew she (the therapist) understood me deeply. It wasn't just that she understood what I was talking about – it was that she understood how it feels to be me. Also, I could see that she understood how powerful her understanding was for me – that it 'took my breath away' as she said. It's funny, it felt like a 'relationship' in which we were *both* sharing. I suppose it was – what she was sharing was not about her own life – what she was sharing was herself, in relation to me.

A superficial empathy understands *what* the client is saying and feeling but it is a deeper empathy and congruence that communicates 'she understood how it feels to be me', and also that the therapist understood the impact on the client of this experience of being understood. Emily's experience of this as a 'relationship' in which they were both sharing offers us a fascinating insight. It really did feel to her like a relationship in which both people were sharing although the content was entirely about Emily and not the therapist. This is a nice reflection of a 'Thou–I' Relationship. It is a relationship with all the shared quality of an I–Thou relationship but its focus is on the client.

Mutuality

Ultimately, an encounter at relational depth is not one that can be neatly partitioned into the experiences of the therapist and the experiences of the client. There is an interpenetration, a complex gestalt of interweaving experiences and perceptions that makes it impossible entirely to disentangle who feels what towards whom. The therapist knows the client; the client knows that she is known; the therapist knows that the client knows that she is known. There is a co-transparency, a co-acceptance, a co-understanding, a co-receiving of each other – a flowing backwards and forwards between therapist and client through the channel that connects them. With respect to this co-transparency, one of the therapists that we spoke to said that these moments of relational depth were like the crystal clear waters of a pool, where both therapist and client can see each other right down to their very depths. It contrasts, she suggested, with the kind of murky pond in which all that can be seen is the surface.

For Stern (2004), this 'mutual interpenetration of minds', in which therapist and client know and feel what the other knows and feels, means that a shared, or 'intersubjective' consciousness, has arisen. Here, for a brief moment of time, two people traverse the same 'feeling-landscape as it unfolds in time': a 'shared feeling voyage'

> During this several-second journey, the participants ride the crest of the present instant as it crosses the span of the present moment, from its horizon of the past to its horizon of the future. As they move, they pass through an emotional narrative landscape with its hills and valleys of vitality affects, along its river of intentionality (which runs throughout), and over its peak of dramatic crisis. It is a voyage taken as the present unfolds. A passing subjective landscape is created and makes up a world in a grain of sand. (p. 172)

This sharing of intentionality is particularly significant for Stern (2004; Stern et al., 1998) and he emphasises the way that, at these moments of meeting, two people momentarily share the same aims (cf. the co-intentionality of infant and caretaker discussed in Chapter 1). They are moving in the same direction, towards the same goals and possibilities, and it is this 'interintentionality' that, for him, lies at the heart of a moment of meeting. At the same time, as both Stern and many of the therapists we talked to emphasised, a moment of meeting is not just about having a common future, but about meeting each other fully in the present: a being together in the right here and right now.

Intimacy

Like the string in a game of cat's cradle, as the interrelating weaves its way around and between the participants, so it draws them ever closer together. Other terms that can be used to describe the relationally deep encounter, then, are 'connection', 'closeness', 'contact' and 'togetherness'. In some of his recent writings, Dave Mearns, and co-author Brian Thorne, has used the term 'intimacy' to describe such a closeness of contact. They write, in relation to the client, Joan:

> In meeting 5 when, in Joan's words, the counsellor was 'willing to just be with me in my hopelessness and depression' we see a moment of intimacy. At times such as these, understanding between client and counsellor exists at many levels, as does acceptance. The outcome is a profound sense of sharing. Such moments, which can be marked simply by a gentle touch, a brief reciprocated glance, or even just sitting silently together, tend to stand out and to be remembered by both client and counsellor long afterwards. For the client whose history of relationships has been disturbed and whose self-acceptance is weak, such intimacy may be a unique experience and is therefore powerfully instrumental in the development of his self-regard. (1999: 144–5)

Meeting Without Words

As can be seen from this example, such moments of intimacy and relational depth often occur without words. Indeed, many of the therapists that we spoke to said that their most in-depth moments of relating occurred in silence: a second of eye-contact, a touch on the shoulder, a laugh shared between themselves and their clients. Stern gives the following example:

> As a regular practice, a therapist I knew shook hands with his patients when they entered the consulting room. It was a way of saying hello before they started to work. And at the end of each session as the patient started to leave, they shook hands again as a goodbye. One day the patient recounted a very moving series of events that affected him (and the therapist) deeply. The patient was sad and almost overwhelmed. At the end of the session, during the 'goodbye' handshake, the therapist brought his left hand up and

laid it on the patient's right hand, which he was already holding, in a two-handed handshake. They looked at each other. Nothing was said. The whole thing lasted several seconds. It was not talked about in subsequent sessions either. Yet, the relationship had shifted on its axis. Something vital was added to whatever had been said in the session – something so vital that the whole session was altered. The moment entered consciousness and was memorable. In fact, that handshake may stand out as one of the most memorable moments in the entire therapy. (2004: 19)

The Therapeutic Value of a Relationally Deep Encounter

In this last part of the chapter, we want to draw together the ideas and arguments presented in the first three chapters of this book to say why we think relationally deep encounters can be of such value to clients and the therapeutic process.

First, we would suggest that an intimate therapeutic encounter can serve as a 'corrective relational experience' (Jordan, 1991b) for clients, a 'counterbalance' to the '"absolute no" of the meeting rejected or withheld in childhood' (Friedman, 1985: 150). As we have argued in Chapter 1, human beings seem to have a basic desire – as well as capacity – to interact with others and when this is frustrated through inadequate or rejecting responses, the result is likely to be a deep sense of pain or loss. So when that person is met with an 'absolute yes', when their yearning for human contact and responsiveness is finally met, there is likely to be a deep sense of fulfilment and realization – in Friedman's terms, an 'existential healing' (p. 134).

Moreover, in experiencing such a sense of connectedness with another, clients may be able to move beyond their feeling of being totally alone, towards a sense that at least one other person knows who they are. And while this is just one person, the difference between feeling entirely alone and feeling one other person beside them can be immense. What is more, even if the contact with the therapist is only for one hour a week, it is something that can carry the client through the rest of their week, a little torch burning inside of them that reminds them that they are not totally alone in the world. Stern (2004) refers to such a moment of human contact as a 'fix', a touchstone of human connectedness that for that brief second reminds the person that they are part of a wider human matrix.

Through such encounters with their therapists, clients can also begin to *hope* that it is possible for them to establish more intimate and meaningful relationships with others. In the words of Darlene

Ehrenberg, 'sometimes just the discovery that certain kinds of intimacy are possible is significant' (1992: 67). This relates to the existentialist argument (see, Cooper, 2003a) that psychological distress is not only about what people currently experience or have experienced, but also about what they *expect* to experience. And if someone expects their life to continue in its isolated vein – or even for those feelings to increase – then feelings of sadness and hopelessness may be impossible to dispel. But if a client, in a moment of relational depth with their therapist, gets a glimmer that closer relationships might be possible, then this can reignite their sense of hope for the future. And just as isolation breeds isolation so a person who is more hopeful about establishing in-depth connections – through exuding a sense of possibility and encouragement to others – may actually be more likely to do so.

Frances, a woman in her late 60s, came to see Mick for over a year. She was deeply distressed that her relationship with her daughter had broken down, and felt that neither her friends nor her husband understood the depths of her pain. Frances made no major 'breakthroughs' over the course of the year, but as her therapy came to an end, she tearfully thanked Mick for the opportunity to talk to somebody, to share with another person all the disappointment and anguish that she was experiencing. 'I wish I could talk to my daughter like I can talk to you' she said to Mick. But although her relationship with her daughter was far from resolved, Frances had begun to make tentative steps to connect with her in a more honest and transparent way, and to begin to hear more of what she felt towards her mother.

This example illustrates another reason why moments of therapeutic connection may be so valuable to clients. Through relating to their therapists at a level of depth, clients may then develop the confidence and skills to relate to others in their lives in this way, and this may make a tremendous change to the quality of their lives as a whole. Clients only spend one hour a week or so with their therapists, but they will often spend many days a week with significant others so any changes in that domain are likely to be of enormous value to clients.

Referring back to the discussion of I–I and I–Me self-relationships in Chapter 2, we would also suggest that a therapeutic meeting at relational depth can help clients transform I–Me ways of relating to themselves into I–I self-relational stances, with all the benefits that this can accrue. What we know from psychology is that the way a person relates to themselves is often an internalised version of how others have related to them (e.g. Vygotsky, 1962). Hence, just as the experiencing of a critical voice in a parent may lead a child to develop their own 'inner critic' (Stinckens et al., 2002) so the experiencing of relational depth with a therapist may lead a client to relate to themselves – or from one configuration of self to another – in a more I–I way. Furthermore, as a therapist engages at depth with different aspects of the client's being, so these different aspects can begin to hear each other more fully. This simple notion of *empathic mediation*, whereby the therapist's empathy with one part helps the other to hear it can have a powerful effect on the rapprochement between the parts. Each begins to understand the other more fully and this, in turn, helps each begin to value the other rather than continuing the historic antagonism. Often the underlying therapeutic agenda is that an older, more protective part needs to accept the challenge of more expansive parts to move on in order not simply to recap the protections of old but to become more open to relating in the present and the future. The effect of the therapist struggling to meet all the parts encourages greater visibility of the parts to each other and a shared 'review' process. Parts may then begin to compare their functions in the past with the needs of the present and begin to move on – to 'reconfigure' (see 'Alexander' in Mearns and Thorne, 2000: 120–6). This gain in fluidity works to remediate problems in the self.

Another, more indirect, reason why meetings at a level of relational depth may be of value to therapy has less to do with the client's experience and more to do with the therapist's. When we asked our interviewees if they thought a meeting at relational depth was of value to therapy – and, if so, why – half of them talked about the fact that, at those times, *they* felt more engaged and invigorated, and this had a knock on benefit for their clients. At these moments, for instance, the therapists described themselves as feeling 'good', 'valued', 'confirmed', 'satisfied' and 'fulfilled'; one of them saying that, at these times, they felt like, 'I'm in the right place, I'm doing what I should be doing with my life at this point'. Another said that, with clients who were difficult to 'engage', 'it gives you the motivation to keep on going'. Such moments of relational depth, then, may also give therapists hope for the therapeutic work, and this may be important in sustaining their in-depth involvement.

Thus far we have been talking about the potency of moments of relational depth, but the clinical significance of the phenomenon also derives from the change these encounters bring to the ongoing therapeutic relationship. Experiencing the therapist at relational depth gives the client a *sense of safety* that far exceeds the norm for therapeutic relationships. Through that sense of safety they can begin to explore aspects of their self that are, for them, the most profound, aspects that they can rarely face themselves and would *never* share with another. There is an argument that, although the therapeutic relationship is characterised as especially open, still it is only the tip of the iceberg that is generally brought into the open – the vast bulk of the client's process lies unexpressed within the 'unspoken relationship' (Mearns, 2003a: 64–73). However, the safety engendered by the deepened relationship we describe allows more of these hitherto 'unspoken' dimensions to be brought into the open, yet still fearfully. Now the therapy may begin to tackle the 90 per cent of material that, in more surface-level therapeutic relationships, never sees the light of day. In this deepened conception of a 'relational' therapy there is the potential to work with clinical populations where the conflicts are so severe that some clinicians would even discount the possibility of establishing a therapeutic relationship (see Chapter 6). In the next chapter we will explore what happens when encounters at relational depth lead to a *continuing*, enduring relational depth and the parts of the client they may help to bring to the fore. In this sense, therapy at relational depth 'reaches the parts that other therapies do not reach'.

4 REACHING THE PARTS...

One of the main reasons why contact at relational depth is important is because it helps to establish a particularly potent therapeutic relationship which, in turn, creates a therapeutic space conducive to the client exploring issues that are of fundamental importance to them – for example, very private questions around their existence, the meaning of their life, their fundamental feelings about their own value and other such 'existential' questions.

The client, Helen, quickly appreciated the differentness of such an engagement at relational depth, seeing the offer of an in-depth understanding as both deeply attractive and deeply terrifying:

> In the first moments of the very first session I knew that I was done for. She (the therapist) met my eyes and did not leave them. I wouldn't be able to fool this person. I wouldn't be able to trick her into thinking that we were making a difference. If I took this person as my therapist she would get beneath all that crap. I did not want that – but I did want it.

Helen had experience of a few other therapists but what was striking for her in this first session was the power of the personal encounter. The contact was intense and immediate. Helen was used to a more superficial relating and a fairly second-hand or 'rehearsed' discussion of her issues. That detachment satisfied the part of her that was scared to make a difference but had wanted to see herself as making a difference. However, the engagement offered by this new therapist appealed to the quieter voice within her that really did want change.

Relational Depth Experienced as a Continuing Relationship

Most of our consideration of relational depth to this point has been in terms of moments of intense contact, often repeated such that the client begins to trust them and the greater depth offered through them. The dimension of relational depth addressed in this chapter picks up from this point and is characterised by a sense of shared commitment to the relationship and the work, a confidence that the Thou–I encounter is achievable at will and welcomed by both. There is a sense of the relationship being reliable over time and a confidence that relationship difficulties will be surmountable. Furthermore, there is a confidence that fluidity will be maintained in the relationship, that it will not atrophy and become stale. In many ways, we can see this more continuous dimension of relational depth as an acceptance by the client of what the therapist has been seeking to offer and, indeed, a reciprocation by the client.

When this enduring relationship is established, the client is offered a truly huge therapeutic space characterised by a strong sense of safety and reliability within the relationship. Also, it is a relationship in which the client, like the therapist, is an active partner (Bohart and Tallman, 1999). This therapeutic relationship is not reflective of a child's trust in the parent – both these persons are engaged in an adult relationship in which the various parts of each have a context to express themselves under the care of both persons. A corollary of this is that the relationship and both the people in it are not threatened by therapeutic endings – it is not a dependency relationship in any shape or form. The therapist may choose to end it just as might the client, and so be it. It is interesting to look at a meeting between this client and therapist some time after they have stopped working together, because there is none of the awkwardness often experienced by both parties. What they had earlier shared had genuinely been themselves, in a context where they knew that they were being fully accepted, so there is no fear that that acceptance will have changed over time.

One of the interesting consequences of this degree of mutuality in the therapeutic relationship is that there are absolutely no transference phenomena at this level of continuing connection (Mearns, 2002). This applies to relational depth in terms of the aforementioned moments of intense contact and also to the continuing dimension of relational depth. The reality is that transference phenomena belong to a much more superficial level of relating where people are still being symbols for each other. Where the client has accepted the relationship with this level of trust and is accessing very fundamental aspects of themselves, all this lies far below the level of transference phenomena. Interestingly, clients frequently comment on transference issues, often intrigued by their absence in this relationship. As one young male client said to his elderly male therapist: 'I am amazed to hear myself talk about all this stuff with an old man like you!'

Equally, at this level of relating, the client *cannot lie*. This may appear to be a somewhat strident assertion, unqualified as it is. Yet, the truth is that, at this level of meeting, lying is simply not possible. It would be interesting to have a philosophical perspective on this from someone like Peter Schmid. But the reality experienced in the therapy room is that when a client has dipped beneath the presentational level of self (see later) to speak from areas closer to his sense of his own existence there is no need for him to present himself in any ways other than how he actually experiences his self. 'Lying' and other forms of deception reflect our wish to present ourself in ways that we want to be seen by the other. In a continuing engagement at relational depth there is no desire to present an image of ourself. In the Preface to this book we noted the fact that a huge amount of the most crucial therapeutic material is often retained in the 'unspoken relationship' between the client and the therapist, that often therapy does not get to deal with the most important material because it remains unspoken. The fault here is that the therapy has failed to establish a continuing contact at relational depth such that the client feels safe to share himself in the way he experiences himself. All these conversations clients and therapists have about how clients 'hide' in therapy could disappear if they could actually establish a sufficient depth of relationship to speak to each other.

This is a qualitatively distinct relationship and recognised as such by both persons. Potentially it can have a particularly positive impact for those clients who started the work by being alienated to relationship. Often a mental health system effectively conspires with such well-protected clients to offer them forms of treatment that are particularly detached in relational terms. What we are describing here is the offering of a intensive and enduring relational contact such that might win the trust of the most fearful and alienated client. To get to this point of a continuing relationship at depth both client and therapist might have had to negotiate fragile process, dissociated process, ego syntonic process, the enormous fears of traumatisation or other forms of social disconnection or alienation. The client might have had to go through a considerable process of facing their fears, while the therapist, equally, had to survive their client's self-protective processes.

Testimonials from clients reveal the depths of safety that they can experience in a therapeutic relationship characterised by such relational depth, and how this can facilitate their therapeutic growth. The client, Jason, said of his therapist:

> I let her into the most private parts of me – the parts that were naked, tortured and so incredibly frightened that I thought I could not exist. Why did I let her in? Because she showed such depth and such peace and such warmth. She would meet me on so many levels at the same time, she would laugh at my joke, crack her own

joke and cock her head and gently smile and warmly show that she also knew the torture I was feeling underneath.

Jason is describing the fact that he let his therapist into his most private self-experiencing – a level of experiencing that is about the person's very existence in the world – how they experience themselves and the meaning, or otherwise, of their living. Jason is partly surprised that he allowed his therapist that most private entry but he also understands the power of the encounter offered by his therapist.

Another client, Bobby, said:

I did not trust *anybody* – certainly not a 'therapist'. Early on, when I saw him with Mary (Bobby's wife) I gave him all sorts of abuse and ridicule. One time I asked him why he continued to see me. He said, 'because you keep coming'. It was a bit glib – he probably could have done better than that. But he was right – there was a small part of me that wanted it. But my God, he had to put up with all the rest of my shit. Instead of being repelled, he even seemed to be interested in my shit, like he tried to *meet* the evil me. In the end that led me to meet that part of me as well and understand how I had become that way.

A client like Jason could respond positively to the encounter offered by his therapist even though there is always a degree of ambivalence about allowing contact at such a profound level of experiencing. However, for some clients, like Bobby, the system of self-protection that they have had to develop is normally very effective in keeping other people out. Bobby's system of self-protection pre-empted even the possibility of an encounter at relational depth by forcing potential 'invaders' out of relationship with him. Most characters like Bobby would not sustain therapy unless, as with Bobby, he began to experience a growing dissonance within his self where a part of him was becoming more and more dissatisfied with the restrictions he had placed on his life and relationships. The important feature of the therapist's behaviour that Bobby highlights is the determination not to fall into the trap of judging and dismissing Bobby but continuing to offer the core conditions, in high degree, to all the 'parts' of Bobby's self, even a part which Bobby himself described as 'evil'. Where clients are chronically governed by a pervasive system of self-protection, the patience and consistency of the therapist's encounter is a critical feature.

The 'Therapeutic Context'

Achieving a continuing, in-depth therapeutic relationship is not simply a question of the therapist offering the quality and consistency of relating illustrated earlier. It is also a matter of working within a therapeutic context which is sufficient for the client to take the risk to join the relationship. Carl Rogers (1957) omitted contextual variables in his evaluation of the power of the therapeutic relationship, suggesting that 'the therapeutic conditions' in themselves would be sufficient for constructive personality change to ensue. One of the difficulties he later ran into was in the Wisconsin Project, a study of psychotherapy with people with schizophrenia, where the contextual variables proved to be of considerable importance. For the long-term hospitalised schizophrenic patients, almost certainly with a considerable degree of institutionalisation, a regular but not particularly frequent therapeutic hour with therapists not of the hospital but coming from outside must have seemed like a pretty thin offer, no matter how relationally engaging the therapists might have been. As Bill Coulson pointed out in his critique: 'what if they [the patients] began to like it? What would they do when the research project was over and the sensitive therapist left? Who would accompany them? I think they believed they would have been foolish to accept the offer of therapy' (1987: 1). It must be said that the therapists involved in the Wisconsin project were extremely creative in the ways in which they sought cooperation and contact with the patients. Finding it frustrating to have only two appointments a week with a patient, many of which were missed, they initiated 'The Ward-Availability Project' which essentially meant therapists just spending time on the wards, meeting patients and looking for possible contacts that might carry on into therapeutic relationships (Rogers et al., 1967: 57–62). The reality is that the amount of contact averaged little more than one session per week and the context was always one in which the therapists were in fact 'visitors' rather than a built-in part of the system. As Bill Coulson observed, visitors are always seen as people who will go away. This contrasts significantly with the therapeutic context described in the work with 'Rick' in Chapter 6. In this hospital setting the aim was to create a therapeutic context that would be 'sufficient' in order to be engaged by the patient, presuming the therapist passed the necessary tests in regard to the therapeutic relationship. The therapy regime was six days per week at a regular hour in a location that was judged to be best for the patient. The patient was not expected to participate at all times but, regardless, the therapist would attend and would be working. Also, the medication regime was designed in such a way that it did not run counter to therapeutic processes.[1]

The 'therapeutic context' is made up of a considerable number of variables including obvious factors such as the frequency, length and physical setting of the sessions. But it also includes other less obvious variables such as whether the venue for the sessions can be altered, whether telephone contact outside sessions is permitted, and the width of 'allowable' client behaviour. In general, an important variable within the therapeutic context is the *flexibility* of the contextual factors. In her work with clients, with 'fragile process' Margaret Warner offers a studied consideration of the importance of both consistency but also flexibility (2000: 150–8). Those who work therapeutically in outpatient mental health projects also know the importance of therapeutic context variables. They know that meaningful work cannot happen if it has to be restricted to the firm boundary of 50 minutes per week in the therapist's office. Many patients simply cannot be restrained to that regime which is transported from a private practice context with a different clientele. Inpatient therapeutic work must be particularly alive to contextual variables. Krietemeyer and Prouty (2003) provide a vivid illustration of how flexible the therapist must be in, for example, being willing to work with the patient in the patient's own room, rather than in the therapy office. Furthermore, the creativity and responsiveness of the therapist is illustrated in this case by Barbara Krietemeyer's willingness at times to position herself outside the entrance to the room when the patient could not bear her closer proximity. Similarly, in Chapter 6, we will see an illustration of inpatient work where the therapist had to be creative with the physical context in order to avoid invasion and promote encounter. Failing to recognise the significance of accommodating the context to the patient would simply have been unprofessional in these examples.

The 'width of allowable client behaviour' is not something that therapists generally consider except play therapists who are disciplined in trying to offer the child as free a context as possible while also being clear to the child and themselves about the necessary boundaries of the context. So, it might be perfectly accepted as part of the process for the child to smash a toy in the playroom but it would probably not be allowed for the child to exit the office to smash things in the waiting room, or for the child to smash the therapist. Generally, play therapists make as few rules as possible but they are very clear about those rules and that is part of the 'holding' therapeutic context (Behr, 2003; Ginsberg, 1984). In working with adults it is equally important for the therapist to consider the boundaries of acceptability. For example, many therapists would automatically refuse to work with an alcoholic client if they presented drunk for the session. Yet, even that 'common sense' judgement is seriously challenged by the case study in Chapter 5.

Considerable research within mental health has been undertaken to evaluate therapeutic 'treatments' in relation to a range of client 'problems'. Equally, a lot of research time has been devoted to examining therapist variables, for example, in relation to the 'core conditions'. Although we have had this wealth of research into client variables and therapist variables, there has been precious little regard to the contextualisation of the work and the variables therein. Also, in recent times, the profession has become less open to experimentation regarding therapeutic contexts. For example, there is less development of therapeutic communities and therapeutic houses. The profession has come to see therapy as boundaried by the practitioner's office. Indeed, there has been an insidious development that has tended to institutionalise the work to that office, seeing anything outside as 'beyond the boundaries'. Practitioners who experiment with the boundaries can now be regarded as 'not doing therapy' or even worse, as doing therapy 'unethically'. This is a disturbing development in the profession because the almost neurotic concern with boundaries, in fact, stems from the empirically untested emphasis with the psychoanalytic method of non-gratification of the analysand in order that they can discover their infantile illusions and desires in relation to the analyst (Syme, 2003: 40–1). Yet, such is the historical power of the analytic community that the norms around boundaries have become a tyranny which judges as deviant all but itself. Indeed, the problem becomes even worse in so far as judgements are made on clients who are 'unsuitable for therapy'. An accurate phrasing of that judgement would be 'unsuitable for the therapeutic context we are prepared to offer'. Many of the clients depicted in this book, either for reasons of their diagnosis (Bobby), their behaviour (Dominic in Chapter 5) or their disconnectedness (Rick in Chapter 6) would be defined as 'unsuitable for therapy'. The reality is that they might be unsuitable for a therapy that needed to boundary itself too tightly, but they may well be 'suitable for therapy' if the context is actively considered and creatively managed. It is not good science to create closure before empirical investigation. Potentially, the therapeutic method can be applied to a much wider ranger of clients if only we were prepared to experiment with contextual variables. The danger is that psychotherapy might end up being narrowed to a few when in fact it could have enormous benefits for many.

Relational Engagement at the 'Presentational Level' of Self

Most relational engagement is at a surface level which, for the present purpose, we call the presentational level of self. At this level of engagement we project a self-image that we judge to be appropriate and strategic for the relational circumstances. The self-image that we project would not be the same in all meetings – the human being is skilled in presenting different 'faces' to the world. However, it would be a mistake to see these projected self-images as so superficial that they do not reflect anything 'real'. They are parts of the person and are just as important as any other dimension of the self that appears to be at a more enduring and fundamental level of experiencing. An adequate definition of self must encompass all of the projected self-images and everything else that underlies them.

It represents enormously skilful human social behaviour to function in relationships at the presentational level. Indeed, traditionally, mental health 'disorders' are symptomised in terms of failures to function adequately at the presentational level of social encounter – psychotic behaviour and manic episodes represent just two of the most obvious examples.

Human beings have a surfeit of social skills that enable them to establish and maintain relational contact with an array of people from perfect strangers, through distant and close friends, to living partners. Even though the degree of affiliation may vary considerably, still the vast bulk of relational engagement is at a presentational level. Indeed, human beings possess such skills of communication and cooperation around the development of 'norms' for behaviour in their relationships that the relating quickly becomes patterned. This norming skill is so important for creating predictability and safety within the relationship – both parties know what to expect from the other in the relationship – that even deception can be accepted as an implicit norm!

Intimacy in relationships is both feared and highly valued because it jumps the boundary from the highly normed presentational level of engagement to one where people are meeting in a more spontaneous and less patterned fashion. Meetings at a less pre-programmed level offer us something different both in terms of experiencing the other person but also in terms of experiencing our self reflected in the encounter with the other person. In interactions at the presentational level we may flirt with the possibility of a deeper engagement, perhaps simultaneously offering both *disguises* and *clues* as to our experiencing at that deeper level (Mearns and Thorne, 1999: 119–21). For example, the addition of humour or a choice of words that defuses the intensity of what we feel or even the transposition of feelings, perhaps from anger to sadness or vice-versa, can all be *disguises* at the presentational level. Disguises help us to 'save face' – if the other person is not able or does not wish to encounter us at a deeper level, then we can save face by continuing to hide behind the disguise and staying at the presenta-tional level. 'I get a bit down about it sometimes' can mean 'I am in com-plete despair' if the other person can meet us there, but if they cannot do so then we can hide behind the relative superficiality of the statement.

However, as mentioned earlier, we often hold simultaneously ambivalent feelings towards being met – wanting it as well as fearing it – and, even along with a disguise, we might also offer a *clue*. As we make our statement 'I get a bit down about it sometimes' we may suddenly and strikingly establish a steady eye contact with the other – a contact that communicates the fact that this an important statement, despite its deluding word choice. The human sophistication with social disguises and clues is such that even an opposite behaviour, like suddenly looking away, can represent exactly the same kind of positive clue. Generally, such non-verbal clues reflect a sudden change in our underlying experiencing and a hope to be encountered there.

These dimensions of social psychology are part of the curriculum of therapists in training. They learn not to seek to identify disguises and clues from their behavioural manifestations, but, rather, to use their developed human sensitivity to notice such changes and offer a response that shows they have noticed and that they are willing to move to another level. Hence, they might respond: 'you say, "I get a bit down about it sometimes", but you looked at me really seriously there. I wondered if you had said it all?' Therapists of all traditions will seek to show the client that they are both able and willing to move beyond the presentational level of relating. Indeed, this is a major difference between what friends have to offer and what the therapist can offer. Friends may sometimes be able and willing to engage us at a deeper level but the therapist should *always* be able to offer that. The therapist offering the possibility of an engagement at *relational depth* is seeking to engage the client at a level that is closer to the client's experience of what is critical to their existence, *as well as* the presentational level of their expressing.

Engagement at a Level of Existential Questioning

Who am I when I am not projecting an image of myself to others or to myself? What is meaningful to me in my life? What is meaningful to me about my life? What do I live for? What would I die for? What are the fears that are too terrible to express? What are the hopes that are too vulnerable to share? What are my most extreme doubts or judgements about myself that might destroy me if I saw them reflected by another person?

Our self-concept includes this deeper sense of our existence as well as our portfolio of projected self-images. This 'sense of our existence' comprises those dimensions of our self-concept that describe our congruent experience of our value and our meaning, as well as our fundamental hopes and fears, as we experience these in an absence of the need to justify or protect ourselves in relation to others. It will contain self experiences reflecting our values, attributes, tendencies, directionality and a range of dynamics interrelating these facets and articulating with our projected self-image. It will also contain what have become introjections about self that did not arise in our self-experience but as definitions of our self given to us by significant others. However, only some introjections will have that fundamental feel about them such that they are experienced by us as belonging to our sense of our existence. Many more introjections are held at the presentational level and frequently 'contained' by self-configurations that give them expression but prevent them from excessively dominating the self (Mearns, 2002). Just one of the reasons why therapeutic engagement at the level of existential questioning is important is that it can reveal some introjections that, although they are evident and 'noisy' at the presentational level, do not have an underlying basis in the self. They are 'ghosts' from the past that do not have substance in the present. Clients give frequent examples of these ghosts and their exorcism:

- 'For years I behaved as though my mother was sitting on my shoulder criticising me. But when I *really* faced my fears she evaporated';
- 'I have always seen myself as lacking ability in almost everything. But when I really "heard" myself there was a strong voice in me that did not accept that. And when I looked at some of the things I really had achieved with a fresh pair of eyes, things really did look different';
- 'My mother called me a "bitch". And I behaved like one. But I am not'.

In order to explore the difference between material that belonged to the presentational level and elements that reflected underlying issues of particular existential significance to the person, the help of an earlier client, Amanda, was enlisted. In an 'Interpersonal Process Recall' (IPR) style method Amanda listened to the audio recording of a 90-minute session from two years earlier and commented specifically on self-referent statements that she had experienced, at the time, as being more congruent to her sense of her existence than others that belonged more to what we are calling here the projected self-image indicative of the presentational level of self-experience.

Early in the session there was a greater proportion of projected self-image statements consistently conforming to the norm of 'social acceptability' and often held together by 'shoulds' and 'oughts', as well as lacking an obvious congruence. Later in the session there was a greater incidence of seemingly more congruent self statements, delivered more powerfully and not necessarily coherent to other narratives, indeed, often contradicting them. One of the interesting aspects of this kind of observation is that the 'existential picture' we get of a person may be quite different from our earlier impression of them based on their social presentation. Earlier they may have been giving us a more readily acceptable picture, perhaps also one that was heavily disguised and adjusted to fit the context of our relationship. Also, these pictures involving the projected self-image tend to be more *coherent*. Rogers (1977) talked about the fact that, early in sessions, there was a tendency for the client to present 'rehearsed' material. Certainly, the presentation of a projected self-image with its socially mediated content would give the material a 'rehearsed' quality with a more consistent narrative. However, when the client feels able to present dimensions of their self as they are experiencing them, without the need to dress them up or make them socially coherent, the picture we obtain is generally much more fragmented, often with apparently inconsistent narratives and evaluations. The growing practice in numerous psychotherapies of taking a pluralist perspective on the self allows this dissonant material to be heard for what it is without the need to impose a unitary structure upon it (see Chapter 2). It is important when working within this domain not to seek coherence or consistency since that simply encourages the other dimensions of the self-concept whose job it is to 'tidy up' experiencing, but perhaps at the expense of 'existential' meaningfulness.

Amanda

The client, Amanda, is a 49-year-old senior business executive. The self-referent statements that she declared to be reflective of her sense of her existence rather than her projected self-image are presented simply in the order in which they appeared during the 90-minute session. One important thing which is, of course, missing from what follows is the therapeutic dialogue and encounter in which these statements emerged. Dialogues such as this are the focus of Chapter 5. Amanda's statements are as follows:

- 'I am worthless... and I am not';
- 'If I use deception, my achievement has no value';
- 'If I use my power, my achievement has no value';
- 'I don't believe myself';
- 'I know that I could *kill*... and that is important to me';
- 'To be good I have to be better';
- 'I have been *good* with most people';
- 'My love for my daughter is the most *whole* part of me';
- 'Secretly, I enjoy the fact that I am boss to so many men. Their frequent discomfort about that amuses me';

- 'One of the things I would never tell anyone is that I am *glad* I put the office before home. I am kind of the person who, on her death bed, might have said, "I wish I had spent more time at the office"';
- 'In the mirror I still see the plain girl';
- 'But it is amazing what £1,000 of designer clothes does to a plain girl!';
- 'I find it difficult to be the plain girl any more – I think she has gone. She was no more "me" then, than I am "me" now';
- 'I am 49 years of age and this is the first time that I would say that I have done a "good job" with my life. But that is *good*. I never believed I would ever get to this point!';
- 'I can now feel *genuine* joy';
- 'I am amazed, and pleased with myself, that I can talk with you like this';
- 'If my husband heard all this stuff I am saying he would not recognise me. He would have to think that I am crazy. That is the only way he could make sense of it!... That is a pity';
- 'Just there, I heard a little voice in my head say "you'll have to try to meet him" (her husband). But, the truth is that I don't think I want to bother. I don't want to make the effort. But, again, if I am different from the way he sees me, perhaps he is different from the way I see him'.

The 'picture' that these statements give of Amanda is radically different from her normal projected self-image ('If my husband heard all this stuff I am saying, he would not recognise me'). Her statements are delivered more stridently, she is less apologetic about herself and there is a much greater presentation of apparent conflicts, e.g. 'I am worthless... and I am not'. The first part of this, 'I am worthless', sounds like a thoroughly integrated introjection within the self-concept but nowadays it is being challenged by its contradiction. She says 'if I use deception, my achievement has no value' and 'if I use my power, my achievement has no value'. However, she juxtaposes those with 'I don't believe myself'. The very untidiness of this presentation allows us to see the developmental process that is in progress. For many years she has devalued any achievements that had been won through her incongruence. However, very recently she has been realising that, secretly, she has actually admired her own use of power. This important dynamic would not have revealed itself through her projected self-image. Another element within her sense of her existence was reflected in 'I know that I could *kill*... and that is important to me'. Although this would have been completely alien to the image projected of herself, it was actually experienced by her as a profound source of strength. It was very important for her that she made contact with and was able to express that apparently dangerous material because it allowed her to symbolise the fact that there was always an alternative to becoming a victim. The statement 'to be good I have to be better', taken on its own sounds very much like an introjection. However, in Amanda's case it is not an introjection but a clearly derived conclusion based on the experience of being a 'plain girl'. Her experience of being a 'plain girl' in the world was reflected in the perfectly logical conclusion – 'to be good I have to be better'.

There is a wealth of other material in Amanda's self statements. Much of it seems to be contradictory, particularly her evaluations of herself and the contributions she has made to life. This rich mixture of material and contradictions is properly reflective of the complexities of the human being. Our perceptions of each other and our presentations of ourself to the other tend to offer consistent and comprehendible pictures but these are not necessarily accurate representations of the human being's sense of their own existence. Pluralist conceptions of the self emanating from a range of therapeutic disciplines have begun to etch a dialogical epistemology through which we can represent different parts and dynamics within the self without needing to remove or rationalise apparent contradictions. This reflects a growing psychology of our time, but one that does not sit easily with the still dominant 'modernist' epistemology that is grounded in Aristotelian logic. That system of knowledge cannot cope with the concurrent existence of opposites, but when we dip beneath the projected self-image that is the kind of process we meet. In earlier social psychology, which rarely saw beneath the projected self-image in relations with others, the observed organising principle was 'internal consistency', variously termed 'balance' (Heider, 1958) or 'dissonance reduction' (Festinger, 1957). In psychology we need to be open to new paradigms – perhaps we even need to be open to the possibility of '*dis*organising principles' within the person, as being important in carrying the function of 'breaking down' old models to allow the growth of the new. That combination of 'organising' functions and 'disorganising' functions represents, at least metaphorically, the kind of homeostatic dialogical process we see in many areas of living, not least in the maintenance of the living organism through a process of not only creating new cells but also destroying old ones and the control of responses through the simultaneous secretion of hormones with competing actions. Just as the movement of a car is more precisely controlled through having brakes as well as a throttle, so too, is the human being more exquisitely governed by having 'organising' *and* 'disorganising' principles.

We are only going to expand psychology in these directions if we can make contact at a level underlying the presentational. Otherwise, our descriptions of human behaviour and experience will remain superficial, will give a false impression of 'order' and will continue to be largely irrelevant to the person at levels they might describe as 'existential', 'fundamental' or 'spiritual'. The challenge, then, to the researcher as well as to the counsellor or therapist is, 'can we encourage a relational context such that the client feels sufficiently "encountered" that they can begin to present themselves as they experience themselves without needing to "tidy themselves up"?'

The Existential Impact of Transition and Trauma

There are times in life when we are brought so close to our sense of our existence that we cannot 'tidy ourselves up'. We become immersed in questions of meaning, of order and of reality to an extent that our whole sense of our existence is profoundly shaken. Commentators on human *transition* note the 'existential dividend' or 'opportunity value' that we may carry forward from such powerful transitional experiences (Adams et al., 1976). At every level of the profession we are aware of this potential dividend. In the selection and training of therapists it is recorded that such powerful prior experiences can offer the therapist a 'touchstone' that assists their own work at depth with clients (Dryden et al., 1995; Mearns, 1997c; see also Chapter 8 of this book).

Transition awakens us to our sense of our existence. Our assumptions about our life, its meaning and the meaning of other people and events to us are challenged. A self-concept that was shaped around relationships or career faces their loss and is challenged to re-evaluate and restructure. That can take the person to new or long-forgotten experiences of themselves, evoking an array of emotions, particularly despair, anger, sadness and guilt. Normative judgements by others on an 'expected' level of experiencing are meaningless – the impact of the event relates individually to the 'hole' that is left after the loss and the degree of restructuring required.

Trauma is also a transition but it is even more existentially shocking. An event has happened, often suddenly, that not only creates loss and the demands for restructuring, but fundamentally disrupts the whole assumptive frame upon which our sense of self is founded. Our assumptions about the world, other people and our self may be violently contradicted by one sudden, catastrophic event.

We make a lot of basic assumptions in order to conduct a social life. We do not even think of them – we take them for granted. A young woman, Mary, walks down the road paying absolutely no attention to whatever is happening behind her. Implicitly she is making the assumption that walking down that busy road on that bright sunny day carries no particular dangers from behind. She does not expect the violent attack that follows. Donald, the train driver, knows that people commit suicide on the line but that does not prepare him for the sight of the man's laughing face running towards him and the detail of the mess that results. Douglas, the mail delivery man, never imagined that anyone would attach razor blades to the inside of that letter box.

Now, Mary only walks down roads in near panic, looking 360 degrees around her all the time. The trauma came totally unexpectedly, out of the 'background' before, so why could it not again? Donald and Douglas have never worked since – their colleagues sympathise, but they do not really understand.

One of the most shocking kinds of trauma is where *we* have been the cause. Jonathan was held at knife-point, robbed and taunted. He would never have seen himself as someone who would fight back. But he did, and with the power that huge anger renders. So, he disarmed the young man who had attacked him. But did he really have to stab him? And why did he stab him four times? Reality is socially constructed and, at the time, it did not seem to Peter to be such a terrible thing to join in the gang's taunting of the girls. Even the sex did not seem to be 'rape'. Later, Peter has considerable difficulty coming to terms with himself as a 'violent rapist'. Nothing socially deconstructs reality as powerfully as war – indeed, it has been described as creating a 'counterfeit universe' (Lifton, 1974). Wayne has never really understood why, with his platoon, he sexually mutilated prisoners before killing them, nor has he been able to live with that reality (Mearns, 1997b).

Trauma is so shocking at an existential level that it can take us completely out of our social world. It can lead to psychological withdrawal and even actual physical withdrawal from contact with others. The trauma victim may find it difficult to perform the simple acts of social living – even shopping in a supermarket can become an impossible task for the trauma victim because of its essential meaninglessness (Mearns, 1997b). Most of our day-to-day life is spent on tasks that, in the larger scheme of things, are not particularly imbued with existential significance. However, the person who is traumatised has had the meaning structure of their life seriously disrupted. It becomes difficult to tolerate insignificance when something so profoundly significant has happened to us.

Another consequence can be that the person finds it extremely difficult to be emotionally 'present' in their social and emotional relationships. Feeling and expressing love towards one's partner used to be such a simple thing but now it feels impossible. Playing with our children was such an easy and natural act but now it has to be forced and the children know the difference.

Conventional psychological thinking on trauma, as epitomised in the *DSM-IV* (American Psychiatric Association, 1994), lists different groups of symptoms required for a diagnosis of post-traumatic stress disorder (PTSD). Yet, this analysis is bizarrely disconnected from the significance of trauma for the client at the existential level. It completely fails to capture the client's experience of the meaningfulness of the event and the consequent meaninglessness of the rest of their life thereafter. The 'search to re-experience' is represented by a list of possible symptoms, yet these completely fail to capture the felt experience of the person who is struggling with the fact that this event was simultaneously the worst thing that ever happened in their life and also the point in their life when they felt most *alive* (sometimes, in war, called 'the buzz').

In working with a client experiencing trauma the therapist is challenged to meet them in the pain of their experiencing. For example, how do we meet Marie as she considers whether she can survive the death of Alexis, her five-year-old daughter, a victim of a school shooting? For six years she sought only the support of others in her community. That is how it usually happens in the early stages: the closer community is more important than external helping agencies. But, generally, our grief lasts longer than our normal life supports. Eventually, Marie felt that she could no longer 'take her grief next door' or even to her husband, Brian. It was time to 'move on', but Marie could not 'move on'. She tells her story, nervously, to her new therapist:

> Alexis was shot three times with an automatic pistol at point-blank range. I pray every day to God that she died right away. I relive her death every day. I see every feature of it. I see her shrivelled little body. I see it every day.
>
> For years I got as much support as anyone could have been given. But the pain is just as great now as ever, and other people have moved on. *How* can I 'move on'? I can't 'move on'. It is totally impossible to 'move on'. Brian does his best. But he *has* moved on and so we are moving further and further apart. Seriously, how *can* someone 'move on'? I would love to do it. I think I'm crazy that I can't do it. But I know that I will *never* be able to do it. There are times when I think I should kill myself – not just to take *my* pain away – but the pain I keep causing to Brian and John [her son].

The most horrific prospect in the profession of counselling and psychotherapy is that Marie may not be met by her therapist at a level of relational depth. The prospect that the preferred 'treatment' might endeavour to get her to reconstrue events such that she might 'move on' is not unthinkable within mental health care, yet from the perspective of this chapter, it is nothing short of abuse. Fortunately, one of the strengths of counselling and psychotherapy is the developed awareness of trauma and, particularly, its existential challenge to the therapist. Meeting Marie *within* her experiencing will be profoundly painful for her therapist – indeed, it will have an enduring impact. Her therapist will know that meeting Marie will have a 'rawness' that will rub off on the therapist – trauma is 'sticky' stuff – and secondary traumatisation is well documented (Sexton, 1999). There will be a danger of the therapist carrying some of that material into the rest of her life. She will need to be prepared for that, but the nature of it is that the form it takes may still take her by surprise. She may find herself feeling sharp/critical/reactive to her own children and her partner. She may find herself thinking about her own existence, the pattern of her current life, and the dissonance between these. Meeting a client within their trauma experiencing places huge demands upon the therapist (see Chapter 6). For some mental health workers, these demands are contradicted by their own vulnerabilities and lack of personal development work in their training. In such circumstances the client cannot be met at a level of relational depth. In fact, in these circumstances, it is extremely important that the mental health worker does *not* seek to engage the client within their trauma experiencing because that would carry considerable threat to both of them.

Fortunately, most of the counselling and psychotherapy profession has placed great store in the personal awareness and development of its practitioners. Marie can expect to be met by a practitioner who will not be trying to 'move her on' but will be prepared to meet her exactly where she is in her process at the present moment. The practitioner will have got her life ready to meet Marie. In the real situation, Marie's therapist immediately added half-an-hour per week to her supervision contract in the first month of working with Marie. The therapist also talked to her partner and her two children about the work she was doing and the fact that it might well impact upon the rest of her life. Her employer (who was not a therapist) wondered about the increased supervision contract – was this a sign of 'weakness'? The therapist's supervisor was able to describe the situation to the employer's satisfaction. But what of the therapist's children? Is this powerful material invasive of their relationship with their mother? Of course it is, and how precious it might be to experience our mothers thus.

To this point in our book we have argued the case for the centrality of 'relationship' in human development and, consequently, in counselling and psychotherapy. We have explored the experience of relational depth in terms of moments of particular human contact and, in this chapter, we have looked at relational depth in terms of an enduring connectedness engendering a particularly facilitative relationship for the client, such that they may feel safe enough to visit areas of their experience that have greatest existential significance for them.

Using notions of the presentational level of self and the level at which more fundamental existential questioning takes place, counselling and psychotherapy contracts can be compared and contrasted. Certainly, some contracts are almost entirely concerned with the presentational level, where it is the way the client presents himself in the world that is the set agenda. If the therapeutic objectives are set at a behavioural level, then the likelihood is that the relational engagement will be focused at the presentational level. Notions such as 'achieving a working alliance' are still relevant, but only at a fairly superficial level of relationship. Indeed, it might be argued that engagement at relational depth, both in terms of moments of contact and also enduring connectedness could be distracting to the set purpose. On the other hand, it is likely that a majority of therapeutic contracts seek to tap material at the more private level of self-questioning. To the extent that it is the relationship that facilitates invited entry to that domain, our notions of relational depth through moments of connection and also through enduring connectedness are relevant. There are also some contracts where the client's relational disconnectedness is so chronic that meaningful and lasting progress can *only* be achieved through the development of an enduring connectedness, generally facilitated by moments of connection, considerable commitment and a sufficient therapeutic context. The case study in Chapter 6 provides an example of this kind of therapeutic work where the relational disconnection is a symptom of the existential trauma and, if a therapeutic avenue is to be created, a particularly trustable enduring connection must be achieved. There are other contracts where the work might proceed at the presentational level of engagement *or* with the aim of offering a depth of relationship. The interesting thing here is that the therapeutic results could be completely different under these two different contracts. The following chapter, featuring 'Dominic', is just such an example. The conventional approach to someone with an alcohol problem is to focus on the problem and the work generally takes place at the presentational level, albeit with the establishment of a good 'working alliance'. But what happens if the therapist totally *ignores* the 'problem' and focuses on the person? What happens if the therapist struggles to connect with Dominic's experiencing, even when that experiencing varies wildly from states of sobriety to drunkenness, bringing out dimensions of questioning at the existential level hitherto unsymbolised? Read on.

Note

1. For example, it is generally inappropriate to prescribe either major or minor tranquilisers to a patient in psychotherapy. The two activities work in counter directions: tranquilisers tend to take a person out of themselves while psychotherapy tends to take the person into themselves. The argument for the prescription of anti-depressants is completely different and research reviews tend to suggest that the optimum condition may be the judicious prescription of anti-depressant medication in conjunction with therapy. (Hammersley, 1995: 31).

5 WORKING WITH DOMINIC: A 'PARTIAL' DRUNK

Introduction

In this chapter Dave Mearns presents, in the first person, an account of a portion of work with the client, Dominic. The bulk of the chapter examines four parts (A, B, C, D) of transcribed dialogue, changed only to clarify moments where the difference between spoken and written language caused confusion. Parts A and B are taken from the third therapy session and C and D from the fourth. Following each part there is a line-by-line commentary which focuses on aspects of relational depth and also other dimensions of the engagement. A particular feature is the criticality of the analysis: the therapist does not get things right all the time, but it can help if we are aware of those responses that 'miss' and if we show our responsibility to the client by seeking to retrieve the situation. To a great extent that effort of the therapist, perceived by the client, contributes to relational depth. After all, it is difficult to relate to perfection. We also find that students appreciate this kind of critical analysis in case studies. It takes pressure off their early fears of 'getting it wrong' by showing that it is the retrieval that is important.

A common 'myth' about relational depth is that it will only happen in long-term therapeutic contracts, once the people have got to know each other. In fact, this assumption is wrong, because it is the *quality* of the contact that is important, not the quantity. These case extracts illustrate that as early as the third and fourth meetings the two people can establish a particular depth of relating, even though Dominic is by no means an 'easy' client to meet at depth.

Readers might wish to go through the chapter as it is presented or they might prefer to read the four parts of the dialogue first to get a sense of the whole before turning to the commentaries.

Dominic

Dominic had sat for an hour on a train line. No trains had come so he went round to a friend's house. He could not go home because he was drunk. His friend, who was a previous client of Dave's, 'made' him phone Dave for a therapy appointment which was arranged for the next day.

Despite this urgent beginning, there had been little urgency in the first two sessions. Dominic had been entirely self critical of his drinking which took a 'binge' format. Some days he would finish one bottle of vodka or more if he could physically reach the off-licence and be served. But, generally, he would begin with a single bottle. Interestingly, his pattern of drinking partially 'meshed' with his life – he chose days when he had found some excuse to be away from home, or was home alone. Dave takes up the commentary.

In the first session I made it clear that I would not base our working around his drinking. I would not keep track of his drinking nor would I try to get him off drinking. Whether he drank or not was up to him. If he turned up drunk we might or might not have the session depending on whether it seemed possible or not. I take this fairly 'detached' position in relation my client's drinking because I do not want our work to become contingent upon his drinking. If that happens it becomes too easy for him, or part of him, to sabotage his therapeutic movement, like everything else, in a bottle of vodka. That would make the therapeutic venture impossibly vulnerable – at some stage there would always be a point when he would have to sabotage the whole thing. Furthermore, as we will discuss in Chapter 7, to have specific aims for a client – particularly where the client may not have those aims himself – makes it highly unlikely that a meeting at relational depth will come about. To fully encounter a client in an in-depth way means letting go of our agenda and being with him, in whichever way he is and in whatever direction he wants to go.

In much of my therapeutic work, subject to the client's agreement, sessions (apart from the first) are taped. This discipline began for my own benefit, as a way of reflecting upon my work in supervision. However, I also found that clients used the facility as much as I did. They would take tapes home to share with their partner, ask for earlier tapes to replay and analyse on their own, or replay parts of the previous week's tape together with me in the fashion of Kagan's (1984) 'Interpersonal Process Recall'. The replay/review would bring us a 'metacommunication' (Rennie, 1998) perspective where we comment on ourselves and each other in a way that inevitably generates significant therapeutic material for the client (and often self-learning for the therapist) and tends to deepen the level of here and now relating in the sessions.

Part A (at the Start of Session 3)

Dominic turned up drunk for session three.

Dominic 1: I shouldn't have come today. I'll go away if you like.

Dave 1: Because you've been drinking?

Dominic 2: Yeah – I've been drinking.

Dave 2: Do you *want* to go or do you *want* to stay?

Dominic 3: I wouldn't mind staying.

Dave 3: I would like that too. But I'd like us to keep the tape on like we did last week. Why I say that is that I want us to have a record of what happens – when you're pissed it's easy to forget.

Dominic 4: Fine. I hadn't realised it was on.

Dave 4: Good that I mentioned it then.

Dominic 5: [Long pause] How do you feel about me... now... here?

Dave 5: Dom, I want to tell you that I feel absolutely *nothing* about the fact that you've been drinking. But you asked how I felt about you, now, here [pauses]. I feel... a bit... scared.

Dominic 6: Scared?

Dave 6: It surprises me too... I guess it *does* matter to me that you've been drinking... I'm scared in case we have to start again. It's like I feel that we've made a really good connection... but will that still be there... today. That's what makes me a bit scared.

Dominic 7: Like it matters to you?

Dave 7: Yes it does Dom.

Dominic 8: Like this isn't just a 'game' to you?

Dave 8: I think you *know* that, Dom. In fact, I *know* you know that Dom.

Dominic 9: Yes, 'sober me' knows it, but does 'drunk me'?

Dave 9: I don't know. Does he? Do you?

Dominic 10: Big question. Maybe I'll need another vodka before I can answer that.

Dave 10: Dom, *be* here, be here *drunk,* but don't play fucking games with me. Neither you nor I deserve that.

Dominic 11: [Silence]

Dave 11: [Silence]

Dominic 12: You're really *serious* about this, aren't you?

Dave 12: As ever.

Dominic 13: I'm sorry.

Dave 13: Apology accepted. Where should we start today?

Dominic 14: We started long ago – this is *me* – this is who I am.

Dave 14: Yes, you're right, I see, we started at the beginning as usual but the start was different because *you* were different. Yes, I missed that.

Commentary on part A

The case material from the work with Dominic is broken into four parts. After each part I will present my own analysis of the work.

Dominic 1: I shouldn't have come today. I'll go away if you like.
Dave 1: Because you've been drinking?
Dominic 2: Yeah – I've been drinking.
Dave 2: Do you *want* to go or do you *want* to stay?

The person-centred therapist and, indeed, therapists of any tradition, will recognise this last question as one that is seeking to centre the decision-making process in the client rather than accept the client's pushing this responsibility on to the therapist. In terms of person-centred theory, the client is being encouraged to internalise rather than externalise their *locus of evaluation* (Mearns, 2003a: 80–3).

Dominic 3: I wouldn't mind staying.
Dave 3: I would like that too. But I'd like us to keep the tape on like we did last week. Why I say that is that I want us to have a record of what happens – when you're pissed it's easy to forget.

It is important to note that 'pissed' is not a derogatory term within the culture in which this work is taking place. In another context the use of this word might well denote the counsellor's denigration of the client. Being able to use the language of the culture in a way that is perfectly congruent for the therapist is an extremely important part of creating the foundations for contact at relational depth. Some therapists have an extremely narrow experiential and communicative range. They will find it difficult to lay the foundations for relational depth except with those clients who happen to fit their own communicative style. Developing that range is part of the *developmental agenda* described in Chapter 8.

Dominic 4: Fine. I hadn't realised it was on.
Dave 4: Good that I mentioned it then.

There is a slight sarcastic edge to my response and that is never ok. I reacted badly to Dom's drunkenness. I was the 'sober' therapist taking the usual care to cover the matter of the taping while he was so 'drunk' that he did not even know the tape was on. I felt uncomfortable with myself but instead of addressing that I made the usual therapist mistake of presuming that the client had not noticed. But he had.

Dominic 5: [Long pause] How do you feel about me… now… here?

Whether drunk or not, it is pretty brave of a client to challenge the therapist's congruence in this way and he deserved a more congruent response than he got.

Dave 5: Dom, I want to tell you that I feel absolutely *nothing* about the fact that you've been drinking. But you asked how I felt about you, now, here [pauses]. I feel… a bit… scared.

The first sentence of this response is completely dreadful. Instead of responding congruently I make the presumption that I knew what was behind his question – that he is scared that I may be judgemental about his drinking. Also, I am so out of touch with my own experiencing in that moment that I proceed to give a denial. Indeed, the degree of incongruence is so profound that, in Gendlin's (1981) language of 'focusing', my 'body talks back' – as I am making that denial I am also realising my own incongruence. A more competent voice within my head tells me to 'answer the client's question for god's sake!'

The second part of *Dave 5* contrasts completely with the first because it is utterly congruent. I am going back to his actual question, having stripped away my own presumptions and I am genuinely looking into myself to get to my congruent response. My own focusing leads me to the entirely new discovery that I am *scared*. This dramatic shift from extreme incongruence to its opposite is an important illustration of the work we do towards establishing the right to meet the client at relational depth. It is not a matter of always being perfect, but it *is* a matter of struggling towards congruence (see Chapter 7). Indeed, it may be our willingness to let the client see that struggle that makes the difference.

Dominic 6: Scared?
Dave 6: It surprises me too… I guess it *does* matter to me that you've been drinking… I'm scared in case we have to start again. It's like I feel that we've made a really good connection… but will that still be there… today? That's what makes me a bit scared.

This continues the flow of congruence: it shows Dominic what is going on in me. I always encourage person-centred therapists and trainers to 'show your working'. Showing your own process not only helps to counter any fantasies the client might have about your process but it tends to be seen by the client as concrete evidence of your valuing of them. In *Dave 6* I am showing that my fear has to do with possibly losing our good connection. It shows that I value that connection we have had and it also shows to Dominic that I value him.

Dominic 7: Like it matters to you?

There is genuine surprise in Dominic's voice. He is drunk in this session and at times his response is glib and superficial, as it was in *Dominic 4*, but at other times he is extremely serious and encountering. He is entertaining the possibility of meeting me at relational depth, but only tentatively.

Dave 7: Yes it does Dom.

This kind of sentence can be said in an off-hand, glib fashion but it was extremely important at this point that it was delivered slowly and strongly to emphasise just how seriously I took this communication.

Dominic 8: Like this isn't just a 'game' to you?

Here, Dominic is, once again, 'checking out' my seriousness about our relationship. He is still entertaining the possibility of our first meeting (involving this part of him) at relational depth.

Dave 8: I think you *know* that, Dom. In fact, I *know* you know that Dom.

This is a difficult response to describe. In our *Dominic 7–8* communication I really *knew* that Dominic was believing my seriousness. Perhaps there were echoes around in him of voices that still did not trust my seriousness but, essentially, I knew that we were encountering each other (Schmid, 2002). This illustrates one very powerful part of the experience of meeting at relational depth – that each person experiences the other's experiencing of that depth (see Chapter 3). Sometimes that experience of meeting at different levels of perspective goes unspoken but it can also be important to the establishing of contact at relational depth that it is made explicit. If Dominic is going to give me invited access into his deepest sense of self, this relationship will need to be a little bit special.

Dominic 9: Yes, 'sober me' knows it, but does 'drunk me'?

This is an absolutely critical point in the therapy. This is the point at which Dominic *separates* two parts of his self, or what we might term 'configurations of self' (see Chapter 2). From the easy way in which he expressed it, it does not sound as though this is a new, 'edge of awareness,' experience but it could be entirely new for him to disclose it to another person.

Dave 9: I don't know. Does he? Do you?

I put this back to Dominic, firstly as 'does he?', then I quickly reframe it as 'do you?' The speed of my reframing reflects the fact that I know I have made a mistake. I have distanced and objectified 'drunk me' using the phrase 'does he?' My client has not indicated that kind of distancing or objectification, so I need to centre it more in himself again. This reflects our discussion in Chapter 2 of the difference between I–Me and I–I self-relating, pointing to the fact that clients sometimes have a distant, objectifying relationship with themselves (I–Me) and that this is different from a relationship where they experience a greater ownership of their different facets, an I–I relationship.

Dominic 10: Big question. Maybe I'll need another vodka before I can answer that.
Dave 10: Dom, *be* here, be here *drunk*, but don't play fucking games with me. Neither you nor I deserve that.

Some therapists will be shocked by this response. It uses bad language; it is an extremely strong expression; and it expresses a powerful judgement in response to Dominic's glib *Dominic 10*. Yet, viewed from the perspective of 'encountering' – of providing a presence that is 'counter' (Schmid, 2002) to the person – the very power of this statement shows Dominic how serious I am about our contact, as he himself reflects in *Dominic 12*.

Dominic 11: [Silence]
Dave 11: [Silence]
Dominic 12: You're really *serious* about this, aren't you?
Dave 12: As ever.
Dominic 13: I'm sorry.

These two words constitute a very big sentence. The 'foray' is over and Dominic is prepared to engage. We have obtained an engagement at a considerable depth of encounter during the third session while Dominic was drunk.

Dave 13: Apology accepted. Where should we start today?
Dominic 14: We started long ago – this is *me* – this is who I am.

Dave 14: Yes, you're right, I see, we started at the beginning as usual but the start was different because *you* were different. Yes, I missed that.

This is a lovely point at which to end this part of the transcript. I had, in the first two sessions, established a therapeutic relationship with one part of Dominic, to the extent that in session three I simply had not recognised the 'drunk Dominic' as a legitimate presence, even though I had actually been relating moderately well to this side of him. Even at the beginning of the session, when Dominic was incredibly glib, that was part of him. That was who he was when he was drunk. We had already been meeting but I had not recognised him as part of the same client I had the met in the first two sessions.

Part B (Later in Session 3)

Dominic 15: It's not easy to live up to a 'holy' name.
Dave 15: 'Dominic'.
Dominic 16: Yes. A good Catholic upbringing kept telling me how important my name was.
Dave 16: Like it told you what you should be?
Dominic 17: Yeah, but it was a fantasy, pure fantasy... pure... fantasy.
Dave 17: *Their* fantasy?
Dominic 18: Yeah... It was like I didn't exist... you know?
Dave 18: Like they had some image of you that was so far from who you were that it was like they were talking about someone else.
Dominic 19: Got it in one. You're good at this shit!
Dave 19: Hope so. What are you *with* just now?
Dominic 20: [Long pause]... [looks directly at Dave]... I don't know what I am about.
Dave 20: [Looks *intensely* at Dominic and moves towards him, speaking slowly] That sounds like a lot, 'you...don't...know...what... you're...about...'
Dominic 21: I'm so full of crap.
Dave 21: ... and ...?
Dominic 22: I don't know whether to believe myself or not.
Dave 22: Say more Dom.
Dominic 23: I'm just so full of crap.
Dave 23: You don't know whether to believe yourself or not.
Dominic 24: I think I'm serious ... sincere. But, *really*, I'm only a drunk ... a fuckin' drunk.
Dave 24: You think that you're serious ... and sincere. But you're really, only, a fuckin' drunk.

Dominic 25: Yes.

Dave 25: A fuckin' drunk – that's all you are.

Dominic 26: [Tears welling up].

Dave 26: A fuckin' drunk.

Dominic 27: [Hits fist on arm of chair in apparent anger... and cries]

Dave 27: Dom, you're angry... and you're crying.

Dominic 28: I'm so fuckin' full of shit [cries].

Dave 28: [Moves to Dominic and puts his arm round him]

Dominic 29: [Cries more and more]

Dave 29: It feels like a lonely place.

Dominic 30: [Looks up at Dave] Yes... [shivers].

Dave 30: Cold, and lonely...

Dominic 31: The only warmth comes through the bottle, whether it's 'single malt' or cheap vodka. It doesn't matter.

Dave 31: It still works, it still gives a *feeling* of warmth.

Dominic 32: It does... I can't describe it... I'm *alive*... but it's killing me... and everything I love.

Dave 32: Dom, can you really help me get hold of this? It sounds really strong, like you feel really 'alive'. That sounds really powerful. But, then, it is also 'killing' you, and everything you love.

Dominic 33: One part of me is really 'hooked' on it. It is the only 'buzz' I get and I can't get enough of it.

Dave 33: And, there is another part...?

Dominic 34: The other part is a loving husband and father...

Dave 34: Yes...?

Dominic 35: Who is killing his family.

Dave 35: You're carrying a lot... a helluva lot.

Dominic 36: And I can't carry it any more.

Dave 36: That sounds serious... No. I don't mean to be 'glib'. It really does sound like you are serious.

Dominic 37: I've got to *do* something.

Dave 37: 'Do'? What would you 'do', Dom?

Dominic 38: Either give it up... or give it up.

Dave 38: I think I understand... one 'part' – the one that is really 'hooked' – would give up on your normal life... and the other 'part' – the one who is a 'loving husband and father' – would give up the booze.

Dominic 39: Most people don't realize how difficult a choice that is.

Dave 39: Is it... does it feel like giving up on living for the life you have?

Dominic 40: Yes.

Dave 40: [Silence]

Dominic 41: It *feels* like 'living' when you're drunk – but it isn't really.

Dave 41: [Silence]

Dominic 42: I've been *scared* of living. All my life I've been scared of living. I've never felt like other people. I've never felt sure of myself the way other people do. If you feel sure of yourself you can go out and do things with your life. If you don't feel sure of yourself you can't. You can't really *do* things with your life. You've always got to make 'safe' choices – choices that don't really test you – choices that aren't really 'living'.

Dave 42: [Silence]

Dominic 43: And so, I have an 'ordinary life' – did you see that film?

Dave 43: *Ordinary Lives* – yes.

Dominic 44: [Long silence]

Dave 44: Are you stuck? Are you thinking about the film?

Dominic 45: Yes, their ordinary lives were blown apart when something terrible happened. They had taken the safe choices for so long that they hadn't developed the strength to deal with real life.

Dave 45: And you... what about *you*?

Dominic 46: Part of me tries to break free, but it also hasn't got experience. It doesn't know how to do it.

Dave 46: [Silence]

Dominic 47: [Silence]

Dave 47: I am feeling sad for it. I think I am seeing it better. It desperately wants to do something, but it has been 'scared of living' for so long it doesn't know what to do.

Dominic 48: So all I can do is to go into that *feeling* of being sad, and get drunk. That's the closest I can get to living.

Commentary on part B

Dominic 15: It's not easy to live up to a 'holy' name.

Dave 15: 'Dominic'.

Dominic 16: Yes. A good Catholic upbringing kept telling me how important my name was.

Dave 16: Like it told you what you should be?

Dominic 17: Yeah, but it was a fantasy, pure fantasy... pure... fantasy.

Dave 17: *Their* fantasy?

Dominic 18: Yeah... It was like I didn't exist... you know?

Dave 18: Like they had some image of you that was so far from who you were that it was like they were talking about someone else.

Once an enduring engagement at relational depth has been achieved, empathy usually comes easily and accurately, as exemplified in this portion of the dialogue. I am alongside Dominic and the responses flow out of a shared understanding of his world. Dominic confirms this in his next response.

Dominic 19: Got it in one. You're good at this shit!
Dave 19: Hope so. What are you *with* just now?

Although it may not be recognised as such by person-centred thera-pists, *Dave 19* is a *process direction* (Rennie, 1998). It does not appear, obviously, as a discontinuity because it is embedded and derived from the ongoing relationship. At other times process directions on the part of the therapist look obviously discontinuous and tend to be avoided by person-centred therapists. At this point in the dialogue, Dominic and I have been looking at material that is not particularly new to him, but it is important because it is the family basis for a major dimension of his self-concept. As well as talking *about* this, I am wondering whether he has any other feelings or reactions to it in the moment. In a sense, I am gently 'knocking on his door' (see Chapter 7) to see if he wants to go to the edge of his awareness.

Dominic 20: [Long pause]... [looks directly at Dave]... I don't know what I am about.

Dominic's looking directly at me was a powerful way to show his engagement at relational depth, as was the very serious way in which he said, 'I don't know what I am about'. This was a serious, wholly gen-uine statement about his core sense of self. The same words, in other circumstances, might be said by someone in a glib fashion. This was not a glib statement on Dominic's part. It was a profound description of his experience of himself in the world.

Dave 20: [Looks *intensely* at Dominic and moves towards him, speaking slowly] That sounds like a lot, 'you...don't...know...what...you're...about...'

When the client is sharing a sense of his very existence the therapist must respond seriously and intensely.

Dominic 21: I'm so full of crap.
Dave 21: ... and ...?

This intervention, *Dave 21*, is entirely unnecessary, as are a few of my later interventions. When we are meeting the client in his core sense of self it is the quality rather than the quantity of our communications that makes the difference. Often we need to say very little but what we do say needs to be showing our quality of presence. In this case my process direction (implying that there should be something else) is likely to disturb the client's flow.

Dominic 22: I don't know whether to believe myself or not.
Dave 22: Say more Dom.
Dominic 23: I'm just so full of crap.
Dave 23: You don't know whether to believe yourself or not.

My 'say more Dom', is a warm contact that is often sufficient to keep in touch with the client and encourage his flow. However, in this case it does not appear to help and in *Dominic 23* he goes backwards. Whenever a client goes backwards then we have to go back to meet them, hence *Dave 23* reflects *Dominic 22*.

Dominic 24: I think I'm serious … sincere. But, *really*, I'm only a drunk… a fuckin' drunk.
Dave 24: You think that you're serious… and sincere. But you're really, only, a fuckin' drunk.

Dominic 24 is a *powerful* statement, but what does it mean? The way he spat out the word 'fuckin'' was, literally, like spitting. I am close enough to his being to know that this statement is really powerful but I have no idea what it means so what I must do is to reflect it accurately and see if he 'focuses' it. Hence, my *Dave 24* more or less repeats his *Dominic 24* with the same kind of emphasis on the word 'fuckin''.

Dominic 25: Yes.
Dave 25: A fuckin' drunk – that's all you are.
Dominic 26: [Tears welling up]
Dave 26: A fuckin' drunk.

My verbatim reflection in *Dave 24* was not enough so I reflect the last part of it again (*Dave 25*) to really show my empathy with the *power* of the statement. *Dominic 26* shows that he has made contact with himself at this deeper level of experiencing. I wish I had left it at that – adding other repetition (*Dave 26*) is unnecessarily dramatic – Dominic is already in touch with his sense of his self.

Dominic 27: [Hits fist on arm of chair in apparent anger… and cries]
Dave 27: Dom, you're angry… and you're crying.

Dominic 27 is in a land beyond words. In *Dave 27* I find myself making a very concrete 'pre-therapy' type of response (Prouty, 1994; Prouty et al., 2002; Van Werde, 2003b).

Dominic 28: I'm so fuckin' full of shit [cries].

This may be as low as a human being can feel about himself.

Dave 28: [Moves to Dominic and puts his arm round him]

Actions often speak better than words. They can also communicate warmth more effectively.

Dominic 29: [Cries more and more]
Dave 29: It feels like a lonely place.
Dominic 30: [Looks up at Dave] Yes... [shivers].
Dave 30: Cold, and lonely...

It would have been better if I had kept my mouth shut and just sat with Dominic. With words I was trying to reach into his experiencing. I may have been right or I may have been wrong but, in any case, it was almost certainly unnecessary. When the client is so fully immersed in their own experiencing they will communicate very fully, in their own time.

Dominic 31: The only warmth comes through the bottle, whether it's 'single malt' or cheap vodka. It doesn't matter.
Dave 31: It still works, it still gives a *feeling* of warmth.

This interaction actually contains much more then may be immediately obvious. This was not a 'glib' statement by Dominic. It was a serious proposition about his fundamental sense of self. We could easily miss this if we simply presumed he was referring to the usual metaphor about the 'warming' effects of spirits. In fact, he was seriously talking about the emotional warmth he experienced when he was drinking.

Dominic 32: It does... I can't describe it... I'm *alive*... but it's killing me... and everything I love.

In retrospect, this may be the key statement in the whole transcript. Dominic is thoroughly in touch with his fundamental sense of his existence. Everything we come across when the client is working at this level is important.

Dave 32: Dom, can you really help me get hold of this? It sounds really strong, like you feel really 'alive'. That sounds really powerful. But, then, it is also 'killing' you, and everything you love.

I know that this is important but I do not understand it in the moment. It is not crucially important that I *do* understand the client. It is more important that I help the client to understand himself – that is my job (see Chapter 7). In any case, a fairly traditional empathic response, but one which emphasises that I have perceived the power of the material, is likely to advance both causes.

Dominic 33: One part of me is really 'hooked' on it. It is the only 'buzz' I get and I can't get enough of it.
Dave 33: And, there is another part…?
Dominic 34: The other part is a loving husband and father…
Dave 34: Yes…?
Dominic 35: Who is killing his family.

Here Dominic expands upon *Dominic 32* to symbolise his core conflict: he only feels fully 'alive' when drinking, yet it is killing his life. It is doubtful whether a therapist who had an agenda with respect to drinking could even hear a conflict like this one. Once again, we need to refer to Chapter 8 for discussion of the developmental processes that therapists often need to go through in order to meet clients within processes very different from their own.

Dave 35: You're carrying a lot… a helluva lot.
Dominic 36: And I can't carry it any more.

Dave 35 is a pretty inadequate statement. It is very superficial and also it talks *about* Dominic's existence rather than meeting him in it. It is in danger of taking him out of contact with his experiencing. When a therapist hears a client saying something like *Dominic 35* the effect is so powerful that they want to respond to it with words. In fact, I would have been better to have kept my mouth shut and *listened*, with the client, to the silence that would have ensued.

Dominic 36: And I can't carry it any more.
Dave 36: That sounds serious… No. I don't mean to be 'glib'. It really does sound like you are serious.

One of the things about having established relational depth with the client is that the client becomes less sensitive to the individual interventions of the therapist. They can roll with inadequacies like *Dave 35* and give the therapist a chance to get back on 'track'.

Dominic 37: I've got to *do* something.
Dave 37: 'Do'? What would you 'do', Dom?
Dominic 38: Either give it up… or give it up.
Dave 38: I think I understand… one 'part' – the one that is really 'hooked' – would give up on your normal life… and the other 'part' – the one who is a 'loving husband and father' – would give up the booze.
Dominic 39: Most people don't realize how difficult a choice that is.
Dave 39: Is it… does it feel like giving up on living for the life you have?

Once again we have an example of how fully we can see our client once engagement at relational depth is achieved and we have gained insight into their process. *Dave 38* is a good example of that: it is showing empathy with what is really quite a complex and highly individual dimension of Dominic's process. Another dimension of this, reflected in *Dominic 39* and *Dave 39*, is how crucial it is that the client is not judged within this realm. Arguably, there is nothing that would be more invasive. Indeed, it is often the fear of judgement at that profound level that makes clients cautious about accepting engagement at relational depth with another person.

Dominic 40: Yes.
Dave 40: [Silence]
Dominic 41: It *feels* like 'living' when you're drunk – but it isn't really.
Dave 41: [Silence]

Dominic 41 is an evaluative statement at the deepest level of Dominic's experiencing. That is a completely different phenomenon from an evaluative statement at a more surface level of experiencing. At a more surface level a statement like *Dominic 41* can be an echo of a parent-like injunction that is not necessarily experienced as congruent by the person. However, the deeper level is far more profound to the person's being than their catalogue of parental injunctions, so a statement like this will be completely accurate for the client. This is an example of the discussion in Chapter 4 on the fact that in meetings at relational depth where the client is in contact with their deepest process, *they cannot lie.*

Dominic 42: I've been *scared* of living. All my life I've been scared of living. I've never felt like other people. I've never felt sure of myself the way other people do. If you feel sure of yourself you can go out and do things with your life. If you don't feel sure of

yourself you can't. You can't really *do* things with your life. You've always got to make 'safe' choices – choices that don't really test you – choices that aren't really 'living'.
Dave 42: [Silence]

My silence in response to *Dominic 42* reflects my experiencing of its enormity.

Dominic 43: And so, I have an 'ordinary life' – did you see that film?
Dave 43: Ordinary Lives – yes.
Dominic 44: [Long silence]
Dave 44: Are you stuck? Are you thinking about the film?
Dominic 45: Yes, their ordinary lives were blown apart when something terrible happened. They had taken the safe choices for so long that they hadn't developed the strength to deal with real life.

I love this little extract because it illustrates how we easily slip from level to level in terms of our experiencing. Dominic gets completely distracted by the film and I eventually spot that change is his manner. We manage to have a conversation about it and yet I am still not sure that we have the right title for the movie!

Dave 45: And you... what about *you*?

After our 'interlude' I invite him to go back into his experiencing, always aware that he may well have had enough for now.

Dominic 46: Part of me tries to break free, but it also hasn't got experience. It does't know how to do it.
Dave 46: [Silence]
Dominic 47: [Silence]
Dave 47: I am feeling sad for it. I think I am seeing it better. It desperately wants to do something, but it has been 'scared of living' for so long it does not know what to do.

Every time I reread *Dave 47* I feel moved by it. I remember as I said it the genuine feeling of being with this person in such a way that I really felt how 'impossible' was his dilemma. Another technical point about *Dave 47* is that I stay true to his present way of symbolising this part of his self as 'it' without changing it to 'you'. It is not my place to *push* him towards more fully owning this part of his self. If that is to happen, it will happen faster if I can stay close to him rather than seek to manipulate his process.

Dominic 48: So all I can do is to go into that *feeling* of being sad, and get drunk. That's the closest I can get to living.

It is doubtful whether this kind of statement from a client relating the 'feeling of being sad' to 'living' can be understood from any theoretical perspective other than the phenomenological. Historically, he had been so 'scared of living' – never going to the edge in anything and always making the safe choices with the result that there was no emotionality, no 'living' in his daily existence. The closest he could get to living was the feeling of being sad, the melancholia he achieved when he had drunk enough to reach it. Dominic's 'problem' was not alcohol but that he had lost touch with living. Alcohol for him was not an act of self-harming as some too readily interpret it. Indeed, it was an act of self-enhancement that had other implications as well.

Part C (Session 4)

Dominic arrived, on time, for the fourth meeting and made no reference to the previous week or any of the content of that session. With apparent pride he talked about the fact that he had been 'clean' for the past seven days, how he had 'got himself together' and was going to be 'off drink forever'. He was extremely critical of himself in regard to his vulnerability for alcohol. Indeed, he produced a written list of ten criticisms of himself which he read out individually and expanded upon them. I sat through this whole process with absolutely no idea where it would go. I found it much more difficult than in any of our previous sessions to make contact with him. He seemed to jump sideways rather than go deeper in response to any empathy and he became more and more agitated. He reached the tenth point of self-criticism on his list and began reading it with great gusto:

Essentially, I am a bastard. I have always been a bastard and will always be a bastard. There is nothing more to me.

Perhaps it was the vehemence with which he spoke the words or perhaps it was the quietness with which I received them but, in any case, he looked directly at me and then burst into tears. My silence had been facilitative, but not through any intent. I had simply been lost for words in my sorrow. I was close to tears in listening to his attempts at his self-destruction. I might have cried, rather than him, and it might have been just as facilitative. In fact, his tears might have been sparked by his empathy for me at that moment. Eventually he said:

I am not convincing you, am I? [I stayed silent] Well, I'm certainly not convincing *me*, anyway. I am running away from who I was last week. It would be nice and easy to say that it was 'only the drink talking' last week and that it wasn't real. I can't remember all of what I said last week but I do remember how it felt. Do you have the tape of last week?

I told him that I did have the tape and he asked me if we could play some of it. I played it on a back-up recorder. After about 10 minutes Dominic put out his hand in a gesture asking me to stop the tape. Our dialogue continued:

Dominic 49: It is difficult to listen to that.
Dave 49: Why is that, Dom?
Dominic 50: Because I'm drunk.
Dave 50: Yes – yes, you are drunk.
Dominic 51: I hate listening to it. It's not me.
Dave 51: It's not you.
Dominic 52: [Silence]
Dave 52: It's not you.
Dominic 53: How can I *be* like that? How can I be a drunk? How can I have let you tape that?
Dave 53: Dom… If you want, I can wipe that tape right now.
Dominic 54: No… No… It's *me*… It *is* me.
Dave 54: It *is* you.
Dominic 55: But not a part of me I want.
Dave 55: Do you recognise him?
Dominic 56: Sure… he's only a bottle of vodka away.
Dave 56: Where should we go with this, Dom? Where should we go with this *right now*? Where *are* you with this right now?
Dominic 57: I've got to meet him.
Dave 57: You 'heard' him, didn't you Dom… you *really* 'heard' him.
Dominic 58: Yes… yes… I heard him.
Dave 58: You are keeping him out… but, *really*, you heard him…
Dominic 59: I heard 'me the drunk'. I hate him. I cry for him. I cry with him. I *am* him. He is part of me.
Dave 59: And you feel you have 'got to meet him'.
Dominic 60: I don't know what made me say that. I *hate* him. When I'm sober I believe he is gone forever. Why did I say that 'I have to meet him'?
Dave 60: [Silence]
      [Dominic meets Dave's eyes]
Dominic 61: I have been running away from him for years but what I need to do is to *meet* him.

Dave 61: [Silence]
Dominic 62: Let's play some more of the tape.

Commentary on part C

Dominic 49: It is difficult to listen to that.
Dave 49: Why is that, Dom?
Dominic 50: Because I'm drunk.
Dave 50: Yes – yes, you are drunk.
Dominic 51: I hate listening to it. It's not me.
Dave 51: It's not you.
Dominic 52: [Silence]

It is *so* difficult for Dominic to accept the part of him that is a drunk. In terms of Rogers' (1951; 1959) theory of personality adjustment Dominic's self-experience of being a drunk is completely outside his self-concept. Facing the absolute reality of his own voice on tape makes it an undeniable part of him, so he is in considerable dissonance. That dissonance is doing the therapeutic work and all I am doing is reflecting what he says about himself.

Dave 52: It's not you.
Dominic 53: How can I *be* like that? How can I be a drunk? How can I have let you tape that?
Dave 53: Dom… If you want, I can wipe that tape right now.

It is with considerable embarrassment that I reproduce *Dave 53*. For just the length of that statement I completely fell out of contact with him. Instead of treating his 'how can I have let you tape that?' as a rhetorical question to himself, I jumped into defensive practice to question my part in the taping process. This was completely and utterly irrelevant to Dominic and was born of the general criticism about taping that was around in the profession at the time. Although I am embarrassed about this response, I like to leave it in because it is the kind of thing that frequently happens to trainees and shows how defensiveness or vulnerabilities on the part of the therapist can disrupt their 'stillness' and their contact with the client. We will explore this more in Chapter 8.

Dominic 54: No… No… It's *me*… It *is* me.

As often happens, my clumsy response did not disrupt his flow to any extent. In fact, Dominic is so close to his experiencing at that point that almost no matter what I did, he would move to the next level of self-awareness.

Dave 54: It *is* you.
Dominic 55: But not a part of me I want.

Between *Dominic 54* and *Dominic 55* we have a crystallisation of the whole issue as far as his self is concerned. Simultaneously, he has given his response to this part of him at different levels of experiencing: at a more superficial level this part of him is 'not a part of me I want' but, at a more profound level 'it *is* me'.

Dave 55: Do you recognise him?
Dominic 56: Sure… he's only a bottle of vodka away.
Dave 56: Where should we go with this, Dom? Where should we go with this *right now*? Where *are* you with this right now?

Dave 56 is a powerful proposition for an encounter. Essentially, it is dipping beneath Dominic's fairly blasé presentational level of self and asking to meet whoever underlies it. Part of its power is the obvious 'congruence' in the proposition: it is a real invitation from someone who is willing to meet whoever may be there. Dominic accepts the invitation to encounter and immediately moves to what may be the most important sentence of his life.

Dominic 57: I've got to meet him.

This was a spine-tingling moment for me, actually to hear Dominic saying that his different parts must meet. Many people spend their life in avoidance of that encounter.

Dave 57: You 'heard' him, didn't you Dom… you *really* 'heard' him.
Dominic 58: Yes… yes… I heard him.

When I first listened to this part of the tape I was amused to see my level of child-like excitement. Dominic tolerates that – perhaps he also liked it.

Dave 58: You are keeping him out… but, *really*, you heard him…
Dominic 59: I heard 'me the drunk'. I hate him. I cry for him. I cry with him. I *am* him. He is part of me.

In this short statement, I–Me becomes I–I (see Chapter 2).

Dave 59: And you feel you have 'got to meet him'.
Dominic 60: I don't know what made me say that. I *hate* him. When I'm sober I believe he is gone forever. Why did I say that 'I have to meet him'?

It is as though his symbolisation of the relationship between his parts just 'happened' – he can see no intentionality and that is confusing for him.

Dave 60: [Silence]
  [Dominic meets Dave's eyes]

In this moment of silence Dominic met my eyes full on. It is possible that he needed to tap that relational engagement we had. Sometimes when we are struggling we need to re-engage that relational depth, just to check that it is still there and to give us the support to continue. Perhaps the eye contact also helps his internal focusing.

Dominic 61: I have been running away from him for years but what I need to do is to *meet* him.

In this short sentence Dominic summarises his sense of self at its deepest level, to which the most respectful response is silence.

Dave 61: [Silence]
Dominic 62: Let's play some more of the tape.

Part D (Later in Session 4)

Dominic 63: [Dominic begins to cry as he listens to the tape – particularly *Dominic 34* – 'the other part is a loving husband and father']
Dave 63: [Silence]
Dominic 64: It's like I'm listening to him – to me – to that part of me, properly, for the first time. I've been locked into antagonism to him – antagonism and denial and hate. I had to deny he was *really* a part of me. He was an 'evil drunk'. But he is a part of me, not just when I am drunk, but every minute of every day. He is a part of me. He is 'sad me', 'lost me', 'desperate me', 'crying me' – though I'm also crying now. It's like he's with me now, and I'm not drunk nor am I going to get drunk… today.
Dave 64: This sounds different – like you are 'meeting' him rather than 'dismissing' him.

Dominic 65: It feels strange – like I am excited but also tense – this feels different. It's not like I imagined it. I came into therapy to kill that drunk and now I am listening to him and crying for him… crying with him. He really is *part* of me, a part that I haven't been open to. We had to be separated by a bottle of vodka.

Dave 65: [Long silence]

Dominic 66: [Long silence]

Dave 66: Where are you in your silence Dom?

Dominic 67: I have suddenly become aware that you are here.

Dave 67: And how is that for you, that I am here with you?

Dominic 68: The first feeling was an acute embarrassment but that quickly passed. Now it feels good that you are here, that you are sharing this with me. I feel so excited but also tense – might this pass? Could I lose it?

Dave 68: 'It'?

Dominic 69: This is the first time that 'sober me' has met 'drunk me' in a way that he can understand him.

Dave 69: Can 'drunk me' also understand 'sober me'?

Dominic 70: Wow – that's a big question – that's too much right now – that panics me.

Dave 70: In case he can't?

Dominic 71: Yes. It's like I've won a lot 'at the tables' today and if we go too far I might lose it.

Dave 71: Fair enough. I thought I might be pushing too far. I knew it was a big step. In fact, part of me told me not to push… and another part – a kind of 'delinquent' part – said, 'go for it'!

Dominic 72: Hah! So the therapist is crazy too. He has different parts too.

Dave 72: I've been found out. Guilty as charged!

Dominic 73: Can we come back to your question when I've lived with this for a while?

Dave 73: Why can't *I* be as wise as that!
SESSION ENDS [in humour].

Commentary on part D

In this part of session 4, Dominic meets himself as he has never done before. Let us go back and look at the process.

Dominic 63: [Dominic begins to cry as he listens to the tape – particularly *Dominic 34* – 'the other part is a loving husband and father']

Listening to oneself on audio tape is a powerfully focusing experience. Quite literally, we cannot fail to 'hear' our self.

Dave 63: [Silence]

When you *know* that the client is immersed in his own experiencing, uninterrupted silence is golden.

Dominic 64: It's like I'm listening to him – to me – to that part of me, properly, for the first time. I've been locked into antagonism to him – antagonism and denial and hate. I had to deny he was *really* a part of me. He was an 'evil drunk'. But he is a part of me, not just when I am drunk, but every minute of every day. He is a part of me. He is 'sad me', 'lost me', 'desperate me', 'crying me' – though I'm also crying now. It's like he's with me now, and I'm not drunk nor am I going to get drunk... today.

This is a significant shift for Dominic. I–Me has very much moved to I–I. The 'drunk' is not just who he was last week – he is a part of his existence, *always*. Dominic is really owning this part of himself and seeing how big it is.

Dave 64: This sounds different – like you are 'meeting' him rather than 'dismissing' him.

This is yet another inane response that is completely unnecessary. In meetings at relational depth the normal 'proofs of understanding' are not needed. This response is, inevitably, a bit partial and also late.

Dominic 65: It feels strange – like I am excited but also tense – this feels different. It's not like I imagined it. I came into therapy to kill that drunk and now I am listening to him and crying for him... crying with him. He really is *part* of me, a part that I haven't been open to. We had to be separated by a bottle of vodka.

Many therapists, of different orientations, will recognise this kind of client statement where a process of self-acceptance and integration is beginning to replace an earlier agenda of self-alienation. It is the kind of process that often happens with the so called 'inner critic' unless the therapeutic approach negatively evaluates the 'critic' and thus blocks the integration (Stinckens et al., 2002).

Dominic 66: [Long silence]
Dave 66: Where are you in your silence Dom?
Dominic 67: I have suddenly become aware that you are here.
Dave 67: And how is that for you, that I am here with you?

Dominic 68: The first feeling was an acute embarrassment but that quickly passed. Now it feels good that you are here, that you are sharing this with me. I feel so excited but also tense – might this pass? Could I lose it?

This is a classic experience for the client engaged at relational depth with the therapist. The therapist is so alongside the client that the client is not aware of him as a separate, independent existence. As Buber puts it: 'I do not experience the man to whom I say *Thou*. But I take my stand in relation to him, in the sanctity of the primary word. Only when I step out of it do I experience him once more' (1958: 22). Now that he explicitly becomes aware of the presence of the therapist that first feeling of embarrassment is very common – it is like realising that you are not alone in your nakedness. The feeling of embarrassment quickly passes, giving way to the continuing security of the relationship.

Dominic 69: This is the first time that 'sober me' has met 'drunk me' in a way that he can understand him.
Dave 69: Can 'drunk me' also understand 'sober me'?

This is another of those cases where I would have preferred to edit out *Dave 69*. It is a wild process-direction not at all centred in the current experiencing of the client nor indeed in my empathy. In *Dominic 69*, Dominic is summarising what has been a huge process for him, in which one part of himself has thoroughly met and understood another part that was previously alienated. For this incompetent therapist to be so smart-arsed as to immediately introduce the opposite proposition steps beyond the bounds of sensibility!

Dominic 70: Wow – that's a big question – that's too much right now – that panics me.
Dave 70: In case he can't?
Dominic 71: Yes. It's like I've won a lot 'at the tables' today and if we go too far I might lose it.
Dave 71: Fair enough. I thought I might be pushing too far. I knew it was a big step. In fact, part of me told me not to push... and another part – a kind of 'delinquent' part – said, 'go for it'!

Fortunately this client and our relationship is strong enough not to be drawn into *Dave 69*. Dominic explains his position and I find a kind of way of apologising. A therapeutic learning from *Dave 69* is that 'delinquent Dave' is not a person-centred therapist!

Dominic 72: Hah! So the therapist is crazy too. He has different parts too.
Dave 72: I've been found out. Guilty as charged!
Dominic 73: Can we come back to your question when I've lived with
　　　　this for a while?
Dave 73: Why can't *I* be as wise as that!

It is amazing how much humour can be involved in work with clients
at relational depth. When people cannot lie to each other they can
openly acknowledge their inadequacies in relation to each other –
what better way to mark such a powerful encounter but with humour.

This fourth session proved to be critical for the therapy. 'Sober
Dominic' had met 'drunk Dominic' and got beyond judgement and denial
to reach genuine understanding. In session five, Dominic went on to
describe himself as a 'partial drunk': 'part' of him was a 'drunk' and part of
him was 'sober'. The problem with those configurations is that the 'drunk'
can generally undermine the whole process and take over the definition of
the person. One wonders how many other people might be described as
'partial' drunks, if only we could be present at the meetings of their parts?

Discussion

Although a lot happened in the first four sessions, Dominic was not, in
fact, an easy person to meet at relational depth. 'Drunk Dominic' was
designed to be in isolation and 'sober Dominic' escaped relatedness by
being offhand, with an easy repertoire of superficial responses. Also 'sober
Dominic's' punitive self-judging created a kind of impenetrable 'babble'
through which he could not normally be met. Neither of Dominic's modes
of being, then, were easy to establish relational depth with, and the lack
of meaningful, in-depth, connection was even more apparent *between*
these two different aspects of Dominic's self. Nevertheless, as discussed in
Chapter 2, as the therapist engaged with each of the different voices, so
the voices began to hear and accept each other more fully.

A number of encounters during the two sessions illustrated moments
or periods of relational depth and contributed to the establishment of
an enduring connectedness at depth. For example, from the last part of
Dave 5, where he moved from acute incongruence to its opposite, 'I feel…
a bit… "scared"' to *Dominic 9*, 'Yes – "sober me" knows it, but does "drunk
me"?', Dave and Dominic are attaining an encounter at relational depth –
their first for 'Dominic the drunk'. Dave has had to fight for the connection
and Dominic has had to fight his cynicism and his fear to give it.

A second connection at relational depth in Part A is made from
Dave 10 where he challenged Dominic in a very congruent way: 'Dom,
be here, be here *drunk*, but don't play fucking games with me. Neither

you nor I deserve that'. Dominic's silent response is his capitulation to their meeting and his apology (*Dominic 13*) is a really striking affirmation of his respect. Dominic and Dave have their second meeting at depth with this particularly slippery part of him (Dominic the drunk) and they are becoming more enduringly connected.

In Part B there is an extended moment of relational depth lasting all the way from *Dominic 20* – 'I don't know what I am about' – where Dominic makes himself entirely exposed, to *Dominic 42*, where Dominic lays his whole previous life on the line. By this time in the developed and continuing relational depth, the moments can equally be initiated by the client – a mutuality has developed. Another interesting aspect illustrated in this encounter is that there are many times when Dave is off track (*Dave 22, 26, 29, 30, 35*) but they have already established their relationship at depth: Dominic *knows* that Dave can, essentially, be trusted, so Dave's 'misses' are not seen as negatives compensated by his accumulated 'credit' – his misses are simply aspects of Dave's personhood in encounter.

Also, in Part B, after dropping out of their encounter at relational depth to discuss a movie, they easily re-establish it between Dave's 'invitation' in *Dave 45*, 'And you... what about *you*?', to which Dominic responds with the powerful statement, 'Part of me tries to break free, but it also hasn't got experience. It doesn't know how to do it'. The contact continues through their silence to *Dominic 48* where he symbolises the essence of his conflict: 'So all I can do is to go into that *feeling* of being sad – and get drunk. That's the closest I can get to living'.

In Part C the first re-establishment of relational depth stems from Dave's silence in response to Dominic's ten self-criticisms. This was not an engineered facilitation into relational depth – it never can be thus. Dave met Dominic's attempt at pre-emptive self-destruction with simple human sorrow and his 'near tears'. Dominic saw himself reflected in Dave's response and he also cried.

Later in Part C, they re-established contact at relational depth from *Dave 56* through *Dominic 61*. This is a lovely illustration of the fact that *both* persons are involved in encounters. Dave is more excited than Dominic, with *Dave 57*, 'You "heard" him, didn't you Dom... you *really* "heard" him', and *Dave 58*, 'You are keeping him out... but, *really*, you heard him...'.

In *Dominic 63*, Dom enters his 'inner' recesses, but not through relational depth, except perhaps, with himself. Essentially, this is a profound example of focusing (Gendlin, 1981) and how it brings a person to meet their self. However, the aspect of established and continuing relational depth is still relevant because Dominic is able to communicate his new symbolisations. He would not be able to do that except in the context of an already established relational depth.

By this time the relationship does not need to be fed by moments of relational depth, yet the continuing established contact will create its own events such as the communication within the long silences of *Dave 65* and *Dominic 66* followed by Dominic's embarrassment when he 'comes out' at *Dominic 67*.

The metaperspective provided by the taping proved useful, but it would be misleading to see that as the 'winning technique'. If the depth of relationship had not been there – and fought for by both parties – it would have been easy for 'sober Dominic' to avoid contact with 'drunk Dominic' in session four. The relationship, at a depth where Dominic could share his most private process, gives a frightening sense of security that enables the client to entertain a new relationship with himself. We use the word 'frightening' because clients often experience that power with considerable ambivalence. There is the 'positive' side of becoming more open to ourself and there is the 'negative' side of that, which is to open the door to huge dissonance. Dominic was moving from a position where he did not have to 'hear' the part of himself that was represented by 'drunk Dominic'. All he needed to do was to *judge* that part as puni- tively as possible. When, in the context of the therapeutic relationship, he dared to step out of that punitive frame and hear himself, he would have to face the dissonance that described his existence.

Most ways of working with clients who have a 'drink problem' are funded to attack the problem rather than meet the person. This is a func- tion of the 'politics of helping' (Mearns, 2004d). In the context of a 'prob- lem' orientation, the position taken by Dominic's therapist – to actively ignore the problem and to take a distinctly phenomenological perspective – could be seen as incompetent. Yet, that phenomenological perspective in session three proved absolutely crucial in getting to the existential sig- nificance to Dominic of his drinking. No one could have guessed that the experiencing Dominic encountered while drinking – especially the pro- found experience of sadness – gave him a powerful sense of 'living' that contrasted with the lack of sensation in the rest of his life since child- hood. Any 'problem-centred' way of working would not have got to that existential significance – in fact, it would still be working on the wrong 'problem'!

The struggle with Dominic was to help 'Dominic the drunk' have a credible voice. However, the challenge of establishing relational depth with the patient, 'Rick', in the next chapter is even greater, because he has no voice at all.

6 EARNING THE RIGHT TO WORK WITH RICK: A TRAUMATISED CLIENT

In Chapter 4 we described the shocking impact that trauma can have on a person's sense of self and the impossible questions it begs of them at an existential level. We challenged the therapy profession to be prepared to offer the traumatised client an engagement at relational depth since that offers him a context where he can explore, in its rawest form, the trauma experience and its impact.

In this chapter Dave Mearns will introduce 'Rick', a patient who had been traumatised in war. Rick was an inpatient in a hospital specialising in the treatment of war veterans. The staff were a mixture of civilians and military personnel and the regime was unusual in that there was a particular emphasis on psychotherapy. The case is presented here because it offers a unique insight into the therapist's efforts to engage at relational depth with Rick who was profoundly cut-off from communication of all kinds. The rest of the chapter is written by Dave mainly in the first person.

The Struggle for Relational Engagement with Rick

Person-centred therapists will often reject the prior reading of case notes before they meet a client. Like all good conventions, it is the exceptions that are particularly interesting. Working in the psychiatric wing of a hospital specialising in a therapeutic regime for profoundly traumatised military personnel, I had got into the habit of reading case notes thoroughly. In fact, they did not usually give a great amount of detail about the events that had led to the traumatisation of the patient but whatever they did contain was gratefully received because it was difficult in the early stages to get a lot from the patient and anything that might possibly lead to a point of connection was valued.

My new patient, Rick, was to be a big assignment. If your working life consists of only three patients but you will meet them for one hour per day, six days a week then any new patient is a big assignment. Brief referral notes recorded the fact that Rick had not spoken since his admission to the hospital one month earlier. About a third of our patients were mute on arrival, either as a consequence of their traumatisation or, quite commonly, as a consequence of the retraumatisation effects of military interrogation. Most of them gradually came around to communicate but that process could be slow and exceptionally challenging. A patient, mute as a response to trauma, is not just verbally silent. Most of the time they are communicatively silent. Their whole expressive and communicative system has closed down – they have separated themselves from the interactive world. In terms of the central, relational, argument of this book, they have seperated themselves from living.

Rick's case notes did not tell the whole story – they never do. He had been hospitalised out of the war following a big fire fight in which a number of his friends had died. But there were signs that his troubles dated further back. His records showed that, with others, he had been involved in what was suspected to be a fatal 'fragging' – the killing of an officer by his men, though nothing could be proved. In war such things happen – a 'counterfeit universe' is established (Lifton, 1974) which creates realities that would not be recognised on the outside. In this therapeutic work you are faced with the easiest content to judge, yet you know that the challenge is not to judge. Your schooling is rapid: can you actually understand how your 18-year-old patient can cut his 70-year-old prisoner into precisely one hundred pieces? Yes, you can, but only if you step out of your world of reality and into a world of unreality. This work cannot be approached with an externally defined reality position. Instead, phenomenology and situational ethics provide the only functional bases. The only way to understand events is to enter the reality of the patient and the only way to come to an ethical judgement is to accept the actual situation where the events took place. The result is that value judgements fall quickly into disuse.

Rick was 24 years of age which made him one of the eldest of our patients. His records showed that he had been on his third tour of duty. Theoretically, three tours should have been impossible – two was the limit because of the known effects of traumatisation. Yet, some veterans had managed to get a third tour. Most of these were already traumatised and the extra tour was motivated by their need to 're-experience' the traumatic context (APA, 1994). Others would find some other conflict as mercenaries, working for pocket money because the real dividend was the potency of the re-experiencing. As was mentioned in Chapter 4, one of the most difficult dimensions sometimes found in traumatisation is that the event, simultaneously, is the worst thing that ever happened to the person and, also, the moment in their life when they had felt most 'alive'. This is a heady cocktail and it is not surprising that many veterans have difficulty in re-entering the 'normal' world thereafter.

Our First Meeting

I first entered Rick's room on a Monday at 3pm. His room was 'L' shaped with his bathroom taking up the remainder of the rectangle on the right as you entered. His bed was at right angles to the point of entry, facing down the short leg of the 'L'. There was a small window beyond the foot of his bed on the left side, so, from his bed he could not see out of the window – patients tended to prefer that. The room furnishings were basic: a small armchair, a straight chair and writing table, a small bed-side table and table lamp, curtains and a small unit that housed a few books and a record player. In all my visits to Rick only one book was ever touched and the record player had never been used. This was in contrast with one of my other patients who played the same record all day, every day. Rick did not have 'family' items in his room to make it more 'homely'. His case records showed that his wife had brought things on her only visit – and Rick had destroyed them. There was no lock on the door, either on the outside or the inside.

Rick was half lying on his bed but in a slightly propped-up position facing the junction of the ceiling and the wall ahead of him. He would be in that position for many of our next 72 meetings. Rick did not acknowledge my entry, except to turn 90 degrees away from me, facing the wall and curling his legs up under him. This 'turning round' of Rick would be the only communication I would get from him for many of our early sessions. Although he would be completely motionless in that position for long periods at a time, I believe that he never ever fell asleep while I was in his room.

The first thing that struck me about Rick was that he was a *huge* man. Being a founder member of 'Runts Lib.', physical size in relation to men is something I have always had to deal with, sometimes constructively and sometimes destructively (for them as well as me). However, in therapy, everyone is the same height (perhaps the reason I got into it). But Rick was something else. I tried to work out how tall he would be standing – he might be 18 inches taller than me. Also his arms were huge: his upper arms were larger and more muscled than my thighs. Despite his inactivity during his time in hospital there was not an inch of fat on him. He was a giant – a giant who was lying, disabled, on his bed. I remember the fleeting and inappropriate thought that I must avoid being hugged by this man!

I began our first meeting by *talking*. In working with a mute patient it is important not to expect them to speak or to reciprocate communication in any way. At the same time, we are always looking for a 'window' for their speech or other communication. My speaking in that first session is to represent who I am and what I am about. That is quite a challenge in the circumstance where we are getting absolutely nothing back from the other person. I must describe 'who I am' and it must be real. Any pretence whatsoever will be a reason for him to keep the door closed. This is a man who is not communicating but he is functioning cognitively and, almost certainly, he is listening acutely. This is my first representation of myself and in it I must show what I am going to be like, consistently. More than anything else I need to offer him a consistent and highly believable reality. Only then will I have the chance that he might begin to engage me relationally. The performance of the actor, Robin Williams, in the movie *Good Will Hunting* is generally berated by people from the psychotherapy profession. Yet, the image of a therapist he depicts accurately reflects the fact that with a client who readily judges our duplicity, we must be especially real. This emphasis on real, believable human contact is one reason why non-military therapists were used in the hospital. It was realised that, potentially, they could offer a quality of human presence that was more difficult for military personnel who had grown more accustomed to a degree of social distance in their relationships within the military. The policy was also a conscious attempt to respond to the fact that a great many patients were ambivalent to say the least about the military. In fact, they often showed a striking 'plurality' in their response. Part of them would, genuinely, be positive towards the military aspect and another part might be so alienated that hospital military personnel were watchful for their own safety. That plurality perfectly reflected their life to that point – the military had been an important part of who they were – it had largely defined their existence (Rogers and Wallen, 1946). Indeed, their training had shown them that their life depended on being unquestioningly positive about the military. As well as all this sustenance for one 'part' there was often another 'part' that knew they had been conned. Self-plurality is nowhere more evident than in the veterans of war – it is needed to try to hold the huge dissonances of war.

So, my 'who I am' speech has to show Rick that I am going to be a real person with him, rather than a representative of the military. I have to present myself exactly as I see myself, warts and all, with all my doubts, fears and, particularly, including how I feel *here and now*. My communication must be excruciatingly congruent because this patient will have a nose for the slightest incongruence. My speech must also cover 'what I am up to'. Patients know that everyone they meet is 'up to' something – we all have an agenda (O'Leary, 1999). The following is the gist of the beginning of my introductory speech in that first meeting:

Rick, my name is Dave. I will be here from 3pm until 4pm every day from Monday to Saturday each week to be with you. If that does not seem to be the right way to do it, we can change it. The basic idea is that I am your shrink and I will be here for you, consistently. If you want someone but I am the shit that is on offer, I can be replaced. That is the system. The idea is that we want to offer you someone to *connect* to. That is what we are about. You may not want that. Our experience is that people often do not want that for a while, even a long while. My job is to hang in for a long while.

Rick, why we do it this way is that, while we do not know *what* you have been through, we feel that the best thing we can offer you is a human contact. I do not know if that makes any sense to you or not, but it does to me.

Rick did not respond to this, nor did I expect him to. We are just at the 'shaking hands' level of relationship, except that he cannot shake hands. Yet, my last phrase was important, '*but it does to me*'. That is the first offering in the direction of relational depth. I am saying to him, '*I am really serious about the human contact I will be offering you*'.

The language of this introduction may not seem to be particularly 'person-centred'. For a start, it is making some assumptions about how he might be experiencing events and I may be missing him by miles. I will have to be extremely sensitive to any minimal responses from him in order, gradually, to meet him. The terse language and tone of the introduction fits fairly well into the military context in which he has existed. My hope is that this very direct style of communication will be more acceptable to him than 'therapist speak'. Of course, the direct-ness of the tone also reflects the straightforwardness that I am trying to communicate in my message.

In that first meeting I told Rick about who I was as a person, in great detail and extremely personally. It is extraordinarily difficult to do that when you are getting nothing back, but what you are actually trying to do is to break that non-communicative cycle. In normal com-munication we 'give' each other enough to sustain the other's giving. If Rick gives nothing back he can normally expect the other to give up. I need to break that 'normal' cycle in order to sustain my offer of engage-ment despite his lack of reciprocation. Included in my statement was my apprehension, my hope and my fears about what we were embark-ing upon. Rick acknowledged absolutely nothing that I had said. That was fine – that was what I had expected. I was pretty sure that he had heard me and I also knew that I had been *real*, so if he had heard me he probably had heard me as a real human being. Twelve weeks later, sitting together outside a military recruitment centre, Rick was able to tell me virtually everything I had said in that first meeting.

Encounter and Invasion

At precisely 3pm the next day I knocked on Rick's door and entered. You do not knock and wait for a response at the door of a patient who has clearly declared himself mute – that would be enormously disrespectful. I noticed right away that Rick did not 'turn round'. So early in our contact I would have expected that response to endure for more sessions and it was pleasing that he did not seem to need to have to do that, at the beginning at least. Of course, he still did not communicate in any other way but stayed looking in front of him. Rick's line of sight was the space at the junction of the ceiling and the wall in front of him. That was not a space I would ever invade unless I was very sure of his engagement with me. If a person is protecting himself we need to be incredibly careful not to invade him. Yet, at the same time, we are also wanting to offer, but not demand, an encounter.

Near the beginning of that second meeting I spoke about the local football team who had had a particularly good result that weekend. From a normal therapeutic perspective this may seem utterly bizarre but if your aim is primarily to connect with someone it is important to keep your communication very broad ranging. We encounter each other not purely through deep emotional or existential connection, but also through a range of different kinds of contacts. Also, an aim in the work was to try to keep the patient grounded in the sense of being familiar with their surroundings. Thus, in our sessions, I would spend some of the time telling him what was happening in the hospital and the local community. At other times my focus was still concrete, but very much centred in the room and on him. Nowadays these would be recognised as 'situational reflections' and 'contact reflections' through the understandings given to us by Gary Prouty and colleagues in the field of 'pre-therapy' (Krietemeyer and Prouty, 2003; Pörtner, 2000; Prouty, 1994; Van Werde, 2003b). As it happens, my talking about the local football team might not have been too clever – much later I discovered that Rick supported a team from another city!

At other times I would introduce more powerful material. In one session, I brought Rick's case notes into the room with me. They represented a moderately large bundle bound with an elastic band. I knew that what I was doing was powerful, so powerful that I had prepared myself by realising that I must not take off the elastic band and actually open the files. There is a very narrow boundary between encountering and invading. With clients who are more communicatively responsive it is easier to sense the danger of invading and pull back. With patients like Rick you develop a general sense of that line between encounter and invasion, but you are never sure. Instead of opening his files what I did was talk about the reactions I had had upon reading parts of his case notes. In this way I made exploratory and empathic probes into his reality while grounding the communication in my experiencing. For example, I said:

> I read in your notes that you rejected a commendation for your part in … That seems to me to a big thing to do in the military. Everyone – all your friends – would expect you to accept a commendation. Yet, you stood out and rejected it. I guess, although it is not recorded, that you told them *why* you had rejected it, too…

My communication was as much carried in my tone as in the content. I was communicating a genuine curiosity and also admiration. I was certainly not expecting a response from him – at the best of times this area was likely to carry too much potency. Rick did not openly respond, yet I could sense from a stiffness in him that he had heard me not just in what I was saying but in the way I was saying it. I recorded this as the first connection I had made that I could really see. It later proved that I had made a number of earlier connections which he had been able to conceal more adeptly.

I was very attentive to the danger of invasion. On the very first meeting I had taken up position in my chair, at right angles to his bed and about eight feet from him. This offered more 'social distance' than with other patients in relation to whom I had already established communicative contact. It felt like a non-invasive distance and I maintained it through most of our first 26 sessions. With the right signs that my presence was not causing fear, I would move to a closer, more normal, distance from a patient, having always started quite a long way away. The same applied whether we were meeting in a therapy room or the patient's room. Even with some patients who were mute I might position myself quite close if I had enough feedback about the fear my presence engendered. With Rick I stayed far back in most of my early working: I had a strong sense of the balance of our relationship in terms of encounter and invasion, in terms of our engagement and his fear.

Although I was careful in respect to invasion, I still made mistakes and one in particular. In one session I made a tiny reference to his wife and child. I could see him 'freezing' before me in an almost catatonic state – I had seriously invaded him. With a mute patient, such an invasion is profound because they cannot respond verbally. I immediately apologised, saying:

> I am very sorry about that Rick. I should not have mentioned that. If I had thought about it for a moment I would have known it was not right for me to bring that up. It is difficult enough for you to have me here at all without me making it more difficult. I am sorry Rick.

As we will discuss in the next chapter, this sensitivity to encounter and invasion is a big part of offering the possibility of a relationally deep encounter. The variation in the power of the material shows a willingness to meet at different levels and also that I am looking for more than a surface-level engagement. Other factors contribute like grounding my comments in my own experience (for example, earlier, in relation to his case records) but also the softness of the tone and the genuine caring for him in whatever pain he might be experiencing are part of the effort to 'earn the right' to engage with him. Paradoxically, that caring may also be communicated by my sincere apology in having invaded him. To encounter we must risk invasion but we must also be able to recognise and work with it. We clean up our own messes and the act of our cleaning can carry a greater impact than if we had 'got it right' in the first place (see Chapter 4).

A useful way to think about encounter and invasion is as a dialectic. Often our act of 'encountering' one part of the self risks 'invading' another part. Even for people who are so severely damaged that they have had to evoke extreme systems of self-protection there is generally, at some level of their experiencing, a wish to be connected. This may be only a very small voice, but if it exists at all, it can potentially be engaged. The smaller the voice the more believable needs to be our offer. We are constantly looking for small indicators of the part that might engage. Even Rick's slowness in 'turning round' during a session is taken as a likely indicator. Also, all the time you are feeling his *need* to turn around. Sometimes that sense was so strong it was tangible. Three times in my work with him I said: 'Rick, it's alright with me if you want to turn round'. It is crucial to have empathy with both dimensions of the dialectic and to honour both. Essentially, encounter and invasion are two faces of the same thing with the plural self.

As suggested in Chapter 4, the most important variable in establishing the encounter may be the *therapeutic context* itself. In most other circumstances Rick would be a patient who would be deemed to be 'unsuitable for therapy'. The reality is that this kind of patient is perfectly suitable for therapy, depending on the therapeutic context we are willing and able to offer. If the therapy he was being offered was a once weekly therapist with a big case load and a habitual pattern of relational detachment, then this patient would certainly be 'unsuitable' for *that* therapy. Yet, here we had a context that offered the patient a consistent one hour per day, six days a week, at the same time and with the same person, where the whole system, including the supportive medication regime, was geared towards establishing therapeutic contact before this person disappeared into themselves more or less permanently.

Sustaining Oneself Without Response

It is extremely difficult to work with a client like Rick. Session after session at some point in the hour he would 'turn round' and I knew that I would no longer get the sight of his face as feedback. Also, even when he was staring ahead, Rick was remarkably still. Some patients are active in their silence though the activity is often not communicative but repetitive, resembling the kind of disconnected repetitiveness sometimes found in autistic spectrum disorders, although certainly quite different in causality.

There are important issues around how we sustain ourself in offering a depth of relational engagement when we are getting very little back. There are four aspects that were important to me. First was what I *did* get back from Rick. When Rick lasted a whole session or most of it without turning round, that would make a big difference to me. Also, now and again, I would get a flicker of his eye and six times in the first 26 sessions he looked me straight in the eye. But I got more than this back from Rick, though it is difficult to describe. I got a strong sense that he was a barometer to my own presence, that his stillness enabled him to detect the quality of my presence with him. I cannot point to specific cues in his non-verbal behaviour but I could sense his awareness of my focus or of my drifting. The best description of this experience in the research literature is offered by Barbara Kreitemeyer who, also working with a communicatively cut-off patient, uses the term 'contact rhythm' (a translation from the German) to describe the unspoken experience of resonance between her and her client, as she says: 'I got the impression that she [her client] was very much aware of how I was present: if I was really with her, or if my attention had diminished' (Kreitemeyer and Prouty, 2003: 155).

A second issue in sustaining myself was the matter of *staying fresh*. One strategy I used was to go back and reread parts of his files. This did not tell me anything new about him but it seemed to help to keep him fresh in my eyes. I would re-experience all the questions I harboured about him and all the awe I had of him. After doing that I could enter his room that day and really be fresh for him. I think I was constantly reminding myself that there was a person in there and that person had probably been through a great deal. Another strategy for staying fresh was to use my *imagination*. This may seem rather strange but I know that my friend Brian Thorne will understand it. I later learned from Brian that stimulating our imagination is a powerful way to freshen up our empathy (see Chapter 8). So, in the absence of a lot of background to Rick, I would use my imagination to consider various possibilities. I would even try to imagine a series of possibilities on what might be going on in him in our sessions. All the time, I was aware that this use of imagination was a kind of exercise: it would never tell me anything about Rick but what it was about was keeping me fresh to a whole range of possibilities. I think it also helped me to stay 'connected' with Rick in between our sessions (Thorne, 2003).

A third experience which helped me to sustain myself was attending an informal discussion group of veterans. Such groups were not for patients as cut off as Rick but they were used voraciously by those who were more able to connect (we estimated that 25–30 per cent of returning veterans were traumatised to an extent that seriously affected their lives thereafter). My group was not formally organised – a number of former patients organised it for themselves and allowed a couple of us to join. I used that group to stay connected with the kinds of experiencing they spoke about, but I also used the group to talk about my patients and my work with them. Me using them to help me to sustain myself was much more important than the niceties of maintaining strict 'boundaries'. I would get a normal mix of reactions but that mix included enough appreciation of what I was doing and how I was doing it. I vividly remember one hardened veteran wiping a tear away when I described a powerful experience with Rick. My experience in the group told me that I was on the right planet and helped me to stay there – it is easy to lose that.

The fourth source of sustenance was my daily supervision with a senior therapist, as well as a three-hour weekly session with other therapists. Both these settings offered the same depth of relational meeting that we were trying to create in therapy. The supervisor and other colleague therapists not only knew my work very well but they also knew *me* very well. Together we would continually explore the boundary between full involvement and over involvement. Inevitably there would be over involvement at times. The purpose of the supervision was not to stop that and make it impossible but to understand it and in that way to control it and make the work safe for both therapist and patient. That was a sustaining kind of support and also one that was particularly encouraging of development. Learning about who we are in terms of our boundaries is such an important part of freeing ourselves to offer clients the possibility of a relationally deep encounter. That is not achieved by having a chronic fear of over involvement but by close monitoring in a trusted context (see Chapter 4).

'Talking the Talk'

One of the important things about working in a specific client context is knowing the common language. I had had a considerable exposure to the language of this conflict some years previously and I was able to maintain and update that through the group. Talking was so important to veterans that they had a sophisticated language for identifying each other and what they had been through without, to the outsider, appearing to talk about much at all.

In four of my first 12 meetings with Rick I spent some time talking about my experiences in the group. It seemed a fair exchange that if I talked about him with them it should also be vice-versa. On one occasion particularly, I could *feel* Rick listening to me. It was an uncanny sensation. I was talking about an experience that one of my friends in the group had described the night before. I was able to talk about it in the language of the culture and about how it had moved me. Particularly, I talked about all the feelings I had had while I listened. I described my friend as a 'gentle giant' and I know that my affection for him was coming over to Rick. Rick and I were, at that moment, in a bizarre situation. We could neither of us express affection for the other: him for obvious reasons and me because it would have been profoundly invasive and also inappropriate to the language of the culture. But, in a sense, we were doing it 'by proxy' through my group friend, for both my friend and Rick were 'gentle giants'.

The 'Flying Book'

In the 15th session Rick threw a book at me. It came entirely out of the blue as far I was concerned and I was so surprised that the book hit me full in the face before I could dodge it. It was a bizarre experience – this huge man throwing a book at me – he could have broken me across his knee if he had wanted to hurt me. I wasn't frightened at all, just surprised. I had no idea what I had done to arouse this response. I tried to reflect it and made a series of guesses but Rick just turned round. Many weeks later I asked him about the thrown book. He blushed, apologised and said that he had 'just got angry with me' – fair enough.

The Day Rick Cried

Again, like the flying book incident, I did not see it coming. In the 23rd session I had been telling Rick about something that had happened on the ward earlier that day. There had been a physical fight and a lot of violent shouting and threats. Also, a knife had been used, though surprisingly ineffectively for this clientele. My rationale for speaking about this was as part of keeping Rick 'in touch'. He would have heard the fracas but would not know what had gone on before or what had followed. I was contextualising the event for him.

I saw his eyes filling and a tear running down his face. I stopped talking abruptly – he would hear that. I stayed silent – he would hear that too. For about a minute he let me see him, then he turned round. And, as always, there was no sound. In a very soft voice, I said, 'I heard you, Rick' and I remained silent and in my position for the last 50 minutes of the hour. That was one of the most powerful 50-minute periods I have ever had in therapy. My feeling was that it held the moment. My experience was that there was considerable relational depth in that period. One thing about it was clear to me: Rick had *let* me see him. He had waited that minute before turning round. Also, I had acknowledged his 'communication'. We had 'met' and we had both acknowledged our meeting.

Part of engaging at relational depth is letting the moments *be*, not endlessly seeking to revisit them and talk them into superficiality. If a depth of communication is achieved, it needs to exist at that level – it does not need to be dissected. The same is true in ordinary life.

Meeting 25

Before meeting 25 a nurse gave me a note he had been given by Rick. It said: 'tell him not to come'. This was a striking moment, because Rick had never used notes before. I did not obey the note: there are two of us in a therapeutic relationship and we both have rights. When I knocked and entered his room that day, in the normal fashion, at precisely 3pm he immediately turned round. But he did it in what seemed to be a much more dramatic way than usual, with what looked like strong irritation. I pulled my seat as far back from its normal position in the room as I could get it. It was right against the door about 15 feet away from Rick. At that moment I decided that I would exert myself in our relationship. I thought that I could do this because Rick had substantially made himself safe by immediately turning round. I said:

> I got your message Rick, but I still wanted to come. I will stay well away from you and I won't ask you to respond. But I just could not not come. It's what I do. I come at 3pm and I go at 4pm. I am nervous about it, because I know that sometimes I make you scared. And that sometimes you would just prefer to be alone *all* the time. But I still wanted to come. It is what I do. It's all I do. I spend this hour with you.

I sat there in silence for the next 57 minutes while Rick remained motionless. It was a powerful meeting between us.

The Day Dave Cried

The next day I was excited as 3pm approached. I could not wait for the start of the session. Usually before sessions I would find a quiet place for five minutes so that I could leave aside the rest of the world and slow down in order to meet my patient (see Chapter 7). This day I did not do that because I was already ready.

When I knocked and entered his room, Rick looked at me and I stood at the door and returned his look. He did not look away and he did not turn away. After 25 hours together, for the very first time, I asked Rick a question. As mentioned earlier, to ask a consciously communicatively disconnected patient a question is one of the most disrespectful things one could do. But after the power of our last meeting and all that had gone before, it seemed natural in terms of our relationship. Without words I held my seat up with one hand and used the other to point to the two areas in the room where I might position it: in its normal place, or at the door. Rick made the smallest shrug of his shoulders. I put my seat into its normal position and I stayed quiet, but I was bursting with excitement. Rick had actually communicated in response to me. He had indicated that he did not mind where I sat. A slight shrug of the shoulders indicating no preference might not seem to represent a huge relational engagement but I knew that for Rick it *was*.

I sat down ready to begin. I knew that I would make no reference to the previous day, because whatever it had been for him, it was in the past. As I sat there, I realised that I could say absolutely *nothing*. This was an extraordinary experience. I sat in silence, looking at him and he half sat, half lay in his usual position staring blindly ahead, not at me. I thought of a dozen things to say and each of them felt wrong, so eventually I succumbed to my silence. As I sat there I gradually felt my chest tightening and I knew I was going to cry. This had happened before, with another patient in the hospital, but it had been in direct response to the pain I knew was tearing him apart (Mearns and Thorne, 1999: 100). In that instance, it had been empathy. But this was not empathy. This was *my* emotion. This was the release of *my* pent-up feelings. This was weeks of putting myself on the edge, weeks of being fully committed, weeks of feeling for Rick and getting little back, until this moment. I had not realised how involved I was. I cried quietly.

Rick turned and looked at me, I think with incredulity. Then he did an amazing thing. He swept his legs off the bed, reached to his bedside table, plucked a Kleenex and handed it to me. Then he resumed his normal position. After another silence, I told him what had been going on for me. He did not respond. He had done more than enough responding for that day.

Meeting 27

The next day I had a message from the nurses that Rick had asked one of them if he could have a coffee maker in his room. The nurse had said 'sure' and set about organising it before he even realised that Rick had actually spoken, so matter of fact had been the request. My first feeling on being told this was irritation. I smiled at myself. We often talked about this in team meetings and in supervision – that when you are working in this way your initial feeling was that key moments should have happened with *you*. The irritation lasted only microseconds.

When I knocked and entered Rick's room he was sitting on the edge of his bed. He said, 'do you take milk and sugar?'

The End of the Beginning or the Beginning of the End?

Those first 27 sessions with Rick had not only been about establishing 'psychological contact' as in the first of Rogers' (1957) six therapeutic conditions. They had chiefly been about establishing *relational* contact at a level that would be needed for work with a person who is profoundly traumatised. For a traumatised person, considerable relational depth is a precondition before they can, really, open up to their experiencing. It sometimes feels as though they look at you, as though they look right *through* you to judge if you can offer them enough for them to take that risk, for it is a terrible risk.

The 27 sessions were not about Rick starting to talk – that is a red herring. The not talking certainly makes communication more difficult, particularly because you do not get as many cues back from the patient to appreciate what is going on inside him. Also, the starting to talk is significant only in so far as it is a sign of Rick's decision to commit to this relationship. For Rick, this was a pretty clear commitment. Other patients would oscillate between communicating and not communicating. Also, other patients were sometimes stronger than Rick in their efforts to push the therapist away.

The title of this section – 'The End of the Beginning or the Beginning of the End?' – is a serious question. On the one hand we may view all that has happened to this point as being a kind of 'pre-therapy' seeking the engagement of the client in a 'normal' therapeutic process. Or, we might alternatively view these first 27 sessions as the essential substance of the therapy, achieving the central goal of helping Rick to re-enter a relational existence. However we view it, having established the relational engagement, the work with Rick could move to another phase. But we could talk about that now and we could more easily share our understandings. My question over coffee in session 27 was: 'where should we begin?' I know as I am sitting there that this will be the beginning of weeks of pain for Rick. I can guess from my experience that in about a third of our sessions he will have to stop to vomit.

I know that he will *feel* the fact that he cannot love his wife or child or any other human being any more. I know that he will describe a pattern, at 24 years of age, of someone who has lived his life already. I know that he will not be able to see any future for himself. I know that he will sob and sob and I will hold him. I know that he will plead to die. I do not know the detail he will disclose of the circumstances leading to his traumatisation. I do not know that one sunny day, sitting in the hospital garden, he will tell me that he machine gunned four children under five and their mother, and that he had laughed.

7 FACILITATING A MEETING AT RELATIONAL DEPTH

In this chapter we will look at ways in which therapists can facilitate an encounter at relational depth with their clients, leading to the kind of ongoing therapeutic relationship that is characterised by a deep sense of trust and safety. We hope this chapter will be of particular value to trainees in the person-centred approach and other relational therapies, helping them to develop their ability to fully meet their clients in this way. In this chapter, we are also hoping to present a new slant on the training and practice of person-centred therapy: one in which the central concern for the therapist is to meet their clients as fully as possible, rather than the implementation of a specific set of skills, or even providing for their client a discrete set of therapeutic conditions.

The use of the term 'facilitate' rather than 'create' or 'make' in the chapter is deliberate, for as we have said in Chapter 3, a relationally deep encounter is not something that a therapist can bring about on their own. This is for a number of reasons. First, as we have emphasised throughout this book, relational depth is not a one-person phenomenon, but something that is fundamentally dyadic. Hence, for instance, however present Dave was with Rick (see Chapter 6), it was only once Rick was willing to reciprocate that presence, at even the most minimal level, that some kind of meeting could come about. Second, for a truly deep relational encounter to happen the therapist must, as we shall see later, let go of her 'aims', 'anticipations' and 'lusts' (Buber, 1958), and this includes a 'lust' for relational depth. This is because, if we are trying to *do* something to someone, we are not genuinely meeting that Other, but rather our own needs and desires. Third, on a very practical level, many clients – like Rick – will sense if we are trying to do something to them, and if they feel forced into relating in ways with which they are not comfortable, they may push it away. This may be particularly the case for clients who are fearful of meeting others at a level of relational depth; clients who, as discussed in Chapter 2, may be most in need of such encounters in their lives.

With respect to this last point, this means that, not only can we not *make* a meeting at relational depth come about, but it is something that we must *earn the right* to enter into. For many clients, the craving to be encountered at a level of relational depth is matched only by their fear of such intimacy; for to be met without pretence or defence means that they can be judged for who they really are without any hiding place. So it is far safer for them to project an image of themselves, perhaps an image that pleases others or at least gives them the comfort of familiarity; and to let down that image and that defence requires a great deal of trust (see Chapter 4). As therapists, then, we cannot simply expect clients to be willing to allow us into the most hidden recesses of their being. However trustworthy and safe we may feel ourselves to be, we should not fall into the myth of self-transparency (see Chapter 2) and assume that others can see our trustworthiness too. It is likely that many of our clients will experience us, initially at least, as a distant and somewhat inscrutable stranger, whose trustworthiness has yet to be proved.

Letting Go of 'Aims' and 'Lusts'

As indicated above, one of the things that often gets in the way of a relationally deep encounter is the desire to do something *to* our clients; for if our attention is orientated towards the outcomes of our work, then it will not be on the client and his experiences. Moreover, if we are trying to do something to, or for, our client, then it is likely that the image we hold of them will be quite different from the image of a capable, volitional, enabled Other – the kind of confirming, respectful attitude that is necessary for a true meeting of human freedoms to come about.

Of course, it is entirely understandable that we will often have aims and goals for our clients. Indeed, to a great extent, this might be unavoidable; and there is no suggestion here that those aims are necessarily malevolent. In many cases, for instance – and particularly in the case of trainee therapists – one of our implicit aims may be to show to ourselves, our clients, or perhaps our supervisors or trainers that we are *competent* practitioners. This is something that we all experience to some extent, but the problem is, the more we are focused on how proficient our therapeutic work is, the less we may be focused on the actual human being in front of us. Rather, they become a medium for our own desires. That is one of the reasons, as we shall see in Chapter 8, why the personal development work of therapists is so important. The aim is not to rid ourselves of any desires, but to ensure that we are aware of those implicit goals that we may have, such that we can put them to one side as best we can – in phenomenological terminology, 'bracket' them (Spinelli, 2005) – and re-engage with the actuality of our clients' lived experiences.

Another well-intentioned agenda that many therapists may have is simply to make their clients feel better. This is often manifested in very subtle ways. In working with a depressed client, for instance, we may tend towards reflecting back their feelings of hope for the future, but not their feelings of despair or hopelessness. Such a bias, again, is totally understandable; indeed, in some therapeutic approaches (such as Brief Solution Focused Therapy; see Miller et al., 1996) it is positively encouraged. Nevertheless, from a person-centred and existential perspective, we would argue that such a response will tend to reduce the likelihood of a relationally deep encounter taking place, because the client is less likely to feel that their therapist is 'with' the totality of who they are.

To fully encounter another at a level of relational depth, we may also need to let go of our desire to *understand* the Other. Here, we can get so caught up in the *content* of what they are experiencing – for instance, 'which sister said what to whom at what time on what day' – that we lose contact with the actuality of the client who is having the experiences. To that end, it may be perfectly possible to provide an intense human contact with the experiencing of the client that in itself creates a safety to explore without ever knowing what the client is talking about. Working with clients whose communications may differ from our own affords useful experience of this discipline of relating with the experiencing rather than the experience (Lambers, 2002; Mearns and Thorne, 2000: 129–30; Van Werde, 2003a; 2003b). For the client exhibiting psychotic process (Prouty, 1994; Van Werde, 2003a), traumatic process (Chapters 4 and 6) or even the client flitting around the only partially symbolised features at the edge of their awareness, there is little possibility of the therapist actually understanding that content in the moment. Indeed, that 'need to know' can lead the new therapist into a series of questions that succeed only in taking the client away from their edge of awareness. Inviting trainee therapists to pay more attention to the client's act of expressing rather than to what the client is actually saying (the expression) can help them to become more at ease with not knowing and to stay connected with the client at the edge of their awareness. This discipline is exemplified by the case study in Chapter 6 and elsewhere (Mearns and Thorne, 2000: 129–31).

In practical terms, how can therapists develop their ability to put their agendas to one side? Perhaps the first and most obvious point here is that the more therapists can be *aware* of their aims the more they will be able to bracket these. Again, personal development work is enormously helpful here: not only so that therapists can become more aware of their needs, but also so that they can become more self-accepting, and hence more able to acknowledge their needs, however distasteful and 'wrong' they may seem (see Chapter 8). A trainee person-centred therapist, for instance, may find it very difficult to acknowledge her need to 'make clients better' because she has come to believe that it is wrong to want to direct clients in any way. However, it is unlikely that such a belief will make her any less directive; indeed, if she simply says to herself that it is wrong to have this need she may be more likely to ignore or justify any times when she acts in a directive way. Far better, then, that she comes to see the intelligibility and concern behind her desire to help out others, such that she can honestly reflect on times when this agenda tends to take over and begin to look at ways in which she might be able to respond in a less agenda-driven way.

In terms of letting go of aims and goals, it can also be useful to remember our limitations as therapists. To think that it should be within our power to 'cure' our client, find the magical 'solution' for them or cause them to change the whole pattern of their life is to embrace omniscience in a fashion that itself resembles 'pathological' thinking. The reality is that our client may have the roots of their present problem located deep in their past existence. Those roots will have later articulations that have enmeshed with their whole world of relationships, achievements and self-concept. It may be that we are working with them at an opportune moment in their life, at a moment when they have become dissatisfied with the developed pattern of their life and are more motivated towards change or at a moment when something dramatic has happened that is causing them to take stock. Perhaps in that circumstance the client will allow us to accompany them for a short time and will invite our different perspective on their life pattern. Perhaps also, in the context of this relationship, they will begin to change the pattern or perhaps not yet. Perhaps this will prove to be simply a period of contemplating a change that will be put into action much later (see Prochaska's (1999) 'cycle of change'). In all of this the client is the agent of their own change (Bohart and Tallman, 1999) and the therapist is just one significant 'other' in their life.

Letting Go of 'Anticipations'

Many of us come into counselling and psychotherapy because we are fascinated with the workings of the human mind and emotions. Even if we are not, it is inevitable that we will have certain assumptions about why people are the way they are; for instance, that people have an innate drive towards actualisation, or that psychological problems are a result of early childhood difficulties. As with our aims for our clients, such assumptions and hypotheses are not 'bad' in themselves, but if we only see our clients through the filter of such theories, then we are not really meeting our clients, but a projection of what we expect and believe. Not unexpectedly, then, when the counsellors we spoke to talked about their experiences of relational depth, none made any mention whatsoever of being aware of theory at that time. At moments of relational depth, they were not thinking things like 'I can really sense the client's "actualising tendency" here'. Rather, there was an immediate contact with their client as another human being, someone who could not be reduced to any set of hypotheses or theory.

Hence, in terms of facilitating a meeting at relational depth, it is important that we encounter our clients from a place of naïvety or 'un-knowing' (Spinelli, 1997), where we try to put our assumptions and expectations to one side and open ourselves up to the client in all their uniqueness and unpredictability. Of course, as with letting go of our aims, this does not mean pretending to ourselves that we have no expectations or assumptions – inevitably we will have. Rather, it means becoming self-accepting and honest enough with ourselves to acknowledge when we do have certain beliefs and biases, and thus having the capacity to bracket them. Paradoxically, too, one of the best ways of developing our capacity to bracket our theoretical assumptions may be by deepening and broadening our theoretical understanding. This is because, by doing so, we increasingly come to realise that the psychological and philosophical theories that we hold – whether explicitly or implicitly – are just *one way* of viewing the world and not some unchallengeable truth. This applied in Dave's work with Rick in Chapter 6 where an awareness of traumatisation in war expanded the imagination making it easier to tolerate uncertainty in the work.

Letting Go of Techniques

Counselling and psychotherapy trainees are often keen to have some technique upon which to hang their practice, but such a way of working can make it more difficult to meet clients at a level of relational depth (see Stern, 2003; Stern et al., 1998). This is for a number of reasons. First, if we try to implement a technique, our attention is likely to be on what we are doing *to* our client and its outcome, rather than on the particular human being present to us. In other words, our relationship with the client is no longer im-mediate, but mediated by certain plans and actions. Second, if we relate to our clients through techniques and therapeutic strategies, we are less likely to be open to them as the unique human beings that they are, but will be looking for particular responses and outcomes from them across particular dimensions. And third, the more we are relating to our clients in a technique-based way, the more we lose *our* own naturalness, spontaneity and uniqueness and start to relate in formulaic and rehearsed ways. This, again, reduces the possibility of an immediate and direct human encounter.

Person-centred trainees and practitioners will be relatively familiar with the arguments above, but what is sometimes overlooked is the fact that even 'person-centred' ways of working can become techniques if implemented in formulaic ways. If we 'reflect' back, for instance, the last few words of everything a client says; or we respond to every question with '… and how do you feel about that?' then our work is no more fluid and spontaneous than that of a technique-orientated cognitive behavioural therapist. Indeed, even non-directivity can become a technique if it is used in inflexible and formulaic ways to *do* something to a client. Barry Grant (2002), an American client-centred therapist and trainer, refers to this as 'instrumental non-directivity', and he distinguishes it from 'principled non-directivity', which is a much deeper and more encompassing commitment to not interfering with others' lives.

Listening… Listening… Listening…

As therapists, when we have things that we want to achieve, theories that we want to prove, or techniques that we want to implement, we often end up trying to rush the therapeutic work. We are anxious, for instance, to help our clients stop feeling depressed, or to find out what has 'caused' their panic attacks, and so we try to hurry them along to the point that we want them to be at. And, in doing so, we will sometimes do one of the things that many clients rate as the most unhelpful of therapists' behaviour: not listening well enough (see Paulson et al., 2001).

Such an unhelpful way of responding to our clients is by no means the prerogative of trainee therapists. As we saw in Dave's work with Dominic, there were a number of times when Dave came in too soon, or said too much, or disturbed the client's flow. It is probably fair to say, then, that all of us as therapists – from the most inexperienced trainee to the most experienced trainer and supervisor – will have times when we want to *do* something to our clients, or get something *from* them, and will consequently provide them with insufficient space to talk.

Why is space and listening so important to the facilitation of a relationally deep encounter? Partly because it ensures that clients will follow their own leads and talk about the things that really matter to them – their core concerns and experiences – rather than those that the therapist deems important. But also, it is essential in allowing clients the time they need to process at the deepest possible level. Many of us can talk about presentational-level issues at a rate of knots, but when we talk about our deeper feelings, we slow down dramatically. When we are trying to talk about these experiences, we generally need much more time to find the 'right' words and phrases. How does someone put into words, for instance, that aching sense of loss, grief and emptiness that they experienced when their husband died; or the utter joy that they felt when they saw their first child being born? As in Dave's work with both Dominic and Rick, then, it is no surprise that many therapists experience their deepest moments of relational depth with clients in silence – when there is a meeting of shared experiencing that is best received without words. Concomitantly, if a therapist is throwing too many words at a client, it can bring the client up from a deeper level of processing and towards a more presentational plane – one in which the words are easily available, but where they actually mean far less.

As a related point, the fact that deep emotional processing often takes time is one reason why it can be so important just to reflect back to clients what they say and in their own words. At *Dominic 24*, for instance, Dominic says, 'I think I'm serious … sincere. But, *really*, I'm only a drunk … a fuckin' drunk'; and Dave repeats this back almost word for word: 'You think that you are serious … and sincere. But you are really, only, a fuckin' drunk'. And then, when Dominic says 'Yes', Dave reflects again, 'A fuckin' drunk – that's all you are'. Sometimes, trainees avoid such word-for-word reflections because they fear that they will be experienced by clients as patronising, repetitive or inane – and, indeed, if implemented as a technique, they can be – but where clients are processing at a deeper level, they often need the time that such reflections provide them to really 'work through' what they are saying. Had Dave, for instance, tried to move on the dialogue by saying something like, 'Well, I experience you as sincere' then Dominic may not have had enough time to really process his self-revelation. Dominic's statement that 'I'm just a fuckin' drunk' could not have been 'worked through' instantaneously: its power needed time to fully sink in, to be felt and thought about; and it is at times such as these that silence or simple reflections are one of the most powerful responses that therapists can make.

'Listening' to clients, however, involves more than providing them with an opportunity to talk. What we mean is really *attending* to the client, and attuning to their being, at an emotional, cognitive and embodied level. This is another reason why it can be so important to provide clients with an uninterrupted space to talk, particularly at the beginning of sessions: because if we come in too early, we do not allow the totality of the client's emotional-cognitive-physical being to emerge. If a client, for instance, starts a session by talking about their anger towards their mother, a therapist's premature reflection of this feeling may stop the client from also expressing their love for their mother, and their concerns over their mother's frailty, and their guilt for not helping their mother more. So, here, the therapist is resonating with only one small part of the client's experienced-whole. To develop a holistic sense of another takes time: people are complex beings, and if therapists come in too soon, they do not allow that complexity – with all its subtleties, interactions, dilemmas and tensions – to emerge.

Another way to think about this is that we, as therapists, need to sense the 'red thread' (Bugental, 1976) of the client's concerns. This is the essence of what they are trying to tell us, their real concern or concerns, the thing or things that are presently most significant for them. And this red thread cannot be sensed if we come in too soon and interrupt the client's telling of their story. Rather, for it to emerge, all the different aspects of the client's narrative must be allowed an opportunity to be aired, such that the thread woven through them begins to materialise. This is what David Rennie (1998) means when he writes about the importance of 'tracking' the client.

Hence, what we are talking about here is a *'holistic listening'*. This is a listening that 'breathes in' the totality of the Other rather than focusing down on one particular element: a kind of 'beholding' or 'circumscribing' of their being. Such a form of taking in another is beautifully described by Buber in his account of contemplating a tree, in which all aspects of the tree, 'picture and movement, species and type, law and number' become 'indivisibly united in the event' (1958: 20). Interestingly, this holistic listening is similar to the attitude of 'evenly hovering attention' that Freud prescribed in the birth years of psychotherapy, a form of attention which 'consists in making no effort to concentrate the attention on anything in particular, and maintaining in regard to all that one hears the same measure of calm, quiet attentiveness' (quoted in Safran and Muran, 2000: 55). Interestingly, too, Freud's justification for listening to clients in such a way is almost identical to that which is presented in this book. He writes:

> As soon as attention is deliberately concentrated in a certain degree, one begins to select from the material before one; one point will be fixed in the mind with particular clearness and some other consequently disregarded, and in this selection one's expectations or one's inclinations will be followed. This is just what must not be done... If one's expectations are following in this selection *there is the danger of never finding anything but what is already known*, and if one follows one's inclinations anything which is to be perceived will most certainly be falsified. (p. 55, emphasis added)

'Knocking on the Door'

Holistic listening means taking in the totality of our clients, but to develop some sense of what that totality is, we may also need to help them explore their lived experiences in a more focused, detailed and in-depth way. In other words, just as Buber (1958) suggests that we will inevitably cycle between I–Thou and I–It modes of relating, and that an I–It relationship can allow us to experience an I–Thou relationship in greater depth, so a focused exploration of the client's lived experiences can help us to engage more fully with the totality of who they are.

When we invite clients to explore their lived experiences and meanings in this way, we can refer to it as 'knocking on the door' of their deeper experiences. In our therapeutic work, there will be moments when our very closeness to their experiencing engages our own sensitivity to something underlying the surface-level expressing and, here, it is perfectly appropriate for us to ask if there is 'anything else there'. Trainees of the person-centred approach sometimes think that person-centred therapists are not *allowed* to ask questions, but this is a myth that comes out of the idea that person-centred therapy is a set of specific techniques or skills. If we think, on the other hand, of person-centred therapy as an approach which is focused around meeting our clients at a level of depth, then the asking of questions is entirely appropriate if it has the potential to facilitate this encounter. At the same time, we would not be so presumptuous as to know what it was or even to be sure of the existence of something as yet unsymbolised at the edge. The metaphor of 'knocking on the door' reflects the gentleness and invitational nature of this encounter. It is indeed a 'Thou–I' encounter: we are with the experiencing of the client and they are the only person who can have any authority in that domain. For us to tip over into being the expert within their experiencing becomes a different therapy more based on the therapist's analytic expertise than their relational encounter.

Such invitations to the client to explore their experiences more deeply can take many forms. At the most basic level, it may simply involve reflecting back to clients a word or phrase they have used. Alternatively, it may take the form of a more direct question like, 'you said that you felt angry, and I was wondering if you could say more about that?' or 'can you say what you meant by "unfair"?' Inviting clients to unpack feeling-words can often be of enormous value. Words like 'angry' or 'sad', sometimes thrown out by clients in an almost casual way, can contain a great richness and complexity of experiences, a 'world in a grain of sand'. So, although asking a question like, 'what do you mean by "sad"?' may seem banal, to a client who is testing the water with their therapist to see whether it is safe to explore this emotion, it can be a very welcomed invitation. Such knocking on the door of the client's felt-experiences mirrors the process of 'focusing' (Gendlin, 1981; 1996; Mearns, 2003a; Mearns and Thorne, 1999; 2000; Purton, 2004), in which clients are invited to explore unclear felt-senses at the edge of their awarenesses. An example of this might be, 'you said you had a sense of deadness in your stomach, and I was wondering if you could stay with that feeling and say a bit more about it'. Here, the therapist will work with the client to fully articulate what is being felt at the bodily level.

As presented above, knocking on the door relies on some level of verbal communication. But even where that is not present, it is still possible to invite the client down to deeper levels of engagement. Some clients may have difficulties with communication for a huge variety of reasons including profound learning difficulties, psychotic process, and as a response to trauma. Indeed, there can be times with any client, for example where they are experiencing considerable distress or confusion at the edge of their awareness, when the symbolisation upon which communication is normally contingent is not happening. In circumstances like these it can be important to be aware of the discipline of 'pre-therapy' which invites the therapist to step out of their normal symbolic level of communication to reflect more concretely on events that may be happening in the client's phenomenal world. Hence 'situational reflections', 'facial reflections', 'body reflections', 'word-for-word reflections' and 'reiterative reflections' become the communicative disciplines through which the therapist makes psychological 'contact' with the client. This method is well described in the writing of the originators (Prouty, 1994; 2001; Prouty et al., 2002; Van Werde, 2002; 2003a; 2003b).

Multidirectional Partiality

To listen to the whole of the client means attending to, and engaging with, the many different 'configurations of self' (Mearns and Thorne, 2000) or 'modes of being' (Cooper, 1999) that the client inhabits – aspects of the client that may be directly opposed to one another. Here, as discussed in Chapter 2, we may talk about adopting an attitude of 'multidirectional partiality' (see Cooper et al., 2004; Stiles and Glick, 2002), a term taken from the family therapy literature (Boszormenyi-Nagy et al., 1991; O'Leary, 1999) that refers to an ability to empathise with a multitude of different voices and positions.

Such multidirectional partiality can be much harder than it sounds because we will inevitably favour certain of the client's voices over others. If we are working with a socially phobic client, for instance, we may have a tendency to side with their 'I want to get over my fears' voice and offer less validation or empathy to their 'I want to steer clear of people' side. In terms of facilitating a meeting at relational depth, however, it would seem crucial that we can engage with both. This was well illustrated in Dave's work with Dominic in Chapter 5, where it seemed essential not simply to establish a therapeutic relationship with 'sober Dominic' but also to be equally willing to welcome, engage and empathise with 'Dominic the drunk'. In naïve approaches to behaviour change, parts that are seen as antithetical to the desired direction of change are often discounted or even ignored. Attention is denied lest it be seen as 'encouraging the bad behaviour'. The theoretical basis of such treatment regimes is grounded more in the politics of the service and in the doctrine of Calvinism than in psychotherapeutics. To work with the dynamics within the person both sides of the conflict need to be engaged, equally. In modern person-centred theory this dialogical emphasis is described in terms of the interaction of 'growthful' configurations and 'not for growth' configurations (Mearns and Thorne, 1999; 2000); or the dynamic formed between the 'actualising tendency' and the need for 'social mediation' (Mearns, 2002).

Another way of looking at this, in psychodynamic terms, is that we need to 'appreciate the wisdom of the resistance' (Hycner, 1991; Hycner and Jacobs, 1995), ally ourselves with it (Safran and Muran, 2000) and embrace it, rather than castigate it or try to break it down. In other words, clients – like all human beings – do not avoid painful feelings out of some self-destructive cowardliness. Rather, we avoid such feelings out of a very human, 'adaptive' (Safran and Muran, 2000) and understandable desire to feel safe, comfortable and non-threatened. Hence, although clients may sometimes need to experience painful or difficult feelings to move on in their lives, we also need to value that part of them that does not want to experience pain and does not see why it should. What from the outside, then, might seem like 'resistance', from the inside of the client's world might seem like a very sensible strategy for not experiencing too much hurt, and unless we can accept and be alongside this need as well as the need for growth, we will not fully be with the whole of the client.

Paradoxically, in terms of facilitating a meeting at a level of relational depth, one of the aspects of the client that it may be particularly important to engage with is that side of them that *does not want* to engage at relational depth. This may be an aspect of the person, as discussed in Chapter 2, that is very afraid of intimacy; or it may be a side of them that carries the message 'keep safe'/'do not take risks'/'opening myself to feeling is dangerous' and so on. In other words, while a more expansive part of the person might welcome a relationally deep encounter, seeing it as a deviation from the norm and a potential 'new dawn', a more protective part might adopt a highly cautious stance, perceiving the offer of contact as a threat to the person's sense of self. Empathising with this latter side of the client may be particularly important because, through it, clients may feel reassured that any desire they express to stop an intimate encounter will be respected. Also, many clients may not be aware that there is part of them pushing away intimacy and closeness; such that, through exploring and accepting this part, clients may feel more enabled to bracket their caution, and risk an in-depth interpersonal encounter. We will explore an example of this later in the chapter.

Thus, for a relationally deep encounter to take place it would seem valuable for therapists to reflect back to clients the multiple – and some-times contradictory – ways in which they experience their world. For instance, rather than reflecting back to a client, 'I get a sense that you really want to meet others', a more helpful response might be, 'I get a sense that you really want to meet others... and that you are also really afraid of it'. Such reflections, it is being suggested, may more accurately reflect the totality of the client's lived world, and help the therapist to attain a more holistic understanding of the web of 'dilemmas' or 'tensions' (van Deurzen, 2002) within which the client lives. Interestingly, however, Bill Stiles (Stiles and Glick, 2002), the eminent person-centred researcher and ther-apist, suggests that it can be confusing to clients to reflect back both voices at once and he argues that it is generally better to work with one voice at a time. Similarly, Dave Mearns, in his advice on person-centred therapy with configurations (Mearns and Thorne, 2000: 132–4) cautions against creating a 'zero sum' by responding to opposed configurations together. So there are still debates here about the best way to work with such multiple voices and needs (see Cooper et al., 2004).

An Openness to Being Affected by the Client

'I urge you to let your patients matter to you', writes the existential psychiatrist Irvin Yalom, 'to let them enter your mind, influence you, change you' (2001: 27). Without such a willingness to be impacted upon by the client, a meeting at relational depth is unlikely to come about, for if a therapist encounters her client from a place of closed-ness or certainty, then she is unlikely to be receptive to the uniqueness and the unpredictability of the client's being. So, for instance, if a ther-apist feels very excited listening to a client (as in Dave's work with Dominic), or if a client's beliefs really challenge a therapist's world-view, then this is not necessarily something 'wrong' or unprofessional, or something that the therapist should avoid. Rather, it might be an indication of just how open the therapist is to the client, and how willing she is to let the client matter to, and impact upon, her. In the example below, one of the therapists that we interviewed talks about her own experience of letting a client in and how she had to overcome her own particular defences to do so:

> During the session, he was telling me how much I mattered to him, not just the counselling mattered to him, but me. And the importance for me, when he was telling me that, was to hear it and take it in fully. I had to counter my past tendency to be shy or avoid; I actually had to do that, because I realised how important it was for me to actually take in everything that he was telling me. There was a real vitality in that, and I knew the vitality of it. And it moved us into a space of deeper knowing and accepting of each other, and who we are to each other.

In terms of facilitating a relationally deep encounter, it may also be valuable to communicate to clients how much they impact upon us, as can be seen in Dave's work with Dominic. When Dominic first asks Dave how he feels about him being drunk at the session, and Dave says that he feels 'nothing' about it, this would seem to have little potential to deepen the therapeutic contact. But once Dave communicates to Dominic that he actually feels scared by it because of the threatened loss of connection, Dominic gets a vivid sense of just how seriously Dave takes him and the therapeutic work. We will return to this process of communicating transparently later on in the chapter.

As in Dave's work with Dominic, letting clients see the impact they have on their therapist does not only apply in the case of a 'positively' experienced impact. A therapist, Kalpana, reports:

> During the first part of the session his [the client's] behaviour had been different. He smiled a lot and appeared quite 'coy' at times. Then he told me how he 'fancied' me and that he would like us to act on that. I paused a moment before responding – I didn't like it. So I told him I didn't like it. I didn't get any sense of substance in what he was saying. It sounded 'sexual' but not relational. It made me feel cold, not warm, like I was an 'object'. I told him the lot. I also asked him how he felt about all that I had said. This took us to amazing new stuff.

This is the kind of situation that many therapists 'fluff'. They feel awkward, smile coyly themselves. Sometimes they may even say something like 'I'm flattered… but of course nothing can happen', all the while feeling profoundly uncomfortable. As we have mentioned many times in this book and as is emphasised by Peter Schmid (2002), 'en-counter' means standing 'counter' to the other person and working therapeutically with the difference. This last point is critical, the therapist must be prepared to *work* with the consequences of their encounter. Their 'counter' to the client is not an act of judgement, aggression or revenge, it is part of the therapeutic engagement. Such an encounter as this is just as likely to lead to a meeting at relational depth as the previous example. Meeting at relational depth is not achieved by being incongruently nice to the client but by being real with him and continuing to work with the difference. There are considerable personal development aspects to this that are reviewed in Chapter 8.

Creating a 'Safe' Space

For many clients, the idea of allowing another person into their deepest, most personal realms is profoundly anxiety-provoking – particularly where previous visitors have left chaos and damage in their wake. Such a client, then, is likely to keep their therapist at arm's length until they feel that they can fully trust that person to do no harm. How can a therapist earn such trust? First, as we discussed earlier, by not trying to force entry into the client's personal realm; in other words, genuinely respecting the client's defences and acknowledging the intelligibility behind them. One of the therapists we spoke to talked about 'treading lightly' in the client's world: moving around with a sensitivity and delicateness, and remembering that, as a guest, he is 'there by invitation only'. Second, by ensuring that our stance towards our clients is a non-judgemental, confirming and valuing one; for the deepest fears of many clients is that, once they are seen for who they are, they will be criticised, humiliated and attacked. Third, by trying to be a relatively stable, dependable and predictable person to our clients, someone who they have a sense will not behave in chaotic or out of control and damaging ways. Hence, while facilitating a meeting at relational depth means being 'real', it also means maintaining appropriate boundaries – such as agreeing contracts, sticking to time limits, and not socialising with clients – for without that, clients may find the therapeutic situation too unpredictable and unsafe to really allow their therapist in. Margaret Warner gives a lucid description of the combination of being open to the client's individual needs while also creating a consistent safe space in her work with clients in 'fragile process' (2000: 150–8).

This idea of creating safety is easily misunderstood. In cultures where incongruence is the norm in engagements at the presentational level of self, there is a tendency to see creating safety in terms of wrapping our client in an 'icing sugar' of effusive and incongruent warmth where there is no challenge, no encounter. This does *not* create safety;

on the contrary this therapist is difficult to trust because we cannot *see* her. In the last example in the previous section, the therapist, Kalpana, did not respond in a fashion the client may have wanted. But her response was not merely her expression of dislike at what her client had said. Her response was to stay close to him and all his different reactions to the rejection for the next 30 minutes and throughout that time to, genuinely, be in relationship with him.

Minimising Distractions

As with the participants in the Geller and Greenberg (2002) study, several of the therapists that we spoke to said that, to prepare the ground for a relationally deep encounter, it was important that they tried to clear their minds from distractions. These distractions could be of an external nature: sounds from the street, a glimpse of people walking past the window, noises from an adjacent room; or they could be of an internal nature, for instance thoughts about what one is going to have for dinner, or whether one will make one's train. Some tips on minimising distractions are given below:

- Give yourself a few minutes before the start of each session to settle yourself;
- Many people find that writing up notes from a previous client, before starting with the next client, helps them to 'put to one side' issues from the previous session;
- Try not to 'squeeze' too many clients into your schedule – we all have limits to our span of concentration;
- If you come to work with salient personal concerns or issues, plan some time after the work when you can address them, so you do not try to deal with them in the session;
- If you become aware of internal or external distractions, do not beat yourself up about it but try to refocus on the client and let the distractions drift away;
- Reflect on why you may have become distracted: does it tell you about a block in yourself, or something about the client's way of being that may be useful to bring back to the therapeutic work?;
- Try to ensure that the room you work in is as sound-proof as possible, and one in which distractions will be at a minimum;
- Know your limits! In the last analysis, if your personal concerns or issues are too overwhelming, it is more ethical and professional to explain this to the client and cancel the session. But this really is only 'in the last analysis' – professional therapists do not cancel sessions readily.

Self-awareness

To this point in the chapter, we have focused primarily on the 'receptivity' side of being present to clients. As Bugental suggests, however, the other side of presence is 'expressivity': a willingness for the therapist to be known by her client in the situation, 'to make available some of the contents of one's subjective awareness without distortion or disguise' (1976: 37). In other words, to prepare the ground for a relationally deep encounter, a therapist must do much more than just passively receive her client. She must also be willing to reach out to the client, and to share something of who she is with them, as Kalpana did earlier in this chapter.

Such expressivity has many parallels with the person-centred notion of 'congruence'. Congruence involves *both* self-awareness and also a willingness to be transparent to the client (Mearns and Thorne, 1999). Sometimes the word is used only to denote the self-awareness aspect (Lietaer, 2001) but this can be confusing to students and practitioners from other disciplines. As Rogers says: 'By this [congruence] we mean that the feelings the counsellor is experiencing are available to him, available to his awareness, that he is able to live these feelings, be them in the relationship, and be able to communicate them if appropriate' (1973: 90).

Before communicating such experiences, however, a therapist must have some awareness of what they are. It was only once Dave, for instance, realised that he felt scared in relation to Dominic's drunkenness, that he could communicate this to Dominic. This, again, highlights the importance of self-development for therapists, for it is through such work that trainees and practitioners can become more aware of their moment-by-moment feelings and thoughts. Such work also helps therapists to identify whether a particular feeling is primarily attributable to them as opposed to their relationship with that particular client, because it helps them to become more aware of their characteristic ways of responding. Had Dave, for instance, come to realise that he had a fear of drunk people, then he might have been less likely to communicate his anxieties to Dominic, knowing that this was more to do with him than with Dominic's state of mind. In terms of becoming more congruent, self-development work is also critical because it tends to lead to greater self-acceptance, or what, in Chapter 2, we have termed an I–I self-relational stance, which then means that therapists will be more able to accept the many different thoughts and feelings that they have when offering therapy.

Transparency

Transparency, itself, can also be seen as having two facets: one of which is about what we *do not* do, and the other about what we *do* do. The first of these, which we might call 'being natural', is simply about not trying to hide or disguise anything that is going on within us. By contrast, the second, which we might call 'immediacy' (Hill and Knox, 2002), is about *actively* communicating our here and now experiences to our clients.

In therapeutic terms, being natural means that we are not trying to be someone that we are not to our clients: of minimising levels of disguise or pretence within the therapeutic relationship. Here, we are talking about things like not pretending to understand a client when we do not, or making gestures that are unnatural to us and awkward. This is relevant to many trainees when they start practising therapy, because there can be a tendency to 'put the counsellor hat on' the moment that they walk into a room with a client. That is, once they start a counselling session – whether actual or practice – it is like they have walked through an invisible veil and changed from 'normal human being' to 'counsellor': their language alters, they hold their bodies in different ways, they make facial expressions that they never would in everyday life. This is not to suggest that, when we are with our clients, we should do exactly the same things as in every other aspect of our lives – for one thing, in this situation we are specifically focused on one person. But if the *person* we are with our clients is noticeably different from the person we are in other aspects of our lives, it suggests that some degree of unnaturalness is coming into our therapeutic practice, and that may make the possibility of a relationally deep encounter less likely.

The more proactive facet of transparency, immediacy, is to do with deliberately disclosing our here and now felt-responses to our clients. For many therapists, from a range of disciplines (e.g. Ehrenberg, 1992; Yalom, 2001), such disclosures are the key to a relationally deep encounter. Indeed, it is often the ability to work with such feelings that distinguishes more experienced therapists from less experienced ones. A willingness to directly communicate our experiences to our client is also, to some extent, what distinguishes the model of person-centred therapy outlined here from a more classical approach (e.g. Brodley, 2001), in which congruent communications tend to be reserved for situations in which the therapist is having an experience counter to the attitudes of empathy or unconditional positive regard.

Disclosure of here and now feelings may take many forms. From a person-centred standpoint, perhaps the most significant of these is disclosure of feelings that seem to emerge from an empathic attunement with the client. Where a therapist, as discussed above, really allows herself to 'breathe in' her client's being, it is likely that some of that way of being will be re-invoked within the therapist. In other words, she may begin to develop an in-depth, advanced empathic sense of what the client is experiencing; and this will not just be a cognitive understanding, but one that is also emotional and bodily in nature. This is what we mean by embodied empathy (Cooper, 2001): an experiencing of how another person is in their world that reaches down to the very depths of our toes, that infuses our body, and that gives us a lived, vital awareness of how it is for them as a cognitive-affective-somatic whole. And when therapists share something of what they are experiencing at this level with clients, this can often have the very powerful effect of helping clients deepen their understanding of how they experience their world. The following is an example of this from one of the therapists that we interviewed:

> This client was telling me about an experience in her youth, and as she was telling me about it, I got an extreme sensation in myself of my energy draining, and I just felt myself suddenly nearly collapsing. It was quite profound. So I told her. I said, 'something has happened to me just now and I'm feeling really depleted'. She, kind of, immediately made a connection for herself and she said that she experienced herself as neglected at that time in her life and of neglecting herself. She talked about that for a wee while and then she moved back to connect with me, and she said, 'you really felt that, didn't you?' and that was a profound experience with the two of us.

In many instances, however, a therapist's here and now disclosures are more a reaction *to*, than an empathic response *with*, her client. When Dave tells Dominic, for instance, not to play games with him, it is a very direct communication in response to how he experiences Dominic's behaviour. As in this instance, the disclosure of such experiences can powerfully deepen the level of relating, because it brings the focus of the work onto the here and now relationship (see below), helps clients see how they may affect other people, and also models for them a genuine and open way of being. As Yalom puts it: 'Therapist disclosure begets patient disclosure' (2001: 29). In the example below, a client has suddenly changed his way of being from quiet and timid to loud and powerful:

Client: I'M JUST NOT GOING TO PUT UP WITH IT FROM HIM ANY MORE. ENOUGH IS ENOUGH – I'VE TAKEN IT LONG ENOUGH!
Therapist: Wow – that took me aback. I felt a sudden shaft of real fear when you said that. Boy, that woke me up pretty smartish.

Client: Did it really? I didn't think I could frighten anyone.

Therapist: Well, for the moment I forgot you weren't angry at *me*, I felt frightened. Maybe it was also the suddenness of it. Suddenly you were quite different from what you usually are.

Client: Yes, *I'm* usually the one that behaves as though I'm constantly frightened.

This is a simple human interchange in which the therapist has expressed her feeling response to her client. What she has offered is a 'reasonable' human response. This is useful to the client because it is different from how he imagines himself. Also, it quickly takes him to the realisation that, usually, he behaves as if he was a frightened person.

The key word in this analysis is 'reasonable'. The therapist's emotional response is potentially useful as a reflection of the client to himself because it is likely to be a common reaction to his expression. It tells him that he has just behaved in a way that some or many people will find frightening. The response would *not* have been useful if it had come from a particularly idiosyncratic position. If the therapist was 'neurotically' disposed to feel fear where there was no particular threatening behaviour, then her reflection of that fear would be confusing indeed to the client. Of course, as discussed earlier, this is yet another example of the 'developmental agenda' (see Chapter 8) for the therapist. During training she will find those areas of particular vulnerability where the reflections she would give to her client are excessively affected by her own personal process. In those areas she will be more guarded because she cannot yet fully trust her transparent response. As well as developing this 'control' she will also address the basis of her vulnerability in this area and perhaps she will be able to remedy it. In fact, the developmental agenda during training is much more concerned with loosening 'controls' than with inserting them. People tend to have developed a lack of trust in the 'reasonableness' of their feeling reactions to others – again, the gradual growth of self-acceptance significantly develops their ability to be transparent.

It is important to emphasise the timeliness of immediacy. It would not be particularly valuable to the above client if the therapist, six weeks later, told him of her earlier fearful reaction. This highlights the most common misunderstanding in regard to therapeutic congruence (see Mearns and Thorne, 1999: 92) as illustrated by the following therapist's statement in supervision:

FINALLY I faced him [the client] with my frustration. It had been building up for weeks and getting worse and worse. He had to be told – so I was 'congruent' with him.

In fact, this therapist has not at all been congruent. She has been decidedly incongruent. Her original feelings are lost in obscurity and have become exaggerated by the passage of time and continued suppression. Her supervisor, if she is transparent, will likely express her own exasperation or even horror that her supervisee should have dumped her own mess on her client.

In some instances the most valuable disclosures that therapists can make may be to reveal their vulnerabilities to their client. As discussed earlier, for example, it is when Dave tells Dominic about his fear of becoming disconnected that the relationship starts to really deepen. Indeed, the existentially informed psychiatrist Leslie Farber (1967) argued that, with some clients, it is only when the therapist reveals their despair at not being able to help the client – and the client starts to *pity* the therapist – that the real therapeutic work can begin. An example of this would seem to be in Dave's work with Rick, where Dave's crying, and Rick's handing him a tissue, seemed to be a real turning point in Rick's willingness to engage with another. Perhaps this is because, once the client starts to see the therapist's vulnerabilities, they begin to experience feelings of care and nurturing towards another person and this opens the door for them back into the inter-human community. Also, once they see the therapist's vulnerabilities, they may come to realise that this person is not a magician who can wave a wand and make them better such that, if they want to improve, they will need to put some effort into it themselves. Disclosures of vulnerability may also be important because they can help clients to see that they really can make an impact upon their world; and if they can change their therapist, they may also come to believe that they can change themselves.

Alongside disclosing vulnerabilities, it can also be very helpful for therapists to 'show their working' to clients. That is, if we are feeling unsure of how to respond to a client, or confused, or if we are pulled in two different directions, these are all things that we can disclose and this may serve to make us more real in the relationship and hence deepen the encounter. An example of this is when Dave apologises to Rick in Chapter 6 for referring to his wife and children, and also at *Dave 51* in Chapter 5, where Dave acknowledges that he might have been trying to push Dominic too far and talks about his own internal conflict between a cautious side and a 'delinquent' part that wanted to push. Here, it is interesting to note how Dave's disclosure seems to facilitate an equalisation of the therapeutic relationship, with Dave no longer the 'one who knows' (*Dominic:* 'So the therapist is crazy too'); and Dominic no longer the 'one who is here to learn' (*Dave:* 'Why can't I be as wise as that!'). Such disclosures, then, may facilitate a more human-to-human encounter, and one that is less dominated by the traditional power roles of authoritative therapist and subservient client (Proctor, 2002).

Needless to say, we are not suggesting here that therapists should disclose all their vulnerabilities and moment-by-moment experiences to their clients. The key question that therapists need to ask themselves is whether the disclosure is *in the service of* the client or whether it is actually more to do with their own needs. We also need to distinguish between our present subject – self-disclosures that communicate the therapist's experiencing in relation to the client – and disclosures about the therapist's life outside the therapy room. Barrett-Lennard (1962), in early research that began to establish the clinical significance of empathy, unconditional positive regard and congruence, also hypothesised that the 'willingness of the therapist to be known' would be of clinical significance. In fact, although the results showed a positive tendency, they did not reach statistical significance and 'willingness to be known' dropped into relative obscurity in research. A more subtle hypothesis might be that there are contexts where the last thing the client needs is the therapist telling them about her own life, yet there are also moments in the process of the therapeutic relationship where the client actively seeks such detail, perhaps as a way to adjust the 'balance' of the relationship. In research into the client's experience of the therapeutic process this phenomenon has often been observed (Dinnage, 1988; Mearns and Dryden, 1989); and, as we have seen in Chapter 1, the contemporary evidence suggests that a limited degree of personal self-disclosure can be helpful in the therapeutic work.

Working in the Here and Now

As suggested above, immediacy statements are often helpful because they bring the attention of the therapeutic work on to the dynamics of the immediate therapeutic encounter and we can speak more generally here of exploring the 'here and now' therapeutic meeting. Such work can facilitate a meeting at a level of relational depth for a number of reasons. First, in many therapy sessions, a client's most pressing concerns will be to do with the therapist–client dynamic, even if they are talking about other issues, such that bringing the focus of the therapeutic work onto this issue can allow clients to be more fully present. A client, for instance, might be talking about her relationship with her daughter, but what she may actually be most concerned about is that her therapist thinks she is a 'bad mother'. So if the therapist asks a question like, 'I wonder how it is for you to talk about these things with me', it provides the client with an opportunity to voice her real and present fears, and thereby become more present.

An exploration of the here and now therapeutic relationship can also help therapist and client identify the kinds of processes that stop the client getting closer to others. As Yalom (2001) points out, a client's strategies for developing, or avoiding, intimacy are likely to emerge in their immediate therapeutic relationships. In the here and now exploration, clients also have an opportunity to find out from a (congruent) other how they are experienced, and this can help them develop their ability to engage with others *as they actually are*, rather than as the client might imagine them to be. The therapist, Kalpana, earlier in this chapter, offered her client just such an opportunity; and another example of this is in Mick's work with Rebecca, discussed at the beginning of Chapter 2, when he shared with her just how much he was struggling to engage with her. As Stern (2004) suggests, then, it is often the crisis points within the therapeutic relationship or the moments of relational disconnection that can be the triggers for a more in-depth encounter, because it is these moments that call for a genuine and spontaneous response from the therapist, rather than a formulaic, role-based one.

Working in the here and now on the dynamics of the therapeutic relationship is explored elsewhere (Mearns, 2003a: 64–73; also see Chapter 4) in terms of 'tapping the unspoken relationship' between the therapist and the client. Although the relationship in therapy tends to be personified as particularly 'open', like any human relationship there will still be much experiencing of each other that goes unvoiced. Potentially, there is huge therapeutic material in that unspoken relationship and some of that can be tapped through the transparency of the therapist and the willingness of both parties to work in the here and now. However, the client's learning about themselves may not be the only learning that arises when the unspoken relationship is tapped. The therapist embarks on such explorations with some courage because it may be her that does the learning. Recently, for instance, a here and now exploration with a client very quickly opened up the fact for Mick that this client experienced him as somewhat cold and detached. It was a surprise for Mick, and not a pleasant one at that, but it did help him to get some insights into how some others might experience him, and consequently that if he wants to engage with others more fully, he needs to communicate more explicitly to them his feelings of warmth and concern.

Conclusion

If we think of relational depth as 'co-presence' – and presence as expressivity and receptivity (Bugental, 1976; see also Chapter 3) – then there are four basic ways in which we can facilitate an in-depth encounter with our clients: enhance our expressivity; enhance our receptivity; help our clients to enhance their expressivity; and help our clients to enhance their receptivity. In this chapter, we have explored a number of different ways in which we can develop our work in each of these areas: becoming more attentive to the whole of our clients, taking the risk of being transparent with them, inviting our clients to express themselves more fully and creating the kind of safe and containing environment in which clients may feel more willing to receive us. In the following chapter, we will explore the first of these two domains in more detail, looking at the kind of personal development work that may be valuable to therapists to help them enhance their ability to be present.

8 THE THERAPIST'S DEVELOPMENTAL AGENDA

In this chapter we shall look at the key developmental aims and structures associated with enhancing the therapist's ability to offer an engagement at relational depth. In this regard we take a fairly generic view of counselling and psychotherapy, expecting that specialists in the various approaches will be able to adapt the language to their own conceptual structure. The likelihood is that even the most inexperienced trainee therapist will grasp the concept of relational depth and, indeed, will have some prior experience of such engagements. The developmental task for the therapist, however, is to become able to offer the possibility of that engagement to *every* client regardless of their individual difference. This is a challenging aim for counsellors and psychotherapists across the range of approaches.

One of the central questions we have been asking in this book is: 'what is it that makes a therapist the kind of person with whom a client – any client – wound be prepared to risk an engagement at relational depth where they would enter these areas experienced as fundamental to their existence?' The answer we have been promoting in these pages is that such a therapist is someone who is not trapped into relating only at the presentational level of self but can respond to the client from their own depths. They are a person who can be both receptive and expressive: they can take people in and they can reach out to people. In both these activities they are not deterred by clients' various systems of self protection. They honour these, but they do not collude with them. They can receive a wide range of others – the client who is incredibly 'fragile', another who protects himself by seeking to put down the other, and someone like Rick (Chapter 6) who has, simply, 'given up' unless someone can offer him a larger presence that the prison he has built around his self. As well as being able to receive they can also reach out to the other. In reaching out they are not deterred by fear – of the other; of how they are seen; of 'getting it wrong'; of losing themselves. They are utterly committed to congruence – to be transparent as well as self-aware – to show the Other what is going on in the therapist; why they are trying; and the feelings they are experiencing in the act of trying.

In all of this, the aim is to offer something truly different to the client, something that the client might begin to accept in moments of relational depth and, as these moments add up, accept in terms of the continuing relationship where they can easily dip into material from the depths of their self-experiencing whether that material is already symbolised or is at the dimmest 'edge of awareness'.

How can we help counsellors and therapists to become that kind of person? Certainly we cannot do it by giving them a manual of interventions, treatment plans and therapeutic 'tools'. The endeavour is so firmly tied to who the therapist is as a person – their personal awareness and security – that it is their self that must be the developmental agenda. We will go on to explore what we consider to be two fundamental aspects of that self agenda: becoming aware of our sense of our existence and the growth of self-acceptance, before considering some of the contexts that can be used to facilitate that developmental agenda.

Becoming Aware of Our Sense of Our Existence

To engage a client at relational depth during moments in therapy and on a continuing basis inevitably involves the therapist being able to be close to their own personal depths. If we can be close to these dimensions of ourself that are of profound significance to our sense of our own existence, then we are at a depth appropriate to that at which we are hoping to meet our client – we enter our own 'depths' to meet our clients in theirs.

What are the significant elements within our sense of our existence? What are the events and self-experiences that are 'touchstones' for us – events and self-experiences from which we draw considerable strength and which help to ground us in relationships as well as making us more open to and comfortable with a diversity of relationships? Presented here is the set of events and self-experiences identified by the therapist, Lesley, along with her commentary on the strength she draws from these and how that helps her to be open in relation to engaging, at depth, a fairly wide range of clients.

Lesley's Existential Touchstones

- One of my earliest memories is sitting on my grandfather's knee. Every time I met him he had a radiant smile and he would plonk me on his knee. What I get from that is huge – it is the experience of completely *unconditional love*. That is a really secure part of me that helps me to feel 'at ease' even in difficult situations;

- No matter what I did, I could never please my father. It happened time after time after time. I would be proud of myself for something and he wouldn't respond or he would nit-pick it and so devalue it. I can feel a child's *frustration* even now, as I talk about it. It is amazing how often that sense of a child's frustration helps me to get a 'flavour' of my client's distress. For some reason, and I'm not quite sure why, this experience is also a source of my *patience* with clients. Perhaps, as a child, I had to be very patient to keep trying so often with my father;

- In primary school I was frequently ridiculed for being thin. The most distressing event happened each year when we would be ceremonially measured and weighed in front of the whole PE class. In a flamboyant way, representing nothing but her own self-importance, the teacher announced: 'watch that Lesley does not fall through the cracks in the floorboards!' The strength I take from this experience is in feeling my own *rage*. At the time it happened I nearly burst into tears but I was determined not to give her the satisfaction so all I felt was the pure rage. It is surprising how often that strong, clean feeling is a source of strength for me with clients. I can enter that 'angry girl' and get a strong sense of my client's anger. I think it would have been much worse for me then and also now if I had burst into tears;

- One year, late in my primary schooling, I came top of the class. Usually I was around tenth place but in this particular year, once all the marks were averaged, I was top. To my enormous pride the teacher invited me to the front of the class. I thought that my considerable achievement was going to be honoured. However, what the teacher did was to ask me to spell the word 'inexplicable'. I was thoroughly confused but I spelled it, accurately I think. Then, with a broad smile and a wave of her arm towards me she said: '*inexplicable!* Yes, that is the best word to describe you coming top of the class!' This time I did not feel angry, what I felt was an intense *humiliation*. That is something I have felt fairly often

(Continued)

(*Continued*)

in my life. It is an absolutely dreadful feeling. It is the feeling
of being stripped naked in public. And that is precisely the
strength I take from it. I have been so severely humiliated so
often that I know what it is. I do not need to fear it because I
know it better than most people. I do not need to be afraid of
looking silly or getting things wrong. I can take risks with my
self-expression because, no matter what happens, I could
never be as humiliated as I have already been;

• Twice in my life I have been bullied by groups of girls. One was
in secondary school and the other was when I was working as
a very junior nurse in a hospital. Both times I was stripped and
the first time I was thoroughly beaten up. It may seem strange
but the second time, in the hospital, what affected me most was
that my very old underwear had been exposed – that was the
greatest *humiliation*. I also took something else from the first
experience. I had an incredibly strong sense of the other girls'
hatred for me. They really were hitting me hard, but still I
fought against them. The more I fought the more I was beaten
and the more I fought. Again, as I am with the incident even
here I get an incredibly strong sense of my *spirit*. I knew that
the more I fought the more they would hit but I still did it.
Near the end one of them threatened to bang my head off the
toilet to 'finish me off' if I did not stop fighting. I spat in her
face and they left me. Although I was covered in blood and
bruises and more or less naked I actually felt that I had won!
That strength of spirit I found then is what helps me get into
unknown territory with my client. I know that I will survive
and I am confident he will too;

• I guess one of the things I also learned from that was that a
very slight girl needed to use her brain rather than her brawn.
I have a few good examples of that, which also give me
strength. One was when I was surrounded pretty late at night
in a dodgy area of town by a group of men. Running was not
an option and fighting certainly wasn't! So, I amazed myself
by taking the initiative. I broke into talking with them and
cracking jokes and making first one and then another and
then another laugh. One of them clapped me on the shoulder
and said: 'you're a good sport' and I was allowed to walk
away. As well as being a self-experience that makes me feel

(*Continued*)

(*Continued*)

good about myself, incidents like this help me to feel that I can make myself pretty *safe* with just about anybody;

- At one time in my life I got into a highly promiscuous pattern. The final straw was finding myself waking up and not knowing who or how many had screwed me. I was at an incredibly low point in my life – I do not think I have ever felt as *low about myself*. That depth of feeling helps me to meet a lot of clients in a very full way;
- 'Being madly in love' has been important for me in lots of ways but I am not going into any detail here!
- Several years after the first bullying incident, the one in which I was badly beaten, I met the ringleader in the street. After the bullying incident I had not told anyone and I had generally avoided that group of girls for most of the rest of my schooling. At times they would mock me from afar but they did not cause me any more trouble. Now, here, the ringleader met me in the street and gave me a cheery, 'Hello Lesley – how are you?' I mumbled, 'Fine' and walked on. Then I became aware of an incredible flood of anger – how dare she speak to me in a 'normal' way! I turned round and ran back down the street, grabbed her, punched her several times very hard, tripped her up and kicked her hard about seven or eight times, four times intentionally in the face. Then I walked, not ran, away. There were plenty of people about, but nobody bothered me and she did not get up too easily. There was nothing 'noble' in what I did. I hit her so hard and fast that she did not have a chance to defend herself. It was pure revenge. It is difficult to explain how that is an important 'touchstone' for me. It has something to do with feeling my *power* but, more than that, it has to do with dispelling any illusions that I am an entirely 'nice' person. It is also an interesting place to go to in order to meet some clients touching their own 'evil';
- 'Believing in something and seeing it seduced' is how I describe my experience of investing a huge amount in political activism and then finding that others were using it for their own self-aggrandisement. The poignancy of that *disappointment* is something I can almost taste. This time it wasn't anger but pure disappointment. It hasn't stopped me believing

(*Continued*)

(*Continued*)

in things but it has helped me to *critique my own motives*, which gives me a fast referent when I am entering unexplored territory with a client;

- There were some particularly poignant events during the time I was a nurse. I remember the little boy 'Ashok' who had leukaemia. Every spare minute I got I would sit with him. I loved that little boy and made it my job to make him laugh. Ashok has given me much more than I ever gave him. A lot of my strong sense of *commitment* and *patience* comes from that long experience with Ashok but, more than anything else, is a sense of my own *love* and a feeling of comfort and trust with my own love;

- Ashok survived but another patient who was one of 'mine' died. It had been a medical 'mistake': he was given ten times the proper dosage of medication. It did not happen on my shift, thank God, but I still carry a lot of guilt about it because I colluded with the cover-up to protect the doctor. At the time it felt that I could not do anything else although I was incredibly angry. The feeling was one of total *powerlessness*. That feeling of powerlessness is an incredibly valuable touchstone for meeting many of my clients;

- Being with someone dying and opening yourself to that helps to develop *depth*. Often the nursing profession runs away from that challenge but I remember a few cases. One was with 'Mary' who was 83 years of age. There was no one to spend her death with her, so I did it. I had finished my shift and I knew that Mary would not be there the next time I clocked on, so I sat with her and she used me to talk about her life. It took two and a half hours and then she died. What Mary left me is useful for me with every single client I meet;

- There are a number of 'touchstones' that have come out of my therapy work, but two come particularly to mind. The first was when I was intensely frightened by the material my client was going into, on the death of her child. It felt like I was only just hanging on by my fingertips because I was *so* distressed. Yet, I knew it was vital for me to hang on and I did it. I really managed to enter that world with her.

(*Continued*)

(*Continued*)

We cried together, and that was okay. Ever after that, it was easier because I knew that I had that *strength to hang on*;

- Another client was quite different. She was 16 years of age and had been put through pretty bad sexual abuse from her father. I had to be incredibly patient, waiting as she put all the elements in place, piece by piece, until she was ready. It could not be hurried because she had to do something that was almost impossible for her, and she could only do it if she got everything in place. When she was ready – ready to take action against her father – she looked me straight in the eye and a tear came into hers. She wiped it away and smiled at me. I do not think I will ever forget that tear and that smile.

Lesley writes about her touchstones as 'places to go' in order to meet her client. When we are seeking to enter our client's experiencing the best way to do that can be to enter a part of our own self that carries the same 'flavour'. So, Lesley can enter her own deep sense of 'humiliation' which puts her on a suitable ground to experience her client at depth and to let her client experience her at depth. As well as Lesley being able to experience the quality of her client's experiencing, it is apparent to her client that Lesley is able to meet herself at a level of depth. This is what is meant by the observation (Bozarth, 2001: 59–75; Mearns and Thorne, 1999: 103–7) that, at high degrees, empathy and congruence are the same thing – the therapist's very being is an accurate reflection of the client. The therapist has got into the right 'territory' to meet the client. She can then, more easily, enter the client's experiencing and with a quality and intensity that exceeds other empathy. Equally, this phenomenon is qualitatively different from the exercises of 'projective identification' (Rowan and Jacobs, 2002: 41–6) or 'cognitive social perspective taking' (Binder, 1998: 219–20) where there is an effort to imagine the world of the other but it is a purely cognitive reach rather than an affective/cognitive one. This level of empathic ability – actually to go into different aspects of the sense of our own existence as 'stepping off' points into our client's experiencing – might seem 'dangerous' to those who are concerned about losing the 'as if' quality of empathy and 'getting lost' in their own self-experiencing. In fact this is the kind of worry that evaporates in the reality of the events. What does 'getting lost' actually mean? If it means finding our own tear for ourself and that being shared with our client while acknowledged as our own, then that can be a most powerful moment in relationship. Our notions of boundaries, proprieties and professionalism are challenged if we are really serious about the concept of meeting our client at relational depth.

'Lesley's touchstones' can readily be used as a stimulus for a training workshop, perhaps even better, as a 'continued professional development' workshop after initial training. But the notion of existential touchstones can also be so crucial as to be retained as an ongoing developmental agenda within the supervision relationship (see later in this chapter).

The Growth of Self-acceptance

Many of Lesley's touchstones had been difficult experiences in her life. For another person, or for Lesley at a different stage of her development, these same events could have had a restricting rather than developing impact. For example, the repeated experiences she had of being humiliated might easily have lain there within her psyche as a RIG (Stern, 2003; see Chapter 2) forever ready to be repeated. She might have become more socially withdrawn, less trusting in relationships and with a developed 'victim' self-configuration ready to play an inhibiting part in her life. Equally, her consistent experience of frustration and disappointment at never being able to please her father might have been a millstone around her neck inhibiting her development in relation to self-worth and leading to continual frustration and disappointment throughout her life. That these experiences, instead, strengthened Lesley's spirit and gave her a great source of patience as well as a touchstone rather than a millstone of sadness, relates mainly to her own general *self-acceptance*.

Self-acceptance, which is a key part of the I–I self-relational stance (see Chapter 2), is the degree to which we see our self as a 'reasonable' human being, capable of a range of actions and reactions, but fundamentally reliable to self and others. We see personal strengths and weaknesses and do not shrink from the development of the latter, yet that implicit self-criticism is not made of the whole person. Self-acceptance should not be confused with an over-vaulting aggrandisement of self over others. That individual's exaggerated positive view of self relies upon a comparison with others – they sustain their own positive self-view, relatively, by maintaining a negative view of others. By contrast, the person who accepts themselves does not have such a fragile base for their self-regard. It is so intrinsic to them that it is largely unthreatened in relationship. They can entertain the other person's difference or even the other person's criticism without needing to protect against the impact that might have on a fragile self. 'Self-acceptance', as we are using it here, is also much more than a passive valuing of ourselves. It represents a strong engagement and dialogue with the self in all its dimensions, such that the whole of the self is potentially available in engagement with others. Even parts that are only in the process of being symbolised are seen as, fundamentally, unthreatening and potentially of value to self and other.

People differ in their degree of self-acceptance. In Rogers' (1951; 1959; 1963) developmental theory and the additional person-centred theory on attachment (Warner, 2000), the development of self-acceptance is seen as relating to a reliable experience of unconditional positive regard during earlier development. Hence, if Lesley's experience with her father had not been offset by other loving relationships or, indeed, if it was also replicated in those other relationships, then she might not have been able to come out of it so positively. Also, even though there might be an early developmental deficit in regard to the roots of self-acceptance, people can make changes through their later life experience of relationships, including therapy, not to mention an effective adolescence.

Therapy training, particularly but not exclusively person-centred training, actively seeks to have a positive impact on a person's self-acceptance and their willingness to encounter themselves. In a training context this is not achieved by surrounding the person in an icing sugar of portrayed unconditional positive regard – quite the opposite. It is about creating contexts where the person genuinely meets their self and experiences themself meeting other people in a direct and immediate fashion. Self-doubts are maintained by keeping our self away from testing them in the encounter with other people. When we actually experience the *reality* of our self in relationship with another, many of the fundamental self-doubts are challenged by that self-experience, as in the case of 'Alison' below.

> ### Alison
>
> Alison was very quiet during the first month of training. She did not look happy with some things, but she never said anything. Eventually she was challenged on her silence in the personal development group. She fielded the challenge without responding to it. The next week she was challenged again, with the same result. Finally, on a third occasion one of her group said, 'Alison, I know we have been pushing you on this and that that may not
>
> *(Continued)*

(*Continued*)

be nice for you but, honestly, some of the time you look so damned angry and yet you say that nothing is going on'. At this point Alison blew up in a tirade about this challenge, the repeated challenges and about a lot of other experiences in that first month. Then she stopped speaking, sat stiffly in her seat with her head firmly facing down towards her lap. After a silence she said, 'I have to go' to which three other people in the group responded with, 'No – *stay*, Alison'; 'If you go, can I come with you?'; and 'Nice to hear from you Alison'. At this point Alison burst into tears. Later she described her feelings in that moment as a mixture of intense embarrassment, relief and joy. She had felt sure that if she expressed her anger, 'a huge cavern would open up in front of me and I would fall into it and disappear forever'. Instead, rather than finding herself annihilated by her expression of anger, she found that it actually opened doors to a stronger engagement with others and, through that, a stronger engagement with her self.

The intense relational environment within therapy training also has a considerable variety of people within it. Our sophisticated ways of protecting and maintaining our self-doubt may fool many of the people most of the time, but they will not fool all of the people all of the time, as 'John' discovered.

John

John was the 'great facilitator'. He exuded empathy, warmth and compassion to anyone in the training group. He soon achieved 'star' status among most of his peers – he even fooled a few trainers. This continued until one day when another trainee, Mary, said:

John, I do not believe you. When you were so supportive of me yesterday I did not feel good. I went quiet. I thought it was *me*, that there was something wrong with me not being able to accept it. Maybe there is, but the reality is that I do not believe you're real.

(*Continued*)

(*Continued*)

Mary's challenge achieved no significant result there and then. John went quiet and his response was that he did not know what she was talking about. One or two other people in the group felt uncomfortable with his response but such was the image he had built up that they did not voice their discomfort. Mary thanked John for not slipping into his 'helper' mode and trying to 'help' her with it. In the next few weeks John was less effusive and eventually he made a statement to the group:

> Mary said something to me a few weeks ago that hurt me a lot. I hated her for saying that and I kind of went into a 'huff'. I harboured a lot of critical thoughts about Mary. But, in fact, I realise she is right. When I go into my 'world-class helper' routine, that's all it is really – it's a 'routine' – it's got no relation to what I feel. It gives an image of how great I am while, all the time, underneath, I really think I'm crap.

And, so, our internalised self-doubt is gradually challenged by new self-experiences reinforced through the challenge and feedback of others. Gradually, the intrinsic negativity is chipped away under the challenge of reality testing and replaced by a growing self-acceptance and willingness to engage with ourselves. Also, once that self-acceptance begins to grow and we experience our self 'for real', the new self-experiences that creates further reinforce the development of our self-acceptance. As John reflected much later:

> Once I 'came clean' about myself and stopped hiding behind an 'act' of being the great counsellor, I found that my fear of being 'no good' gradually diminished. I stopped acting and did it for real. Most of the time people liked it and this time I could believe myself.

As John says, this process is about the diminishing of fear. If we harbour self-doubt we will be afraid of being exposed to others and to our self. If we consider our self to be, fundamentally, a person lacking in ability, motivation, dedication, inspiration, or love, we will have developed sophisticated skills in regard to protecting our self from being exposed. The disguises mentioned in Chapter 4 will offer façades to hide behind if we feel we need to. But we can be even more sophisticated in protecting our self from being exposed. One way is to be never quite engaged – never 'really' spontaneous – always, at a fundamental level, guarded. In this protected condition we can display many of the signs of relational engagement. We can behave warmly, we can speak personally, we can even show a considerable range of emotion. Yet, we are never really able to engage in a fully congruent fashion. Our empathy may be accurate, but seldom 'additive' (Mearns and Thorne, 1999) and our valuing of the Other is strictly conditional upon them not challenging our status quo. In particularly distressing examples we even deceive ourselves into believing that the icing sugar we have added as our topping is our genuine substance.

Stripping away the icing sugar can be a painful process. We are accepting the fundamental challenge of being prepared to see who we are beneath our protective portrayals while we actually harbour the fear that we are 'incompetent', 'unacceptable' or even 'evil'. It is to the enormous credit of developing counsellors and psychotherapists that they face up to this challenge, the fear of which is generally stronger than the reality. They face it down and find that while they are not competent at everything they are by no means incompetent; that while some others may have difficulties with them they are not generally 'unacceptable'; that the 'evil' tag was never something of their own making but a 'present' from a significant other earlier in their life. When we find that we have less to defend against than we thought, our fear diminishes and that allows us to be more open to ourselves and also more open to encounter with others. Indeed we may, for a time, become voracious feeders on encounter having been starved for so long.

While we can consider self-acceptance as a generalised appraisal of our self, it can also be useful to differentiate it in terms of different 'parts' of the self. In a person's own description of their self-structure some parts will be accepted but others may not. With some parts they will have an I–I relationship but with others it will be I–Me. Part of the therapist's developmental agenda will be an acceptance of, and willingness to engage with, *all* the parts, for parts that become accepted can obtain a licence to be present in the therapy room. Even then, the initial licence is usually a provisional one, with the part subject to close supervision. This process of engaging with and accepting the parts is crucial for the advanced development of the therapist, for it expands the 'person' she can offer at relational depth. Some parts are important because of the quality of presence they offer and others are critical because they offer particular 'places' to use in order to meet the client, as in the previous section. Dave Mearns offers illustrations of both of these in the following commentary.

It was about 10 or 12 years into my practice before my 'little boy' was allowed entry to the therapy room except under the closest supervision. He had an enormous warmth and tenderness as well as humour. He also had a *passion* that could be an incredibly powerful place to meet a client. But it took me a long time fully to trust him and his passion so he was closely 'supervised' at first. Another part is more difficult to describe – I don't have a single label for this part of me. This is a part of me that can exist in total isolation. It can be in incredibly fearful situations and be completely calm. It can witness atrocity and survive. Probably it is my 'darkest forest'. Many people would find it frightening and even distasteful, probably because they would not readily understand it. Yet, to me, it is anything but frightening. It has its origins in my development as an 'only child' but its real depth comes from facing, alone, some powerful situations. To me it is my closest internal friend, even more than my 'little boy'. With most clients it is not involved in the therapy room but with some it is virtually essential to our achieving an unlikely meeting at relational depth. For example, it affords a rare safety to the young man in profound existential trauma, for questions of meaning are its essence and it is, essentially, unthreatened by them. It can exist in the 'not knowing' response to such questions. It took some years to move from being frightened of this part to seeing it for what it was – an old and fundamental friend. As a therapist this part has been central to me in my work with 'Rick' (Chapter 6) and many other young men in particular.

An engaging account of Dave's 'little boy' in the therapy room is offered in Mearns and Thorne (Mearns and Thorne, 2000: 141–3).

Contexts in Which the Developmental Agenda May Be Furthered

Any approaches to the development of counsellors and psychotherapists must be student-centred. The self curriculum is so personal and individualised that it could never be predetermined by trainers or supervisors. This can be challenging for institutions such as universities, counselling and psychotherapy centres, employers and professional bodies if they need to stay in control to the extent that they cannot allow the student a central position in regard to the detail of the self curriculum and how to achieve it (Mearns, 1997a; 1997c).

The developmental agenda can be furthered using a wide variety of learning and experiential contexts. 'Life experience' is indeed a great teacher but it is not the only teacher. In the psychotherapy profession some contexts have been used more than others to further the developmental agenda. In this section we will look at the opportunities offered by personal therapy, encounter group experience, training and supervision.

Personal therapy

Personal therapy offers a context that is wholly focused on the individual and is made safe by the confidentiality offered. It may not be as powerful as group settings for raising awareness of the developmental agenda but it provides a particularly focused context for working on issues once they are raised.

One of the difficulties with personal therapy as it has historically been envisioned is that it tends to be relatively unfocused. There is a case (Mearns, 1997a) for entering into a personal therapy experience that is exclusively focused upon the self curriculum as that is being uncovered during training and thereafter. This is properly called the 'training therapy' because it articulates with the ongoing training experience, with feedback from one to the other. For example, a personal discovery made in the context of the training group is referred to the training therapy and, later, referred back to, perhaps, the personal development group within the training context. Thus the work remains focused and it also encourages the ongoing support of the training colleagues. However, in practice, the personal therapy experience tends to grow much bigger (and more expensive) than this, with other needs only peripherally related to the developmental agenda, taking precedence. The result can be hugely uneconomic in terms of the developmental needs met against the expense of time and money. It can resemble the 'Dissertation upon Roast Pig' whereby the whole village has to be burned down every time the villagers want roast pig! If it could be more focused upon the developmental agenda then it could become more economic as well as meaningful. Until recently, the accrediting organisations within Great Britain – the British Association for Counselling and Psychotherapy (BACP),[1] COSCA and the British Psychological Society – have all set a personal therapy requirement for accreditation of between 40 and 90 hours of personal therapy (adding at least 30 per cent to the cost of training). Many people think these figures are much too low and others believe that personal therapy should not be seen as the essential required structure through which to achieve the developmental agenda. But, that criterion could at least be made relevant if the hours were indeed focused upon the self curriculum as that becomes evident during training. In fact, none of these organisations require that kind of focus – indeed barriers argued in terms of 'boundaries' are erected actively to prohibit articulation between personal therapy and training. So it is likely that personal therapy will remain an expensive but not well-focused structure.

Encounter group experience

Although not as prolific as the other contexts described in this section, the encounter group experience is highly relevant to the developmental agenda in regard to working at relational depth. Encounter groups consist of approximately 12–14 people who get together for the express purpose of creating a context whereby people can learn about self and others through their interactions in the group. The experiential process is helped if three further suggestions are adopted. First, a suggestion is to focus more on '*here and now*' experiencing rather than on events in the past or the future. A second suggestion is not to become totally embroiled in a cognitive discussion but also to give attention to people's *feeling* reactions to whatever is going on. The third suggestion is particularly important as it invites the members to be aware of the fact that the normal process of groups is to work towards '*norming*'. Human beings, when in a group, conspire together to create a definition of what should happen in the group and what should not. This process of norming tends to make the group feel safer but it also limits severely what can happen and introduces a system of value-judging people's contributions. The third suggestion, then, is that people try to stay aware of this norming process as it evolves in their group and be prepared to challenge that process when it seems to be establishing. For example, a frequent early 'norm' that develops is that people should be 'warm' in their expressions to each other, whatever the content of those expressions. The early result of this norm feels sweet and nutritious – like icing sugar! But it soon makes the process sticky and then stuck. Indeed, as the time in contact with each other increases and people, naturally, become aware of a variety of responses, including negative ones, towards each other, the level of incongruence either increases and is challenged or another norm – silence – develops. Generally boredom will facilitate a challenging of that norm and the process can move on. Every time a norm is challenged and people inspect their incongruence to that point, considerable learning about our self and also about how our self comes over to others, results. Of course, these three 'suggestions' are not to be seen as 'rules'. They are designed to open up communication and make it more diverse – if they were expressed as rules that would achieve the opposite.

The communication that takes place in encounter groups can be powerful and the personal learnings considerable. It is a particularly potent context for bringing to awareness elements of the developmental agenda. It can also be a useful context for working on those elements. Personal therapy might offer more individual attention and a place that is experienced as 'safer' but the group can give a much wider range of human experience and feedback. For example, Dave, who clocked up exactly 1000 hours of encounter group experience between 1972 and 1995 (when he stopped counting!) recounts an important early experience in groups as far as tackling the developmental agenda to engage at relational depth is concerned:

> Encounter groups were where I 'won' my congruence. It feels like a 'victory' because it was a long, hard battle. I went through early years in groups of getting repeated feedback on my incongruence. There followed the normal responses of denial and strategic 'adjustment'. But the early adjustments didn't improve the feedback I got – now it was in terms of how 'subtle' my incongruence was! They were right of course, so eventually I took it on. I decided that I would *only* be congruent. That agenda, of course, meant that I had to announce it to the group in order to 'show my working'. The early stages were weird until I could discriminate what was genuinely a response to others and what was not. I fondly remember a regular evening 'men's group' at that time – how these good men put up with my internal battle I do not know – but they helped me through the early stages. Soon it improved, because I developed my own 'bullshit sensor'. Now, I can still 'bullshit' people, but at least I know when I am doing it!

Just as the personal therapy context can lose its focus on the developmental agenda, so too can the encounter group. The most common way to subvert the encounter group is to make it into a therapy group. Often group members and even sometimes the facilitator conspire to slip into this kind of norming whereby one by one the group members take up an hour of the group to explore their current or historic issues. These experiences can be powerful if they do indeed represent edge of awareness material or they can be extremely boring for others if they are simply going over 'rehearsed material' (Rogers, 1977). However, in either case, the living learning encounter group process has been subverted. If the encounter group transmutes into a therapy group it can be extremely difficult to challenge a process thus subverted because creating a therapy context is something that therapists or even therapists in training are particularly skilful at achieving together! The person who would challenge the 'therapy group' norm risks the definition of being a 'philistine'! The encounter group process has failed to become established as a recognised medium for the developmental agenda in Britain, particularly – perhaps the cultural norms of incongruence are too well established to tolerate it.

There are three powerful movie documentaries on the encounter group process available from film libraries: *Journey into Self; Because That's My Way*; and *The Steel Shutter*. The first of these won an Oscar, the second is, arguably, the most revealing about encounter groups and the third was made in 1972 at the height of the 'Troubles' in Northern Ireland. It comprised equal numbers of people from the Roman Catholic and Protestant divides in Belfast spending three days together in an encounter group in Pittsburg. (Dave helped to edit the soundtrack in La Jolla, California – because he was the only one present that could comprehend the Belfast accent!) The producer and director of all three of these documentaries is Bill McGaw, who once said of the encounter group: 'it shows we humans up for what we really are – desperate to *really* meet each other and shit scared of doing that'. The Oscar on his mantelpiece symbolised at least part of what he was saying: that the encountering process is a phenomenon that carries considerable significance for human beings.

Training

The connotation of the word 'training' includes the implication that the 'trainer' sets the course of study which is then rigidly followed by the 'trainee'. That cannot be the case in respect of the self curriculum. Certainly, the trainer can illustrate the range of personal development objectives that might commonly be found among a cohort of students (Dryden et al., 1995: 98–100; Mearns, 1997c: 97–9) but the actual self curriculum will be quite different for every student. Hence, it is important that the preconception of the trainer laying down the curriculum does not become established either in the minds of trainers or trainees. Crucial to the endeavour is that each understands and accepts their responsibilities. The trainer's responsibility is to create a variety of meaningful learning contexts. These include structures such as counselling practice settings, personal development groups, supervision groups, large group experiences, specific personal development workshops and actual clinical practice. However, from the outset, it is the trainee's responsibility to use these structures towards identifying and furthering their self curriculum. There is a whole range of issues here around the 'responsibility dynamic' within the training course (Mearns, 1997c) and the selection of trainees, particularly in regard to their readiness to accept appropriate responsibility for their own development. The essential requirement of the trainee is both a willingness to put themselves into a variety of fairly challenging learning situations while also, substantially, looking after themselves in those contexts. A training course that has to create huge 'safety' for very vulnerable participants is doomed from the outset. One way to symbolise the situation is to borrow from the basic concepts of Transactional Analysis. When a person comes along to be a client in therapy it is perfectly appropriate for them to be in their 'Child'. When they go along to a training course to be a trainee they are also expected to bring their Child but their Adult is expected to come along as well. If this solidity in terms of recruitment falters, the endeavour slips into a pattern that is largely Parent–Child in nature and is not conducive to the student taking responsibility in regard to their self curriculum.

Equally, trainers have a responsibility to maintain the responsibility dynamic. One of the main demands this places upon trainers is the ability to work within 'open process' without feeling the need to close it. For example, a trainer who needs to create a warm, unchallenging environment for reasons of their own insecurity may well be loved by the vulnerable trainee in the early stages because they appear to create such safety. However, in the longer term, such early closure of human interactive processes will seriously erode the developmental opportunities. Indeed, this phenomenon can have such a paralysing impact upon training that it can actually lead to a negative result whereby trainees exit the process having had considerable experience in exercising and further developing their systems of self-protection. The demanding challenge of self-acceptance has been subverted and early closure provided, generally with the collusion of the trainer, such that, instead of developing self-acceptance, the self-protections have stayed in place and become ever more sophisticated. Some of the potentially most powerful developmental contexts in training such as the 'learning group' in psychodynamic training and the 'personal development group' in person-centred and other forms of training have been survived not by engaging the challenges but by becoming more sophisticated in the defence against them. Often the graduates of such failed trainings look like clones of their adopted approach. They appear to say all the right things and do all the right things but they never feel quite 'real' and the prospects of them being able to meet clients at relational depth are slim.

Supervision

The end of initial training is only the end of the beginning of the developmental agenda for working at relational depth. Indeed, that ending can be suddenly disorienting (Blaxter et al., 2001; Buchanan and Hughes, 2000), moving from a highly supported environment into a virtual vacuum. Supervision, previously just one of many supports, now takes on particular importance because the developmental agenda is only just begun.

One of the strengths of the psychotherapy and counselling profession is its maintenance of the essentially *developmental* function of ongoing supervision. This is well described, in the person-centred tradition, by Elke Lambers:

In person-centred supervision, the supervision relationship can be conceptualised as parallel to the therapy relationship: offering a context where the therapist can become aware of the processes taking place in herself in the relationship with the client and enabling her to become more congruent in that relationship. This is a developmental view of supervision in an accurate sense, the supervisor has no other concern, no other agenda than to facilitate the therapist's ability to be open to her experience so that she can become fully present and engaged in the relationship with the client. The person-centred supervisor accepts the supervisee as a person *in process* and trusts the supervisee's potential for growth. The person-centred therapist who is willing to fully engage with the client on an existential level will be changed by the experience – the supervisor is a witness to that change. (2000: 197)

The supervisee can powerfully use developmentally oriented supervision to assist them with the ongoing agenda in regard to working at relational depth. Indeed, most of this development tends to occur after initial training, so supervision combined with continuing personal development (CPD) is critical.

Within supervision there is a tendency for the work to go in one direction: ongoing practice is examined and issues arising are explored so that they may facilitate further personal development that feeds back into future practice. This is great – it is real learning from ongoing experience, well supported. However, it also makes sense to make the ongoing developmental agenda explicit within supervision. The supervisor, then, becomes the confederate, helping the therapist to lay out the ongoing developmental agenda, monitor it and further develop it though practice and CPD as in the following example of the counsellor, 'Inge', three years out of initial training.

Inge's Agenda

- I 'missed' a client, 'Lee', a while back. He looked at me so hard but I blinked his invitation into obscurity. I couldn't meet him. I couldn't find a place in me to meet him. He wasn't asking a lot – just for someone to put to one side the fact that he has hit his wife and meet the person – the desperate person that was underneath. I need to find a way to meet people like Lee;
- Earlier, I could not have even begun to meet Mary. She is just *so* 'needy' that I would have felt suffocated. Now, I am doing

(Continued)

(*Continued*)

better. Margaret Warner's stuff on 'fragile process' has been great for me. It has helped me to understand the simultaneous need for this client to be in a structured situation and also to have power to challenge the structure. I am beginning to get to points where Mary and I make *real* contact – I am no longer just 'confused' and I am becoming more patient. Also, I have stopped my much earlier tendency to 'withdraw' myself. I am beginning to wonder whether it will be Mary or I who learns more from our work together!

- I have some depths within me that are ready for a challenge. I used to be fearful of power – power from the other person. I always 'blanked out' with a client like that. Now I feel that I have become more OK with that part of myself and it's time to see if I can really be good for that kind of client;
- I am on a campaign to reduce my smiling. This is something that has annoyed me about me forever. When a client is on the 'edge' of going to a deeper place he doesn't need a smile. My smile is saying, 'you can see I am a really nice person'. If he is maybe going to that deep place he doesn't need that superficiality. He needs my serious sensing of what is going on for him.
- Next week I am going to a meeting of lesbians. I am not sure if I have expressed that appropriately and that shows my inadequacy. Finally, I have recognised that I have a difficulty in this area. I am pretty frightened. But I had a lesbian client a while ago – quite common in my service – and I was so stiff that the woman actually told me! In fact, it was lovely what she did. Despite her own torment, she took care with me in my difficulty. It's like she met me although I couldn't meet her. So, she has helped me to get the courage to step into the unknown. I have been perfectly open to the group about what I am doing and the woman I spoke to seemed OK about it. So, here goes!

Inge uses her supervision as the focal point for reviewing her ongoing developmental agenda. Some traditional views on supervision would only define it in terms of reviewing issues arising from practice. That is a limited perspective on supervision – it is only half the story. To tackle the ongoing self curriculum there needs to be an interplay between practice and self-development with supervision as the focal review point for both. This perspective does not confuse supervision with personal therapy. Personal therapy is a milieu where parts of the self curriculum can be explored in great breadth and depth. Supervision is where the products of that work and other learnings from CPD and elsewhere can be brought together to inform, stimulate and inspire future practice. This is part of what Elke Lambers (2003) describes as the role of supervision enhancing the therapist's 'fitness to practice' in a similar fashion to the 'physical fitness coach'. She argues that the duty of the supervisor is to 'pay attention to the humanity of the therapist'. In this regard she takes the same view as ourselves, that the therapist's humanity is the basis of their ability to connect at relational depth. Paying attention to the therapist's humanity might be exemplified by the following extract (paraphrased from Lambers, 2003):

> My supervisee is talking about work he is doing with a client who has just lost his parent. My supervisee has also recently lost his parent and finds this to be both a poignant and a difficult experience. On the one hand this commonality of experience has given my supervisee a tender acuity to the experiencing of his client. It is easy for him to touch a depth where he can meet his client. My supervisee is also somewhat nervous in talking about this: 'some people would automatically see this as a situation to be avoided, in case of over involvement'. Issues of over involvement can certainly be part of this process but that is not the only thing supervision is concerned with. As the supervisor I am intent on honouring my supervisee's experience of this situation. I want to stay with that a while because his humanity is a big part of who he is as a therapist.

This illustration is timely, coming as it does at the end of this chapter on the developmental agenda for the therapist. In this example the supervisor is intent on working in a fashion that reflects the *potentiality model* where the aim is to help the supervisee in this case to develop further the skills and sensitivities they have. The opposite to that would be the *deficiency model* which could be exemplified, like in the above extract, by solely focusing on the dangers of over involvement. The deficiency model sees the person only in terms of their deficits. In the deficiency model, 'therapy' is only about remediating those deficits – it is not about developing 'potentialities' – thus the political dialectic is set. The deficiency model is negatively rather than positively oriented but it largely defines the paradigm that is reflected in most of our public institutions including education, social services and health. In defiance of the mainstream 'deficiency model' the profession of counselling and psychotherapy has distinguished itself by pursuing a potentiality model both in its working with clients and also in its approach to professional supervision. Supervision within psychotherapy serves a developmental function rather than a policing function. However, there is a constant danger that both supervision and also therapy could gradually drift into a deficiency orientation where the major role for the supervisor is the policing function (Dryden et al., 2000; Mearns, 2004b). Policing and potentiality are opposites that do not mix. If the profession allows an insidious movement towards the deficiency model, books like this that endeavour to trace a form of working emphasising relational depth will have to become seen as 'unethical' as the profession drifts into an excessively detached, defensive non-presence.

At this point we are nearing the end of our book. Yet, it is a somewhat frightening ending. We have traced the essence of working at relational depth in counselling and psychotherapy, yet we are approaching the end with the ogre of the psychotherapy relationship in the future perhaps being 'policed'. It is, therefore, opportune, if our concluding chapter is distinctly 'political' in nature. For that we make no apology.

Note

1. Very recently BACP has abandoned the requirement of personal therapy, recognising that this is not the exclusive way of obtaining the personal development agenda.

9 TOWARDS A REVOLUTION

In our eight chapters to this point we have argued the centrality of relationship in psychotherapy research findings (Chapter 1) and in the development of psychological distress of all kinds (Chapter 2). In Chapter 3 we presented our understanding of what it is to encounter a client at relational depth in counselling and psychotherapy. Here, we have not been talking about that fairly superficial level of relationship that can be required to establish a therapeutic alliance, but a relationship which offers a particular depth of human engagement with each other, one that is experienced by the client as so genuine and so profound that they can, sometimes only gradually and fearfully, face their own sense of their existence and be met there by the therapist (Chapter 4). The transition from Chapter 3 to Chapter 4 is from moments of encounter at relational depth to the winning of a particular quality of trust that deepens the continuing relationship. In Chapters 5 and 6 we used case examples to illustrate both moments of meeting and the importance of winning depth in the continuing relationship. Chapter 7 explored the therapist's role in facilitating moments of meeting and Chapter 8 outlined the key personal development agenda, emphasising that this continues long after training.

Although we have taken many of our examples from person-centred therapy and existential psychotherapy, our argument is not restricted to these approaches because the kind of relational contact we have been exploring depends more on the person of the therapist than the approach with which they identify. One of the most respected psychotherapists in Great Britain in the past 30 years has been John Foskett. John's background is Kleinian and he sees a lot of situations in terms of 'families'. But it is not his 'family' interpretations and metaphors that impact upon those with whom he works. It is the tenderness with which he 'holds' people and the depth of personal engagement he offers. From a previous generation, the famous behaviour therapist, John Krumboltz (Krumboltz and Thoresen, 1969), based his work entirely upon learning theory. However it was not that fact which enthralled the participants of the 1974 International Round Table for the Advancement of Counselling in Cambridge, England. What enthralled the audience was the humanity of this man, his patience and respect for his clients and the intimacy that was so obviously engendered. In the early 1970s, the Center for Studies of the Person (CSP) in La Jolla, California would, at times, receive visitors from the Gestalt Institute further north. The first question asked of these visitors was, invariably, whether they had been trained by Laura Perls or by Fritz Perls. If trained by Laura, the person-centred practitioners of CSP would know that they would find an almost perfect correlate to the way they worked. They would know that, while these Gestalt colleagues would use some different concepts, when it came to their actual engagement with clients they would show Laura Perls' emphasis on the delicacy of interactions and the contiguity of the therapist's interventions with the client's process. However, if trained by Fritz there would be almost nothing in common and the encounter was likely to be boringly competitive. The psychoanalytic tradition is equally difficult to categorise. On the one hand there is a clear impression that much of classical analysis is based on a relatively superficial relationship maintained by the analyst at a level of transference process that actively blocks an engagement at relational depth. We can witness the dreadful human carnage created by this tautological system in a book such as *One to One* by Rosemary Dinnage (1988) where she presents the accounts of 20 clients who had undergone up to 31 years of analysis and who were, virtually unanimously, screaming out their frustration at the lack of relational contact, endured only because of the disempowering pathologies engendered by the therapy itself. Anna Sands' *Falling for Therapy* (2000) is another example of how a detached, impersonal psychoanalytic style can scar, rather than heal, clients. Yet, as we have seen in Chapter 1, many contemporary psychoanalysts and psychodynamic practitioners are moving towards their clients, which, in embracing the 'real relationship' in psychoanalysis (Stern et al., 1998), is actually reflecting much better the earlier practices of its originator (see Boss, 1963; Stadlen, 2005).

Nor can we assume that because the relationship is centrally featured in person-centred therapy and existential psychotherapy, all therapists adopting these labels will be able, consistently, to offer the experience of relational depth to their clients. Certainly, that is the aim of professional training (Mearns, 1997c) but it is by no means universally attained. For a considerable time before the requirement for in-depth training, numerous practitioners simply adopted the 'person-centred' label, perhaps because it sounded easy, defined, as it tended to be, simply in terms of three core conditions. Here, there was a failure to realise that it is, arguably, one of the most difficult therapeutic approaches to develop coherently (Spinelli, 2004).

Perhaps it is time to move away from the old labels. It is said that there have been in excess of 500 separate therapeutic approaches identified

(Spinelli, 2004). This could just as well be a multiple of all therapists and all their clients insofar as each therapeutic relationship is unique. One of the most fascinating findings from empirical research going back as far as Fiedler (1950) and consistently found thereafter (e.g. Howe, 1993; Raskin, 1974) is that while inexperienced therapists tend to differ quite widely and are easily identifiable by their adopted approach, experienced therapists tend to have become more close in their working and are not so easily identified by approach. We should, perhaps, be delighted by this kind of finding because it probably means that therapists are learning from their clients and gradually being shaped by their clients to offer a relationship that is meaningful. In a relationship, both people contribute and both are shaped by the influence of the other. In a similar vein, verbally violent debates are easily engendered by bringing therapists together to contrast their various ideas (for such debates in the person-centred field, see Greenberg, 2004; Mearns, 2004d; Sachse, 2004; Schmid, 2004; Swildens, 2004). Yet, when practitioners, apparently working from very different theoretical models, get together to describe their actual practice and compare their experiences of relationship, it is the similarities that are more noticeable than the differences (Mearns, 2004a; Mearns and Jacobs, 2003).

In this book we have grasped what we believe to be a fundamental dimension of relatedness. It seems to us that this judgement follows from the empirical evidence (Chapter 1) and from the experiences of therapists across a range of traditions. Even more important are the accumulated reports of clients consistently pointing out that relationally oriented therapies gain superior patient evaluations (King et al., 2000; Seligman, 1995). This centrality of relationship is not simply because 'relationship is a good vehicle for communication', it is because relationship is fundamental to the existence of the human being – we are governed and defined by relationship. Even the person who appears pathologically to reject relationship is, in fact, governed by relationship – so governed, in fact, that he feels he needs to protect himself from it.

Yet, politically, relationally oriented counsellors and psychotherapists have a considerable challenge to meet. The current 'politics of helping' (Mearns, 2004b), on which decisions about service provision are made, continues to be founded on 'modern' rather than 'postmodern' assumptions and logic: assumptions which stand in direct contrast to the holistic and systemic principles on which a relational therapy is based. In this frame, therapeutic work is not seen as being with 'people' and 'processes' but with 'problems' and 'treatments': problem A needs to be dealt with by treatment B to produce outcome C. Within the postmodern and relational frame the assumptions and the logic are entirely different. The view from within that frame is that psychological change in the human being is much more complex than this A-B-C. For a start, 'A' (a 'problem') is not the starting point. The starting point is a person, embedded within a network of relationships, and influenced by tendencies related to past, present and future events, with ever-changing dissonances (not pathologies) among the tendencies. These dissonances are potentially life-enhancing. Often they are not comfortable but they engender the ability to protect, to adjust and to develop. They are derived from relationships in the person's life and continue to be worked out in relationships in therapy. While, in the A-B-C model, a problem can be seen in unitary terms as the same across different 'patients', that simplistic logic cannot be applied to a person.

From a postmodern standpoint, even the therapeutic relationship (which, from our perspective, comes closest to the notion of a treatment, 'B') cannot be considered a unitary phenomenon. In the early days of Rogers' research he, understandably, investigated the therapeutic relationship in terms of the unitary epistemology of his time and reported the therapeutic relationship 'conditions' that were necessary and sufficient for therapeutic personality change. However, like ourselves, increasing numbers of thinkers in the person-centred field are now putting the conditions back together again (see Chapter 3) in an interactive and mutually enhancing fashion offering a potency of *relating*. This powerful therapeutic relationship offers the client a striking context for growth. However, this power of the relationship will not create a smooth, unitary path towards whatever the client calls improvement. There is no direct relationship between this 'treatment' and a predictable therapeutic outcome because the therapist has entered into and relationally engaged the client's variable process rather than sought to reduce that process to a unitary problem. In this regard the dissonances of the client are not seen in terms of 'resistance', 'procrastination', 'denial' or even 'stuckness' but as normal, indeed 'healthy' aspects of a person in process. Equally, but much more difficult for the medical model to tolerate, the side of the relationship offered by the therapist will be affected by the person of the therapist and the judgements they make. At times the therapist will find that they 'invade' albeit through an effort to 'encounter' (see Chapter 6). Or, in their effort to be fully involved with the client there will be times when particular aspects of the therapist are touched and they will become 'over-involved'. While these are 'mistakes' in the A-B-C model, they are 'parts of the process' in the relational paradigm. If our aim must be never to make a mistake in relation to our client then, basically, we must withdraw 90 per cent of our self-in-relation and rely only on the 10 per cent that can be properly sterilised. That is not psychotherapy in the model that we are describing. So called 'mistakes' will happen and they will become parts of the process of the working. In our university Dave Mearns does the initial discussion sessions with students on 'overinvolvement'. Every year he urges students not to be too frightened by the notion of overinvolvement. Indeed he even goes so far as to say that the best time to get overinvolved is during the training period when one has greatest support. In fact, it can be really important to experience that boundary between full involvement and overinvolvement if we are to learn the incredibly demanding skills of using ourselves fully to work with the client at relational depth. In the profession of counselling and psychotherapy there is an increasing tendency to see the work as defined by ever-narrowing boundaries. While boundaries are important in every professional endeavour, if they continue to shrink they need to be challenged, else the work, and its impact, will become sterile. (Just in case anyone takes this discussion of 'overinvolvement' to indicate a willingness to accept sexual overinvolvement – we do not!)

The therapeutic relationship is not the only set of variables at 'B' – the therapeutic context represents another powerful set of variables. Again, as described in Chapter 4, there is a danger of ever narrowing what is regarded as an acceptable therapeutic context to 50 minutes a week in the private practitioner's office. The reality is that such narrowing is essentially for the comfort and the security of the practitioner. It would be fascinating to see what new heights the profession could reach if it became more 'fieldwork' oriented and challenged itself to offer the service in contexts more sculpted to the needs of the client. Clinical populations that are currently judged as inappropriate for counselling and psychotherapy might well be appropriate if we can be creative in forming meaningful contexts (see Chapter 6).

From a postmodern standpoint, the results of our therapeutic endeavour with our client may indeed be the relief of an initial symptom, but not always. Relationship-oriented therapies are not aimed at specific symptom reduction which, if it occurs, is a by-product of other changes. The interesting thing is how often such symptom reduction *is* one of the consequences of a holistic therapy even though none of the therapeutic process has actively worked on the symptom. For example, an anxiety-related symptom tends to disappear once the basis of the anxiety becomes symbolised. Also, after Dominic's fourth session (Chapter 5), it is going to be really difficult for him to retain his alcohol problem particularly in the context of his continuing relationship-at-depth with his therapist. The work with Rick was not targeted at reducing his symptoms of trauma. Indeed, it must be said that Rick's symptoms were much more pronounced once a continued relationship at depth was obtained from session 27. Between then and session 61 Rick's experiencing of his trauma was rabid. In his own, later, words, he 'went to Hell' – and Dave went with him. Generally, the results of a relationship-oriented therapy are much more than symptom reduction. The relationship may have helped the person become less fearful of their own process, more aware of that process, less afraid of their dissonances and of their changing. They may have become more positive about facing future life contexts and, more important than anything else, more confident about themself and others in relationship.

So, the principle behind an A-B-C, unitary approach to therapy is quite different to a postmodern, relational paradigm. Of course, there is a present political difficulty insofar as mental health provision tends to be seen in terms of modernist, unitary, A-B-C theory. Probably, in the greater scheme of things, this only represents a momentary point of stuckness until the A-B-C unitary paradigm is recognised for what it is: a self-replicating system. If the epistemology by which systems are evaluated is oriented only to the A-B-C model, then only the A-B-C model can be proved effective.

The majority of psychotherapists, across all traditions, know that the A-B-C paradigm is, essentially, flawed. However, in the political mainstream there is no place for the person who would point out that the emperor is, in fact, naked. The fallacy of the A-B-C paradigm is a kind of 'controlled folly' (Casteneda, 1973). We all know it is, really, a folly, within mental health at least. However, it is a nice simple definition of existence, so why do we not just go along with it, like everyone else? Of course we cannot go along with it but, equally, we must find a way of 'articulating' with it, albeit in constructive defiance (Mearns, 2003b).

Perhaps there will, sometime, be a 'revolution' and the unitary A-B-C paradigm will be exposed. Let us not presume that the revolution will be initiated by the involved professions of psychology, psychotherapy and psychiatry – the revolution might, in fact, be inspired by the commissioners of services. Indeed, it might have already begun. It is interesting to note the static nature and even the depletion of mental health funding for conventional services in recent years, compared with other sectors of the health service. The A-B-C paradigm in mental health is not being well fed. Commissioners of services and key stakeholders, particularly GPs, know that patients value relationship-oriented therapies. We can develop these beginnings, particularly through our research, continuing the work of recent years to examine counselling and psychotherapy in a wider fashion than the A-B-C model, to trace the impact upon the person in terms of their understanding of their own process, becoming less fearful of that process including their dissonances and their changing and, most particularly, the remediation in their ability to use relationship.

Whether the change happens by revolution or by evolution, it is inevitable, because it is an essentially untenable position for human beings to seek to deny the centrality of human relationship in their dealings with each other. Constantly there is the leakage of humanity that catches all our breaths. It touches everyone, just as we hope some of the people in this book have touched the reader.

REFERENCES

Adams, J., Hayes, J. and Hopson, B. (1976) *Transition: Understanding and Managing Personal Change*. London: Martin Robertson.

American Psychiatric Association (APA) (1994) *Diagnostic and Statistical Manual of Mental Disorders IV*. Washington, DC: APA.

Anderson, R. and Cissna, K.N. (1997) *The Martin Buber – Carl Rogers Dialogue: A New Transcript with Commentary*. Albany, NY: State University of New York Press.

Aronson, E., Wilson, T.D. and Akert, R.M. (1999) *Social Psychology*. New York: Longman.

Asay, T.P. and Lambert, M.J. (1999) 'Therapist relational variables', in D.J. Cain and J. Seeman (eds), *Humanistic Psychotherapies: Handbook of Theory and Practice*. Washington, DC: APA. pp. 531–57.

Bachelor, A. and Hovarth, A. (1999) 'The therapeutic relationship', in M. Hubble, B.L. Duncan and S.D. Miller (eds), *The Heart and Soul of Change: What Works in Therapy*. Washington, DC: APA. pp. 133–78.

Barrett-Lennard, G.T. (1962) 'Dimensions of therapist response as causal factors in therapeutic change', *Psychological Monographs*, 76 (43): whole no. 562.

Barrett-Lennard, G.T. (2005) *Relationship at the Centre: Healing in a Troubled World*. London: Whurr.

Bateson, G., Jackson, D.D., Haley, J. and Weakland, J. (1956) 'Towards a theory of schizophrenia', *Behavioral Science*, 1: 251–64.

Beebe, B., Rustin, J., Sorter, D. and Knoblauch, S. (2003a) 'An expanded view of intersubjectivity in infancy and its application to psychoanalysis', *Psychoanalytic Dialogues*, 13 (6): 805–41.

Beebe, B., Sorter, D., Rustin, J. and Knoblauch, S. (2003b) 'A comparison of Meltzoff, Trevarthen, and Stern', *Psychoanalytic Dialogues*, 13 (6): 777–804.

Behr, M. (2003) 'Interactive resonance in work with children and adolescents: A theory-based concept of interpersonal relationship through play and the use of toys', *Person-Centered and Experiential Psychotherapies*, 2 (2): 89–103.

Benjamin, J. (1990) 'An outline of intersubjectivity: The development of recognition', *Psychoanalytic Psychology*, 7: 33–46.

Beutler, L.E., Malik, M., Alimohamed, S., Harwood, M.T., Talebi, H., Noble, S. et al. (2004) 'Therapist Variables', in M.J. Lambert (ed.), *Bergin and Garfield's Handbook of Psychotherapy and Behavior Change* (5th ed.). Chicago: John Wiley and Sons. pp. 227–306.

Binder, U. (1998) 'Empathy and empathy development with psychotic clients', in B. Thorne and E. Lambers (eds), *Person-Centred Therapy: A European Perspective*. London: Sage. pp. 216–30.

Birtchnell, J. (1999) *Relating in Psychotherapy: The Application of a New Theory*. Hove: Brunner-Routledge.

Blaxter, L., Hughes, C. and Tight, M. (2001) *How to Research*. Buckingham: Open University Press.

Bohart, A.C., Elliott, R., Greenberg, L.S. and Watson, J.C. (2002) 'Empathy', in J.C. Norcross (ed.), *Psychotherapy Relationships That Work: Therapist Contributions and Responsiveness to Patients*. Oxford: Oxford University Press. pp. 89–108.

Bohart, A.C. and Tallman, K. (1999) *How Clients Make Therapy Work: The Process of Active Self-Healing*. Washington, DC: APA.

Bohm, D. (1996) *On Dialogue*. London: Routledge.

Boss, M. (1963) *Psychoanalysis and Daseinsanalysis*. New York: Basic Books.

Boszormenyi-Nagy, I., Grunebaum, J. and Ulrich, D. (1991) 'Contextual therapy', in A.S. Gurman and D. Kniskern (eds), *Handbook of Family Therapy* (Vol. 2). New York: Brunner-Mazel.

Bott, D. (2001) 'Client-centred therapy and family therapy: a review and commentary', *Journal of Family Therapy*, 23 (4): 361–77.

Bowlby, J. (1969) *Attachment*. New York: Basic Books.

Bozarth, J.D. (2001) 'Beyond reflection: Emergent modes of empathy', in S. Haugh and T. Merry (eds), *Empathy*. Ross-on-Wye: PCCS Books. pp. 131–43.

Brazier, D. (1993) 'The necessary condition is love: Going beyond self in the person-centred approach', in D. Brazier (ed.), *Beyond Carl Rogers*. London: Constable. pp. 72–91.

Brodley, B.T. (2001) 'Congruence and its relation to communication in client-centred therapy', in G. Wyatt (ed.), *Congruence*. Ross-on-Wye: PCCS Books. pp. 55–78.

Brown, G.W. and Harris, T.O. (1978) *Social Origins of Depression: A Study of Psychiatric Disorders in Women*. London: Tavistock.

Buber, M. (1947) *Between Man and Man*. London: Fontana.

Buber, M. (1958) *I and Thou*. Edinburgh: T & T Clark.

Buber, M. (1988) *The Knowledge of Man: Selected Essays*. Atlantic Highlands, NJ: Humanities Press International.

Buchanan, L. and Hughes, R. (2000) *Experiences of Person-Centred Counselling Training*. Ross-on-Wye: PCCS Books.

Bugental, J.F.T. (1976) *The Search for Existential Identity: Patient-Therapist Dialogues in Humanistic Psychotherapy*. San Fransisco: Jossey-Bass.

Casteneda, C. (1973) *A Seperate Reality*. Harmondsworth: Penguin.

Claiborn, C.D., Goodyear, R.K. and Horner, P.A. (2002) 'Feedback', in J.C. Norcross (ed.), *Psychotherapy Relationships That Work: Therapist Contributions and Responsiveness to Patients*. Oxford: Oxford University Press. pp. 217–33.

Comer, R.J. (1998) *Abnormal Psychology* (3rd ed.). New York: W.H. Freeman.

Cooper, M. (1999) 'If you can't be Jekyll be Hyde: An existential-phenomenological exploration on lived-plurality', in J. Rowan and M. Cooper (eds), *The Plural Self: Multiplicity in Everyday Life*. London: Sage. pp. 51–70.

Cooper, M. (2001) 'Embodied empathy', in S. Haugh and T. Merry (eds), *Empathy*. Ross-on-Wye: PCCS Books. pp. 218–29.

Cooper, M. (2003a) *Existential Therapies*. London: Sage.

Cooper, M. (2003b) '"I–I" and "I–Me"': Transposing Buber's interpersonal attitudes to the intrapersonal plane', *Journal of Constructivist Psychology*, 16 (2): 131–53.

Cooper, M. (2004) 'Encountering self-otherness: "I–I" and "I–Me" modes of self-relating', in H.J.M. Hermans and G. Dimaggio (eds), *Dialogical Self in Psychotherapy*. Hove: Brunner-Routledge. pp. 60–73.

Cooper, M. (2005) 'The inter-experiential field: Perceptions and metaperceptions in person-centered and experiential psychotherapy and counseling', *Person-Centered and Experiential Psychotherapies*, 4 (1): 54–68.

Cooper, M., Mearns, D., Stiles, W.B., Warner, M.S. and Elliott, R. (2004) 'Developing self-pluralistic perspectives within the person-centered and experiential approaches: A round table dialogue', *Person-Centered and Experiential Psychotherapies*, 3 (3): 176–91.

Coulson, W. (1987) 'Reclaiming client-centered counseling from the person-centered movement'. Comptche, CA: Centre for Enterprising Families.

Crits-Christoph, P. and Gibbons, M.B.C. (2002) 'Relational interpretations', in J.C. Norcross (ed.), *Psychotherapy Relationships That Work: Therapist Contributions and Responsiveness to Patients*. Oxford: Oxford University Press. pp. 285–300.

Crossley, N. (1996) *Intersubjectivity: The Fabric of Social Becoming*. London: Sage.

Csikszentmihalyi, M. (2002) *Flow: The Classic Work on How to Achieve Happiness*. London: Rider.

Curtis, R.C. and Hirsch, I. (2003) 'Relational approaches to psychoanalytic psychotherapy', in A.S. Gurman and S.B. Messer (eds), *Essential Psychotherapies: Theory and Practice* (2nd ed.). New York: Guilford Press. pp. 69–106.

Derrida, J. (1974) *Of Grammatology*. Baltimore, MDY: The Johns Hopkins University Press.

Dimaggio, G., Salvatore, G. and Catania, D. (2004) 'Strategies for the treatment of dialogical dysfunction', in H.J.M. Hermans and G. Dimaggio (eds), *Dialogical Self in Psychotherapy*. Hove: Brunner-Routledge. pp. 190–204.

Dinnage, R. (1988) *One to One: Experiences of Psychotherapy*. London: Viking.

Dryden, W., Horton, I. and Mearns, D. (1995) *Issues in Professional Counsellor Training*. London: Cassell.

Dryden, W., Horton, I. and Mearns, D. (2000) 'Counselling: past, present and future', *British Journal of Guidance and Counselling*, 28 (4): 467–83.

Duck, S. (1998) *Human Relationships*. London: Sage.

Dziurawiec, S. (1987) 'Neonates' attention to faces', in V. Bruce, H. Ellis and A. Young (eds), *Developmental Aspects of Face Recognition*. Grange-over-Sands: Unpublished Report on ESRC Workshop.

Ehrenberg, D.B. (1992) *The Intimate Edge: Extending the Reach of Psychoanalytic Interaction*. New York: W.W. Norton.

Elkin, I., Shea, M.T., Watkins, J.T., Imber, S.D., Sotsky, S.M., Collins, J.F. et al. (1989) 'National Institute of Mental Health treatment of depression collaborative research program – General effectiveness of treatments', *Archives of General Psychiatry*, 46 (11): 971–82.

Elliott, R., Watson, J.C., Goldman, R. and Greenberg, L.S. (2004) *Learning Emotion-Focused Therapy: The Process-Experiential Approach to Change*. Washington, DC: APA.

Farber, B.A. and Lane, J.S. (2002) 'Positive regard', in J.C. Norcross (ed.), *Psychotherapy Relationships That Work: Therapist Contributions and Responsiveness to Patients*. Oxford: Oxford University Press. pp. 175–94.

Farber, L.H. (1967) 'Martin Buber and psychotherapy', in P.A. Schlipp and M. Friedman (eds), *The Philosophy of Martin Buber*. London: Cambridge University Press. pp. 577–601.

Festinger, L. (1957) *A Theory of Cognitive Dissonance*. Evanston, IL: Row Peterson.

Fiedler, F.E. (1950) 'A comparison of therapeutic relationship in psychoanalytic, non-directive and Adlerian therapy', *Journal of Consulting Psychology*, 14: 436–45.

Friedman, M. (1985) *The Healing Dialogue in Psychotherapy*. New York: Jason Aronson.

Geller, S.M. and Greenberg, L.S. (2002) 'Therapeutic presence: Therapist's experience of presence in the psychotherapy encounter', *Person-Centered and Experiential Psychotherapies*, 1 (1–2): 71–86.

Gelso, C.J. and Hayes, J.A. (2002) 'The management of countertransference', in J.C. Norcross (ed.), *Psychotherapy Relationships That Work: Therapist Contributions and Responsiveness to Patients*. Oxford: Oxford University Press. pp. 267–83.

Gendlin, E. (1981) *Focusing*. New York: Bantam Books.

Gendlin, E. (1996) *Focusing-Oriented Psychotherapy: A Manual of the Experiential Method*. New York: Guilford Press.

Gergen, K. (1999) *An Invitation to Social Construction*. London: Sage.

Gerhardt, S. (2004) *Why Love Matters*. London: Routledge.

Ginsberg, B. (1984) 'Beyond behavior modification: Client-centered play therapy with the retarded', *American Psychology Bulletin*, 6 (3): 321–34.

Giovazolias, T. (2004) 'The therapeutic relationship in cognitive-behavioural therapy', *Counselling Psychology Review*, 19 (2): 14–20.

Goren, C.C., Sarty, M. and Wu, R.W.K. (1975) 'Visual following and pattern discrimination of face-like stimuli by newborn infants', *Paediatrics*, 56: 544–9.

Grant, A., Mills, J., Mulhern, R. and Short, N. (2004) *Cognitive Behavioural Therapy in Mental Health Care*. London: Sage.

Grant, B. (2002) 'Principled and instrumental non-directiveness in person-centered and client-centered therapy', in D.J. Cain (ed.), *Classics in the Person-Centered Approach*. Ross-on-Wye: PCCS Books. pp. 371–7.

Grant, B. (2004) 'The imperative of ethical justification in psychotherapy: The special case of client-centered therapy', *Person-Centered and Experiential Psychotherapies*, 3 (3): 152–65.

Greenberg, L.S. (2004) 'Being and doing: Person-centeredness, process guidance and differential treatment', *Person-Centered and Experiential Psychotherapies*, 3 (1): 52–64.

Greenberg, L.S. (2005) 'Foreword', in G.T. Barrett-Lennard (ed.), *Relationship at the Centre: Healing in a Troubled World*. London: Whurr. pp. vii–iii.

Greenberg, L.S., Rice, L.N. and Elliott, R. (1993) *Facilitating Emotional Change: The Moment-by-Moment Process*. New York: Guilford Press.

Hammersley, D. (1995) *Counselling People on Prescribed Drugs*. London: Sage.

Hargaden, H. and Sills, C. (2002) *Transactional Analysis in Psychotherapy: A Relational Perspective*. London: Routledge.

Heidegger, M. (1962) *Being and Time*. Oxford: Blackwell.

Heider, F. (1958) *The Psychology of Interpersonal Relations*. New York: Wiley.

Hermans, H.J.M. and Dimaggio, G. (eds) (2004) *Dialogical Self in Psychotherapy*. Hove: Brunner-Routledge.

Hermans, H.J.M. and Kempen, H.J.G. (1993) *The Dialogical Self: Meaning As Movement*. San Diego, CA: Academic Press.

Hill, C.E. and Knox, S. (2002) 'Self-disclosure', in J.C. Norcross (ed.), *Psychotherapy Relationships That Work: Therapist Contributions and Responsiveness to Patients*. Oxford: Oxford University Press. pp. 255–65.

Holdstock, L. (1993) 'Can we afford not to revision the person-centred concept of self?', in D. Brazier (ed.), *Beyond Carl Rogers*. London: Constable.

Hovarth, A.O. and Bedi, R.P. (2002) 'The alliance', in J.C. Norcross (ed.), *Psychotherapy Relationships That Work: Therapist Contributions and Responsiveness to Patients*. Oxford: Oxford University Press. pp. 37–69.

Howe, D. (1993) *On Being a Client*. London: Sage.

Hubble, M., Duncan, B.L. and Miller, S.D. (1999) *The Heart and Soul of Change: What Works in Therapy*. Washington, DC: APA.

Hycner, R. (1991) *Between Person and Person: Towards a Dialogical Psychotherapy*. Highland, NY: Gestalt Journal Press.

Hycner, R. and Jacobs, L. (1995) *The Healing Relationship in Gestalt Therapy*. Highland, NY: Gestalt Journal Publications.

Jordan, J.V. (1991a) 'The development of women's sense of self', in J.V. Jordan, A.G. Kaplan, J.B. Miller, I.P. Stiver and J.L. Surrey (eds), *Women's Growth in Connection: Writings from the Stone Centre*. New York: Guilford Press. pp. 81–96.

Jordan, J.V. (1991b) 'Empathy, mutuality and therapeutic change: Clinical implications of a relational model', in J.V. Jordan, A.G. Kaplan, J.B. Miller, I.P. Stiver and

J.L. Surrey (eds), *Women's Growth in Connection: Writings from the Stone Centre.* New York: Guilford Press. pp. 283–9.

Jordan, J.V. (2000) 'The role of mutual empathy in relational/cultural therapy', *Journal of Clinical Psychology*, 56 (8): 1005–16.

Jordan, J.V., Kaplan, A.G., Miller, J.B., Stiver, I.P. and Surrey, J.L. (eds) (1991) *Women's Growth in Connection: Writings from the Stone Centre.* New York: Guilford Press.

Kagan, N. (1984) 'Interpersonal process recall: Basic methods and recent research', in D. Larson (ed.), *Teaching Psychological Skills: Models for Giving Psychology Away.* Monterey, CA: Brooks/Cole.

Kaslow, N.J., Dausch, B.M. and Celano, M. (2003) 'Family therapies', in A.S. Gurman and S.B. Messer (eds), *Essential Psychotherapies.* New York: Guilford Press. pp. 400–62.

Keijsers, G.P.J., Schaap, C.P.D.R. and Hoogduin, C.A.L. (2000) 'The impact of interpersonal patient and therapist behaviour on outcome in cognitive-behavior therapy', *Behaviour Modification*, 24 (2): 264–97.

King, M., Sibbald, B., Ward, E., Bower, P., Lloyd, M., Gabbay, M. et al. (2000) 'Randomised controlled trial of non-directive counselling, cognitive-behaviour therapy and usual general practitioner care in the management of depression as well as mixed anxiety and depression in primary care', *Health Technology Assessment*, 4 (19).

Krietemeyer, B. and Prouty, G. (2003) 'The art of psychological contact: The psychotherapy of a mentally retarded psychotic client', in *Person-Centered and Experiential Psychotherapies*, 2 (3): pp. 151–61.

Krumboltz, J.D. and Thoresen, C.E. (eds) (1969) *Behavioral Counseling.* San Francisco: Holt, Rinehart and Winston.

Krupnick, J.L., Sotsky, S.M., Simmens, S., Moyer, J., Elkin, I., Watkins, J. et al. (1996) 'The role of the therapeutic alliance in psychotherapy and pharmacotherapy outcome: Findings in the national institute of mental health treatment of depression collaborative research program', *Journal of Consulting and Clinical Psychology*, 64 (3): 532–9.

Kvale, S. (1996) *InterViews.* London: Sage.

Laing, R.D. (1965) *The Divided Self: An Existential Study in Sanity and Madness.* Harmondsworth: Penguin.

Laing, R.D. (1967) *The Politics of Experience and the Bird of Paradise.* Harmondsworth: Penguin.

Laing, R.D. (1969) *Self and Others* (2nd ed.). Harmondsworth: Penguin.

Laing, R.D. and Esterson, A. (1964) *Sanity, Madness and the Family.* Harmondsworth: Penguin.

Lambers, E. (2000) 'Supervision in person-centred therapy: facilitating congruence', in D. Mearns and B. Thorne (eds), *Person-Centred Therapy Today: New Frontiers in Theory and Practice.* London: Sage. pp. 196–211.

Lambers, E. (2002) Personal Communication.

Lambers, E. (2003) *Looking After Ourselves: Keeping Fit to Practice.* Paper presented at the Cruse Conference, Perth, Scotland.

Lambert, M.J. (1992) 'Implications of outcome research for psychotherapy integration', in J.C. Norcross and M.R. Goldstein (eds), *Handbook of Psychotherapy Integration.* New York: Basic Books. pp. 94–129.

Leiman, M. (2004) 'Dialogical sequence analysis', in H.J.M. Hermans and G. Dimaggio (eds), *Dialogical Self in Psychotherapy.* Hove: Brunner-Routledge. pp. 255–69.

Levinas, E. (1969) *Totality and Infinity: An Essay on Exteriority.* Pittsburgh, PA: Duquesne University Press.

Lietaer, G. (2001) 'Being genuine as a therapist: congruence and transparency', in G. Wyatt (ed.), *Congruence.* Ross-on-Wye: PCCS Books. pp. 36–54.

Lietaer, G. (2002) 'The united colours of person-centered and experiential psychotherapies', *Person-Centered and Experiential Psychotherapies*, 1 (1–2): 4–13.

Lifton, R.J. (1974) *Home from the War*. London: Wildwood House.

Lysaker, P.H. and Lysaker, J.T. (2002) 'Narrative structure in psychosis – Schizophrenia and disruptions in the dialogical self', *Theory & Psychology*, 12 (2): 207–20.

Lysaker, P.H. and Lysaker, J.T. (2004) 'Dialogical transformation in the psychotherapy of schizophrenia', in H.J.M. Hermans and G. Dimaggio (eds), *Dialogical Self in Psychotherapy*. Hove: Brunner-Routledge. pp. 205–19.

Mahler, M.S., Pine, F. and Bergman, A. (1975) *The Psychological Birth of the Human Infant*. New York: Basic Books.

Mearns, D. (1994) *Developing Person-Centred Counselling*. London: Sage.

Mearns, D. (1997a) 'Achieving the personal development dimension in professional counsellor training', *Counselling*, 8 (2): 113–20.

Mearns, D. (1997b) 'The future of individual counselling'. Paper presented at the 1997 Ben Hartop Memorial Lecture, School of Education, University of Durham.

Mearns, D. (1997c) *Person-Centred Counselling Training*. London: Sage.

Mearns, D. (2002) 'Further theoretical propositions in regard to self theory within person-centered therapy', *Person-Centered and Experiential Psychotherapies*, 1 (1–2): 14–27.

Mearns, D. (2003a) *Developing Person-Centred Counselling* (2nd ed.). London: Sage.

Mearns, D. (2003b) 'The humanistic agenda: Articulation', *Journal of Humanistic Psychology*, 43 (3): 53–65.

Mearns, D. (2004a) *Dave Mearns in Conversation* (video). Newport: University of Wales.

Mearns, D. (2004b) 'The human curriculum'. Paper presented at the Annual Conference of the British Association for Counselling and Psychotherapy.

Mearns, D. (2004c) 'Person-centred therapy: The leading edge'. Paper presented at the North West Counselling Association, Manchester.

Mearns, D. (2004d) 'Problem-centered is not person-centered', *Person-Centered and Experiential Psychotherapies*, 3 (2): 86–98.

Mearns, D. and Dryden, W. (eds) (1989) *Experiences of Counselling in Action*. London: Sage.

Mearns, D. and Jacobs, M. (2003) *Person-Centred and Psychodynamic Therapy: Colleagues or Opponents?* Video. Birmingham: CSCT.

Mearns, D. and Thorne, B. (1999) *Person-Centred Counselling in Action* (2nd ed.). London: Sage.

Mearns, D. and Thorne, B. (2000) *Person-Centred Therapy Today: New Frontiers in Theory and Practice*. London: Sage.

Meltzoff, A.N. and Moore, M.K. (1998) 'Infant intersubjectivity: Broadening the dialogue to include imitation, identity and intention', in S. Braten (ed.), *Intersubjective Communication and Emotion in Early Ontogeny*. Cambridge: Cambridge University Press. pp. 47–62.

Merry, T. (2003) 'The actualisation conundrum', *Person-Centred Practice*, 11 (2): 83–91.

Merry, T. (2004) 'Classical client-centred therapy', in P. Sanders (ed.), *The Tribes of the Person-Centred Nation: An Introduction to the Schools of Therapy Related to the Person-Centred Approach*. Ross-on-Wye: PCCS Books. pp. 21–44.

Miller, S.D., Hubble, M. and Duncan, B.L. (eds) (1996) *Handbook of Solution-Focused Brief Therapy*. San Fransisco: Jossey Bass.

Mitchell, S.A. (2000) *Relationality: From Attachment to Intersubjectivity*. Hillsdale, NJ: The Analytic Press.

Moustakas, C. (1961) *Loneliness*. New York: Prentice-Hall.

Newson, J. (1978) 'Dialogue and development', in A. Lock (ed.), *Action, Gesture and Symbol: The Emergence of Language*. London: Academic Press. pp. 31–42.

O'Leary, C. (1999) *Counselling Couples and Families: A Person-Centred Approach.* London: Sage.

Paulson, B.L., Everall, R.D. and Janice, S. (2001) 'Client perception of hindering experiences in counselling', *Counselling and Psychotherapy Research*, 1 (1): 53–61.

Plomin, R., DeFries, J.C., McClearn, G.E. and McGuffin, P. (2001) *Behavioral Genetics* (4th ed.). New York: Worth Publishers.

Pörtner, M. (2000) *Trust and Understanding: The Person-Centred Approach to Everyday Care for People with Special Needs.* Ross-on-Wye: PCCS.

Prochaska, J.O. (1999) 'How do people change, and how can we change to help many more people?', in M. Hubble, B.L. Duncan and S.D. Miller (eds), *The Heart and Soul of Change: What Works in Therapy.* Washington, DC: APA. pp. 227–55.

Proctor, G. (2002) *The Dynamics of Power in Psychotherapy: Ethics, Politics and Practice.* Ross-on-Wye: PCCS.

Prouty, G. (1994) *Theoretical Evolutions in Person-Centered/Experiential Therapy: Applications to Schizophrenic and Retarded Psychosis.* Westport, CT: Praeger.

Prouty, G. (2001) 'A new mode of empathy: empathic contact', in S. Haugh and T. Merry (eds), *Empathy.* Ross-on-Wye: PCCS Books. pp. 155–62.

Prouty, G., Pörtner, M. and Van Werde, D. (2002) *Pre-Therapy: Reaching Contact Impaired Clients.* Ross-on-Wye: PCCS Books.

Purton, C. (2004) *Person-Centred Therapy: The Focussing-Oriented Approach.* London: Palgrave Macmillan.

Raskin, N. (1974) 'Studies on psychotherapeutic orientation: ideology in practice', *American Academy of Psychotherapists Psychotherapy Research Monographs.*

Reinecke, M.A. and Freeman, A. (2003) 'Cognitive therapy', in A.S. Gurman and S.B. Messer (eds), *Essential Psychotherapies.* New York: Guilford Press. pp. 224–71.

Rennie, D.L. (1998) *Person-Centered Counselling: An Experiential Approach.* London: Sage.

Rogers, C.R. (1951) *Client-Centered Therapy.* Boston: Houghton and Mifflin.

Rogers, C.R. (1957) 'The necessary and sufficient conditions of therapeutic personality change', *Journal of Consulting Psychology*, 21 (2): 95–103.

Rogers, C.R. (1959) 'A theory of therapy, personality and interpersonal relationships as developed in the client-centered framework', in S. Koch (ed.), *Psychology: A Study of Science* (Vol. 3). New York: McGraw-Hill. pp. 184–256.

Rogers, C.R. (1961) *On Becoming a Person: A Therapist's View of Therapy.* London: Constable.

Rogers, C.R. (1963) 'The actualizing tendency in relation to "motives" and to consciousness', in M. Jones (ed.), *Nebraska Symposium on Motivation.* Lincoln, NE: University of Nebraska Press. pp. 1–24.

Rogers, C.R. (1973) 'The interpersonal relationship: the core of guidance', in C.R. Rogers and B. Stevens (eds), *Person to Person: The problem of Being Human.* London: Souvenir Press. pp. 89–103.

Rogers, C.R. (1977) *Carl Rogers on Personal Power.* London: Constable.

Rogers, C.R. (1986) 'A client-centered/person-centered approach to therapy', in I.L. Kutash and A. Wolf (eds), *Psychotherapist's Casebook.* San Francisco, CA: Jossey-Bass. pp. 197–208.

Rogers, C.R. and Wallen, J.L. (1946) *Counseling with Returned Servicemen.* New York: McGraw-Hill.

Rogers, C.R., Gendlin, E., Kiesler, D.B. and Truax, C.B. (eds) (1967) *The Therapeutic Relationship and Its Impact: A Study of Psychotherapy with Schizophrenics.* Madison, WI: University of Wisconsin Press.

Rowan, J. (1990) *Subpersonalities: The People Inside Us.* London: Routledge.

Rowan, J. and Cooper, M. (eds) (1999) *The Plural Self: Multiplicity in Everyday Life.* London: Sage.

Rowan, J. and Jacobs, M. (2002) *The Therapist's Use of Self*. Buckingham: Open University Press.

Sachse, R. (2004) 'From client-centered to clarification-oriented psychotherapy', *Person-Centered and Experiential Psychotherapies*, 3 (1): 19–35.

Safran, J.D. and Muran, J.C. (2000) *Negotiating the Therapeutic Alliance: A Relational Treatment Guide*. New York: Guilford Press.

Sands, A. (2000) *Falling for Therapy: Psychotherapy from a Client's Point of View*. London: Macmillan.

Sartre, J.-P. (1958) *Being and Nothingness: An Essay on Phenomenological Ontology*. London: Routledge.

Schmid, P.F. (2001a) 'Authenticity: the person as his or her own author. Dialogical and ethical perspectives on therapy as an encounter relationship. And beyond', in G. Wyatt (ed.), *Congruence*. Ross-on-Wye: PCCS Books. pp. 213–28.

Schmid, P.F. (2001b) 'Comprehension: The art of not knowing. Dialogical and ethical perspectives in personal and person-centred relationships', in S. Haugh and T. Merry (eds), *Empathy*. Ross-on-Wye: PCCS Books. pp. 53–71.

Schmid, P.F. (2002) 'Knowledge of acknowledgement? Psychotherapy as "the art of not-knowing" – prospects on further developments of a radical paradigm', *Person-Centered and Experiential Psychotherapies*, 1 (1–2): 56–70.

Schmid, P.F. (2003) 'The characteristics of a person-centered approach to therapy and counseling: Critiera for identity and coherence', *Person-Centered and Experiential Psychotherapies*, 2 (2): 104–20.

Schmid, P.F. (2004) 'Back to the client: A phenomenological approach to the process of understanding and diagnosis', *Person-Centered and Experiential Psychotherapies*, 3 (1): 36–51.

Schneider, K.J. (2003) 'Existential-humanistic psychotherapies', in A.S. Gurman and S.B. Messer (eds), *Essential Psychotherapies*. New York: Guilford Press. pp. 149–81.

Segrin, C. (2001) *Interpersonal Processes in Psychological Problems*. New York: Guilford.

Seligman, M.E.P. (1995) 'The effectiveness of psychotherapy: The Consumer Reports Study', *American Psychologist*, 50: 965–74.

Semerari, A., Carcione, A., Dimaggio, G., Nicolo, G. and Procacci, M. (2004) 'A dialogical approach to patients with personality disorders', in H.J.M. Hermans and G. Dimaggio (eds), *Dialogical Self in Psychotherapy*. Hove: Brunner-Routledge. pp. 220–34.

Sexton, L. (1999) 'Vicarious traumatisation of counsellors and effects on their work-places', *British Journal of Guidance & Counselling*, 27 (3): 393–403.

Shaffer, D.R. (1996) *Developmental Psychology: Childhood and Adolescence*. London: Brooks/Cole.

Spinelli, E. (1997) *Tales of Un-Knowing: Therapeutic Encounters from an Existential Perspective*. London: Duckworth.

Spinelli, E. (2001) *The Mirror and the Hammer: Challenges to Therapeutic Orthodoxy*. London: Continuum.

Spinelli, E. (2004) *Conversation*. Glasgow: Kinharvie Institute of Facilitation.

Spinelli, E. (2005) *The Interpreted World: An Introduction to Phenomenological Psychology* (2nd ed.) London: Sage.

Stadlen, A. (2005) Personal Communication.

Standal, Stanley W. (1954) *The Need for Positive Regard: A Contribution to Client-Centered Theory*. Chicago: Unpublished dissertation.

Steering Committee (2002) 'Empirically supported therapy relationships: Conclusions and recommendations on the Division 29 task force', in J.C. Norcross (ed.), *Psychotherapy*

Relationships That Work: Therapist Contributions and Responsiveness to Patients. Oxford: Oxford University Press. pp. 441–3.

Stern, D.N. (2003) *The Interpersonal World of the Infant: A View from Psychoanalysis and Developmental Theory.* London: Karnac.

Stern, D.N. (2004) *The Present Moment in Psychotherapy and Everyday Life.* New York: W.W. Norton.

Stern, D.N., Sander, L.W., Nahum, J.P., Harrison, A.M., Lyons-Ruth, K., Morgan, A.C. et al. (1998) 'Non-interpretive mechanisms in psychoanalytic therapy – The "something more" than interpretation', *International Journal of Psycho-Analysis*, 79: 903–21.

Stiles, W.B. and Glick, M.J. (2002) 'Client-centered therapy with multi-voiced clients: Empathy with whom?', in J.C. Watson, R. Goldman and M.S. Warner (eds), *Client-centered and Experiential Psychotherapy in the Twenty-first Century.* Ross-on-Wye: PCCS Books.

Stinckens, N., Lietaer, G. and Leijssen, M. (2002) 'The valuing process and the inner critic in the classic and current client-centered/experiential literature', *Person-Centered and Experiential Psychotherapies*, 1 (1–2): 41–55.

Stolorow, R.D., Brandchaft, B. and Atwood, G.E. (1987) *Psychoanalytic Treatment: An Intersubjective Approach.* Hillsdale, NJ: The Analytic Press.

Stone, H. and Winkelman, S. (1989) *Embracing our Selves: The Voice Dialogue Manual.* Mill Valley, CA: Nataraj Publishing.

Stuart, S. and Robertson, M. (2003) *Interpersonal Psychotherapy: A Clinician's Guide.* London: Arnold.

Swildens, H. (2004) 'Self-pathology and postmodern humanity: Challenges for person-centered psychotherapy', *Person-Centered and Experiential Psychotherapies*, 3 (1): 4–18.

Syme, G. (2003) *Dual Relationships in Counselling and Psychotherapy: Exploring the Limits.* London: Sage.

Thorne, B. (1992) *Carl Rogers.* London: Sage.

Thorne, B. (2003) 'Developing a spiritual discipline', in D. Mearns, *Developing Person-Centred Counselling* (2nd ed.). London: Sage. pp. 45–8.

Tillich, P. (2000) *The Courage to Be* (2nd ed.). New Haven, CT: Yale University Press.

Trevarthen, C. (1979) 'Communication and cooperation in early infancy: A description of primary intersubjectivity', in M. Bullowa (ed.), *Before Speech: The Beginning of Interpersonal Communication.* Cambridge: Cambridge University Press. pp. 321–47.

Trevarthen, C. (1980) 'The foundations of intersubjectivity: Development of interpersonal and cooperative understanding in infants', in D. Olson (ed.), *The Social Foundations of Language and Thought.* New York: W.W. Norton. pp. 316–42.

Trevarthen, C. (1998) 'The concept and foundations of infant intersubjectivity', in S. Braten (ed.), *Intersubjective Communication and Emotion in Early Ontogeny.* Cambridge: Cambridge University Press. pp. 15–46.

Trevarthen, C. and Hubley, P. (1978) 'Secondary intersubjectivity: Confidence, confiding and acts of meaning in the first year', in A. Lock (ed.), *Action, Gesture and Symbol: The Emergence of Language.* London: Academic Press. pp. 183–229.

Trüb, H. (1964) 'Selected readings', in M. Friedman (ed.), *The Worlds of Existentialism: A Critical Reader.* Chicago: University of Chicago Press. pp. 497–505.

Tryon, G.S. and Winograd, G. (2002) 'Goal consensus and collaboration', in J.C. Norcross (ed.), *Psychotherapy Relationships That Work: Therapist Contributions and Responsiveness to Patients.* Oxford: Oxford University Press. pp. 109–25.

van Deurzen, E. (2002) *Existential Counselling and Psychotherapy in Practice* (2nd ed.). London: Sage.

van Kessel, W. and Lietaer, G. (1998) 'Interpersonal processes', in L.S. Greenber J.C. Watson and G. Lietaer (eds), *Handbook of Experiential Psychotherapy*. New Yor Guilford Press. pp. 155–77.

Van Werde, D. (2002) 'Prouty's pre-therapy and contact work with a broad range persons' pre-expressive functioning', in G. Wyatt and P. Sanders (eds), *Contact a Perception*. Ross-on-Wye: PCCS Books. pp. 168–81.

Van Werde, D. (2003a) 'Dealing with the possibility of psychotic content in a seeming congruent communication', in D. Mearns, *Developing Person-Centred Counselling* (2r ed.) London: Sage. pp. 125–8.

Van Werde, D. (2003b) 'An introduction to client-centred pre-therapy', in D. Mearn *Developing Person-Centred Counselling* (2nd ed.). London: Sage. pp. 120–4.

von Weizsäcker, V. (1964) 'Selected readings', in M. Friedman (ed.), *The Worlds Existentialism: A Critical Reader*. Chicago: University of Chicago Press.

Vygotsky, L.S. (1962) *Thought and Language*. Cambridge, MA: MIT Press.

Warner, M. (2000) 'Person-centred therapy at the difficult edge: a developmentall based model of fragile and dissociated process', in D. Mearns and B. Thorne, *Perso Centered Therapy Today: New Frontiers in Theory and Practice*. London: Sag pp. 144–71.

Whiffen, V.E., Judd, M.E. and Aube, J.A. (1999) 'Intimate relationships moderate th association between childhood sexual abuse and depression', *Journal of Interperson Violence*, 14 (9): 940–54.

Williams, J.H.G., Whiten, A., Suddendorf, T. and Perrett, D.I. (2001) 'Imitation, mirrc neurons and autism', *Neuroscience and Biobehavioral Reviews*, 25 (4): 287–95.

Wittgenstein, L. (1967) *Philosophical Investigations*. Oxford: Blackwell.

Witty, M.C. (2004) 'The difference directiveness makes: The ethics and consequences guidance in psychotherapy', *The Person-Centered Journal*, 11 (1–2): 22–32.

Wolf, N.S., Gales, M.E., Shane, E. and Shane, M. (2001) 'The developmental trajector from amodal perception to empathy and communication: The role of mirror neuron in this process', *Psychoanalytic Inquiry*, 21 (1): 94–112.

Wolitzky, D. (2003) 'The theory and practice of traditional psychoanalytic treatment', i A.S. Gurman and S.B. Messer (eds), *Essential Psychotherapies: Theory and Practic* (2nd ed.). New York: Guilford Press. pp. 69–106.

Wyatt, G. (2001) 'Congruence: A synthesis and implications', in G. Wyatt (ed.), *Congruenc* Ross-on-Wye: PCCS Books. pp. 229–37.

Wyatt, G. and Sanders, P. (eds) (2002) *Contact and Perception*. Ross-on-Wye: PCC Books.

Yalom, I. (1980) *Existential Psychotherapy*. New York: Basic Books.

Yalom, I. (2001) *The Gift of Therapy: Reflections on Being a Therapist*. London: Piatkus

AUTHOR INDEX

SUBJECT INDEX